IN SEARCH OF TRUTH

In Search of Truth

From the Creation to the Restoration
An Overview of the
History of Christianity

Robert L. Smith

CFI
An Imprint of Cedar Fort, Inc.
Springville, Utah

ISBN 13: 978-1-4621-1051-3

Published by CFI, an imprint of Cedar Fort, Inc.
2373 W. 700 S., Springville, UT, 84663
Distributed by Cedar Fort, Inc., www.cedarfort.com

LIBRARY OF CONGRESS CATALOGING-IN-PUBLICATION DATA

Smith, Robert L. (Robert Leroy), 1946- , author.
In search of truth / Robert L. Smith.
pages cm
Summary: Combines a study of the doctrines of the Old and New Testaments, with an overview of the history of Judaism and Christianity, to show how God has always revealed His will to men through prophets. Also discusses how the predicted apostasy was fulfilled, which established the need for the Restoration of the gospel by a modern prophet.
Includes bibliographical references and index.
ISBN 978-1-4621-1051-3 (alk. paper)
1. Great Apostasy (Mormon doctrine) 2. Bible--Criticism, interpretation, etc. 3. Prophets (Mormon theology) 4. Restoration of the gospel (Mormon doctrine) I. Title.

BX8643.G74S63 2012
230'.9332--dc23

2012010784

Cover design by Angela D. Olsen
Cover design © 2012 by Lyle Mortimer
Edited and typeset by Kelley Konzak

Printed in the United States of America

10 9 8 7 6 5 4 3 2 1

Printed on acid-free paper

Contents

Author's Note .... **vii**
Introduction **1**

Section 1: A Synopsis of the Old Testament and a Brief History of the Hebrews

Chapter 1: The Hebrew Bible of the Old Testament 7
Chapter 2: Biblical Manuscripts of the Old Testament 21
Chapter 3: The Dead Sea Scrolls 31
Chapter 4: Doctrines Taught in the Old Testament 39
Chapter 5: The Clay Tablets of Ebla 57

Section 2: The New Testament and Historical Evidence of Jesus

Chapter 6: The Ministry of Christ and the Establishment of His Church 65
Chapter 7: The Ministry of the Apostles 89
Chapter 8: The Writing and Canonization of the New Testament 101
Chapter 9: The Predicted Apostasy in the Primitive Church 115
Chapter 10: The Primitive Church After the Apostles 125
Chapter 11: The Church Established by Constantine 155
Chapter 12: The Church in the Middle Ages 171
Chapter 13: The Protestant Reformation 183

Section 3: The Restitution of All Things

Chapter 14: Heavenly Visitations 195
Chapter 15: Voices from the Dust 213
Chapter 16: Evidences of the Book of Mormon 217
Chapter 17: In Search of Truth 231

About the Author 237

Author's Note

In Search of Truth: From the Creation to the Restoration is an overview of the history of Christianity. It begins with a synopsis of the Old Testament, including a brief history of the Hebrews, and then provides a review of the lost five hundred years between the Old and New Testaments. It describes the church established by Jesus and his Apostles, the ministry of the Apostles, and the apostasy following the death of the Apostles. Next it examines the persecutions of the early Christians, the formation of the Universal Catholic Church by Constantine, and the struggle for supremacy between Rome and Constantinople. Then, it provides information on the church in the Middle Ages and the Protestant Reformation, and it concludes with the Restoration of the Church of Jesus Christ in the latter days.

In Search of Truth: From the Creation to the Restoration describes the biblical manuscripts of the Old Testament, the Old Testament Apocrypha, and missing books of the Old and New Testaments, the Dead Sea Scrolls, and the influence of the Greek and Roman domination of Israel. Included is a summary of the doctrines taught in the Old and New Testaments as a continuing theme of a promised Messiah, who was the God of the Old Testament and the Savior and Resurrected Lord of the New Testament. The ministry and demise of the Apostles is discussed as far as there is historical knowledge, and the locations and periods of the ministries of the Early Church Fathers are tabulated. The recently translated Nag Hammadi codices reveal the writings of the Gnostics, whom the Early Church Fathers battled as heretics, giving new insights to the chaos and apostasy in the early Church.

The historical development of the New Testament books is explored, including questions by Bible scholars about the real authors and the dates that the books were written. Variant New Testament manuscripts are reviewed, and considerations are given to errors in translations or changes made by scribes who inserted their own interpretations. The biblical predictions of the Apostasy are cited, and the fulfillment of these prophecies is shown in the changes wrought in the church of the Middle Ages, which brought about the Protestant Reformation.

Finally, the Restoration of the primitive Church and the fulness of the gospel in the latter days is presented through the words of Joseph Smith Jr., who describes his vision of Heavenly Father and Jesus Christ. These heavenly beings called him as a prophet of the latter days to restore many lost truths of the gospel of Jesus Christ, which were taken from the scriptures or misunderstood as a result of the Apostasy. The Book of Mormon is introduced as another witness of Jesus Christ and as a history of the ancient inhabitants of Central America.

In Search of Truth: From the Creation to the Restoration outlines doctrines of The Church of Jesus Christ of Latter-day Saints, including continuing revelation and the belief that Jesus Christ appeared to the ancient inhabitants of the Americas and to modern prophets. It explores hidden messages in the Bible that have been lost to the understanding of the modern world and that have been brought to light by revelation to a modern prophet, Joseph Smith Jr. Many scriptures in the Bible, whose meanings have been obscured by loss of continuing revelation, are discussed from the LDS perspective without an attempt to prove their revealed messages.

Introduction

SINCE THE BEGINNING OF TIME ON THIS EARTH, MEN AND WOMEN have stood in awe of the majesty of the creation, gazing into the starlit heavens; pondering the motion of the sun, the moon, and the stars; participating in procreation and the miracle of birth and life itself; experiencing the changing of seasons, the food chain of the animal kingdom, the foliage and vegetation that provide food and shelter, and the refreshment of mighty rivers and small streams; experiencing joy; and suffering sickness, pain, and eventual death.

From the beginning of time, mankind has pondered his very existence and longed for a deeper understanding of it all. What does it mean? Who am I? Where did I come from? What is my purpose? Various civilizations of the earth have tried to develop theories to answer these questions, some worshipping the sun, moon, stars, and other gods of their own imaginations. Some created their own gods, made of the elements of the earth, and worshiped them in vain hopes of pleasing inanimate creations of their own hands. History records many of these religious systems in the temples, mounds, or pyramids built by these civilizations, and in their attempts to prepare their departed loved ones for a safe journey into the life after death.

For many in this modern world, the answers to these questions are found in the Bible, which describes a powerful God of the Old Testament who created the heavens and the earth and formed man from the dust of the earth and a woman from the rib of the man. According to the book of Genesis, this first couple was expelled from the Garden of Eden into the world, where they were compelled to work for their living and seek answers to these age-old questions about the purpose of life. But the Bible tells that the first man and woman were not left without help from God. The entire premise of the Bible is that the God who created the earth called men as prophets to reveal his will to his people and teach them of his ways. The Bible, as a history of the ancient Hebrew people, chronicles mankind's rebellions against God and God's continuing effort to bless them through the preaching of prophets.

The accounts of the Old Testament prophets were handed down through word of mouth for centuries before being recorded in written scriptures. And when they were finally recorded, the difficulty of copying everything by hand meant that few copies of these scriptures were available.

The New Testament chronicles the fulfillment of Old Testament prophecies of Jehovah, the spirit God of Abraham, Isaac, and Jacob, who became Jesus Christ. Jesus Christ, the Son of God, was born of a virgin, lived with both mortal and immortal characteristics, performed miracles of healing, and led men and women to God. He was then crucified and resurrected to bring about the eternal life of all mankind. Like the Old Testament, the New Testament books after the resurrection are based on revelation of the Lord to apostles and prophets on the earth, who organized the Early Church and prophesied in his name.

Modern theologians, however, have begun to question the accuracy, authorship, and completeness of the scriptures that have been published in our Bibles of today. The Apocrypha, Pseudepigrapha, and lost and missing books of the Bible are attracting new attention. Bible scholars are looking at ancient records more critically to determine their validity. Certainly, not all of the revelations to the prophets have been preserved in writing, and of those that have been preserved, we find many variations due to scribal errors or intentional changes inserted by those whose interpretation differed from the original texts. Where multiple copies exist, Bible scholars labor diligently to decipher the correct transmission and translation of variant texts. They also consider the possible alteration or interpretation of the text based on the philosophy of the scribe who copied the text from the original.

This book reviews the history of the Bible, the Hebrews, and the Christians and their foreign rulers. In doing so, it looks for clues about the Lord's message to his prophets by examining the sources of the records and how they were preserved. It examines ancient preserved or buried records such as the Dead Sea Scrolls, Apocryphal or Pseudopigraphic documents, letters written by the Early Church

Fathers, the Nag Hammadi codices or Gnostic gospels, and the Book of Mormon: Another Testament of Jesus Christ, which is believed by The Church of Jesus Christ of Latter-day Saints to be the same gospel of Jesus Christ revealed to ancient prophets on the American continent. It explores the techniques used by Bible scholars to critically examine variant texts and the means by which the Old and New Testament teachings can be harmonized to understand the word of God.

This book also summarizes historical events that led to the formation of the early Christian church; the persecutions of the early Christians by the Romans; the Apostasy, or falling away from the true teachings of Christ; the efforts of the Early Church Fathers to refute the heretics who composed the Gnostic gospels; and the formation of the early Catholic church. It chronicles the medieval church, including the Crusades, the institution of the Knights Templar, and subsequent inquisitions; the Protestant Reformation; and finally the story of the Restoration of the Church of Jesus Christ to the earth in the latter days and the publication of the Book of Mormon.

The original records from which the Book of Mormon was translated are not available today for analysis like the parchments of the Dead Sea Scrolls or the Nag Hammadi codices, but the evidences for the Book of Mormon will be explored by examination of archaeological and traditional historical evidence of the most significant event recorded in the book: the visit of Jesus Christ to the Americas after his resurrection in Jerusalem. A complete exploration of this evidence is beyond the scope of this book, but the primary purpose of this discussion is to show the Latter-day Saint answers to "purpose of life" questions through theology contained in the Book of Mormon and revelations to the Prophet Joseph Smith, and to show the need for a prophet today to dispel the confusion of men who try to interpret ancient records that have not come to us in unaltered form.

Many ancient records have been lost through the ravages of time and the elements, due to their intentional destruction by religious zealots who tried to suppress what they believed were pagan beliefs, or by Roman Emperors who sought to stamp out Christianity. Many ancient records were buried to preserve them for future generations, such as the Dead Sea Scrolls and the Nag Hammadi texts, and many Apocryphal documents exist that never made it into the Bible. But could there be hidden records—hidden in plain sight—simply because the interpretation of their original messages has been lost to our understanding?

The Bible is filled with hidden messages whose meanings have been lost to most people because the prophets who recorded them were killed and the spirit of revelation and prophecy was lost to the people because they rejected the prophets. The Judeo-Christian religions were founded upon the belief that God reveals his will to prophets, who, by the Holy Spirit, reveal the will of God to the people.

Members of The Church of Jesus Christ of Latter-day Saints believe that the Lord speaks again to a prophet on the earth and that these modern revelations have provided answers in the age-old quest for knowledge about the true nature of God and our relationship to him.

The purpose of this book is to give a high-level overview, showing the pattern of God's revelations to prophets on earth, man's rejection of prophecy, and God's willingness to continue to call prophets in each dispensation of time, in spite of man's rejection of him. Each chapter ends with conclusions, which are the conclusions of the author based partly on the discussions presented but also on opinions of the author that have not been fully discussed due to the limitations of space and given the wide range of the subject material. The author does not intend each conclusion to be a complete summary of the chapter, and no effort is made to prove the material presented, but the conclusions introduce new concepts and topics to be presented in subsequent chapters and hint at lost or hidden doctrines, hidden in plain sight but misunderstood because of man's rejection of prophecy in favor of human reasoning.

SECTION 1

A SYNOPSIS OF THE OLD TESTAMENT AND A BRIEF HISTORY OF THE HEBREWS

CHAPTER 1

THE HEBREW BIBLE OF THE OLD TESTAMENT

THE CREATION STORY

So God created man in his own image, in the image of God created he him; male and female created he them.

Genesis 1:27

HUNDREDS OF DIFFERENT CHRISTIAN AND JEWISH DENOMINATIONS base their faith in God on the Holy Bible, but there are as many variations of doctrines as there are distinct churches or congregations. However, a fundamental theme resonates from the pages of the Old Testament: a supreme being, variously called God, Gods, Heavenly Father, Jehovah, or Elohim, created the earth and all its elements and living creatures, including plants, animals, and finally humans, who are identified as the children of God. Throughout this book, God spoke to prophets and commanded them to preach to his children to prepare them to return to live with him.

The creation story of the book of Genesis tells of Adam and Eve, who awoke to find themselves in what seemed to be eternal bliss in the Garden of Eden, a place of peace and beauty, where food and water were abundant and life was without pain, worry, stress, sickness, or sin. The Creator, God, gave Adam and Eve dominion over all the earth, with only one restriction. They were not to partake of the fruit of the tree of knowledge of good and evil. If they did so, they were told that they would surely die. But Satan, or Lucifer, seduced Eve into breaking this commandment and then enticed her to get Adam to do the same. As punishment, Adam and Eve were cast out of that beautiful garden into the real world, where they would have to work for their living, suffering pain, hunger, sorrow, and eventually death.

REVELATION FROM GOD TO PROPHETS

With only this simplistic, seemingly mythical introduction to the beginning of the human race, one might well wonder about the true purpose of life and consider this story to be more fable than fact. However, the Bible goes on to tell that God continued to speak to Adam and Eve and their children after they were cast out of the Garden of Eden. He taught them what was required to return to his presence. Not everyone listened, of course, including Cain, who killed his brother Abel and became the first murderer on earth. Since not all of God's children were obedient, God called certain of those who did obey him to be prophets to teach the others to repent and worship him.

Jehovah, the God of the Old Testament, taught the prophets to offer sacrifices of lambs as a similitude of the sacrifice that would one day be offered by the Son of God for the sins of all the world. Without further understanding of the scriptures, this practice seems strange, but many followers of Abraham, Isaac, and Jacob (whose name was changed by the Lord to Israel) faithfully offered these sacrifices throughout the centuries of the Old Testament record.

GOD'S COVENANT WITH THE CHOSEN PEOPLE

Abraham, who was willing to obey God's every commandment, was even willing to sacrifice his only son. This was a type and symbol of the sacrifice God himself would make by offering his Only Begotten Son as a sacrifice for the sins of all the world. Because of Abraham's faithfulness, God established a covenant with him that through his seed all the world would be blessed. The physical sign of the covenant was circumcision of all males, which seems today to be a strange symbol, but the real sign of the covenant was obedience and worship of the only true God and not idols or worldly gods. Because of this Abrahamic covenant, the children of Israel became known as the chosen people of God. God blessed the prophet Abraham that through his lineage all of the earth would be blessed, but alas, many of his descendents failed to live up to the covenants that he made with God. History would show that they were chosen only as long as they obeyed their part of the covenant to worship the true God and not worldly idols.

IDOL WORSHIP

Through the prophet Moses, God gave his children the ten commandments. One of the most fundamental commandments was to refrain from worshiping idols. Yet, from the account of Moses to the end of the Old Testament, we read a continuing chronicle of the struggles of the children of Israel (the descendents of the twelve sons of Jacob, grandson of Abraham) to keep this commandment. For four hundred years, the children of Israel were enslaved by the Egyptians and learned to worship their idols, and when they were miraculously set free from their bondage, they soon returned to idol worship even without pressure from the Egyptians.

The Old Testament is replete with accounts of Jehovah's efforts to save his children from destruction if they would only repent and worship him. It is also filled with stories of devastation when they failed to do so.

THE KINGDOMS OF ISRAEL

The children of Israel lived in a patriarchal order for many generations, with God as their king who directed their prophets, but they eventually coveted the governmental pattern of the rest of the world and wanted worldly kings to be their leaders. Through the prophet Samuel, God predicted the results of this rebellion against him as their king, but he allowed the people to exercise their free will to choose to have an earthly king. After the reign of the wicked king Saul, David, who as a youth slew Goliath to defend the God of Israel, became a righteous king, only to fall victim to his lusts. Solomon, the son of David, inherited his father's throne and was blessed by God with such wisdom and wealth that he was renowned throughout the ancient world as the wealthiest and wisest king ever known. But Solomon too fell from the grace of God by having hundreds of wives from pagan nations, who caused him to allow the worship of idols in the kingdom of Judah. The successors to Solomon also fell into sin and idolatry, and rebellion eventually led to the house of Israel splitting into two kingdoms. The tribes of Judah and Benjamin, known as the kingdom of Judah, made up the southern kingdom in Jerusalem, and the other ten tribes, called the kingdom of Israel, made up the northern kingdom in Samaria.

THE LOST TEN TRIBES

In about 721 BC, Sargon, king of Assyria, destroyed Samaria, the capital of the northern ten tribes of Israel, and carried the people away captive into Assyria. Because the people were not faithful in keeping the commandments of God, it is probable that most of them assimilated into the culture of the Assyrians and thus became lost as to their identity as Israelites.[1]

However, according to one apocryphal book, 2 Esdras, one group of the captives repented of their evil ways and sought forgiveness of the Lord.

> But they took this counsel among themselves, that they would leave the multitude of the heathen, and go forth into a further country, where never mankind dwelt, that they might there keep their statutes, which they never kept in their own land. And they entered into Euphrates by the narrow passages of the river. For the most High then shewed signs for them, and held still the flood, till they were passed over. For through that country there was a great way to go, namely, of a year and a half: and the same region is called Arsareth. Then dwelt they there until the latter time.[2]

THE BABYLONIAN CAPTIVITY

In about 608 BC, Nebuchadnezzar, king of Babylon, invaded Jerusalem and took more than three thousand prisoners to Babylon. Among those taken captive were Daniel and Ezekiel, whose lives are detailed in their respective books of the Old Testament. Beginning in 597 BC, Nebuchadnezzar returned to Jerusalem, spoiled and sacked the temple of Solomon three times, and finally conquered Judah and Israel. This resulted in the historic Babylonian captivity of Israel in about 580 BC, at which time most of the nation of Israel was carried away captive into Babylon.[3]

"And he carried away all Jerusalem, and all the princes, and all the mighty men of valour, even ten thousand captives, and all the craftsmen and smiths: none remained, save the poorest sort of the people of the land" (2 Kings 24:14).

At the time, Zedekiah was the king of Judah. Josephus, the Jewish Roman historian, recorded the following account of the capture of Zedekiah:

> Now as to Zedekiah himself, while he heard the prophet [Jeremiah] speak, he believed him, and agreed to everything as true, and supposed it was for his advantage; but then his friends perverted him and dissuaded him to do what they pleased. Ezekiel also foretold in Babylon what calamities were coming upon the people, which when he heard, he sent accounts of them unto Jerusalem. But Zedekiah did not believe their prophecies, for the reason following: It happened that the two prophets agreed with one another in what they said as in all other things, that the city should be taken, and Zedekiah should be taken captive; but Ezekiel disagreed with him [Jeremiah], and said that Zedekiah should not see Babylon [see Ezekiel 12:13], while Jeremiah said to him, that the king of Babylon should carry him away thither in bonds [see Jeremiah 34:3]; and because they did not say the same thing as to this circumstance, he disbelieved what they both appeared to agree in, and condemned them as not speaking the truth therein, although the things foretold him did come to pass according to their prophecies, as we shall show upon a fitter opportunity.[4]

Both prophets were vindicated by subsequent events as recorded in 2 Kings 25:7. Regarding Zedekiah, Nebuchadnezzar commanded his sons and his friends to be slain,

> while Zedekiah and the rest of his captains looked on; after which he put out the eyes of Zedekiah, and bound him and carried him to Babylon. And these things happened, which Jeremiah and Ezekiel had foretold to him, that he should be caught and brought before the king of Babylon, and should speak to him face to face, and should see with his own eyes; and thus far did Jeremiah prophesy. But he was also made blind, and brought to Babylon, but did not see it, according to the prediction of Ezekiel.[5]

Nebuchadnezzar put to death the leaders of Judah, and all of the healthy people were carried captive into Babylon (see 2 Kings 25:18–26), but "the poor of the land" (v. 12) were allowed to remain.

The Babylonian captivity had a dramatic impact on the descendents of Abraham. Dr. Foakes-Jackson (in Biblical History of the Hebrews) says that the captivity of Judah "is one of the greatest events in the history of religion. . . . With the captivity, the history of Israel ends, and the history of the Jews commences." While some of the captive Israelites adopted the pagan practices of their captors, the majority "recoiled from the abominations of their neighbors and clung to the faith of . . . Abraham." Without their temple, they could no longer offer animal sacrifices, so "the rabbi and the scribe took the place of the sacrificing priest. The synagogue and the Sabbath came to occupy a new place in the religious practice of the people."[6]

RETURN FROM THE BABYLONIAN CAPTIVITY

When the Persians overthrew the Babylonian empire in 539 BC, Cyrus gave permission for the Jews to return to their native land after seventy years in exile. Since the northern tribes had been taken captive by Assyria and never returned, the survivors of the Babylonian exile were all that remained of the children of Israel. Since only the poorest of persons remained in the land after the captivity by Nebuchadnezzar, their descendants still inhabited Samaria when over forty-two thousand of the Babylonian Jews returned. Cultural differences between the Samaritans and the returning exiles resulted in hostilities. The Samaritan Jews had intermarried with the Assyrians, which was forbidden by Mosaic law, and their practice of religion had not followed the strict observance of the law of Moses, which was the glue that had bound the captive Jews together in the midst of the Babylonian abominations.

> This period saw the last high point of biblical prophecy in the person of Ezekiel, followed by the emergence of the central role of the Torah in Jewish life; according to many historical-critical scholars, it was edited and redacted during this time, and saw the beginning of the canonization of the Bible, which provided a central text for Jews.
>
> This process coincided with the emergence of scribes and sages as Jewish leaders. Prior to exile, the people of Israel had been organized according to tribe; afterwards they were organized by clans, only the tribe of Levi continuing in its "special role." After this time, there were always sizable numbers of Jews living outside Eretz Israel; thus, it also marks the beginning of the "Jewish diaspora."[7]

SELF-RULE UNDER THE PERSIAN KINGS

Cyrus, the Persian king, gave the returning Jews the charge to rebuild the temple and even restored some of the temple treasure, which had been looted during the Babylonian captivity. Despite these acts of apparent goodwill, Cyrus wanted "no descendent of David on the throne of Israel or Judah." He and his successors appointed Jewish governors, who reported to them. Consequently, the Jews viewed their high priests, rather than the governor, as "the most powerful person in Judah's society."[8]

According to Josephus, Nehemiah arrived in Jerusalem from Babylon in 440 BC.[9] He brought with him a royal commission from the Persian king to rebuild the city. Some years later, about 428 BC, Ezra was also sent by the Persian king with a letter that empowered him to spend treasury money to rebuild the temple. Ezra was a priest who emphasized strict adherence to the laws of God. Since the returning exiles had lost the ability to read their ancestral language, he had the law of Moses translated from Hebrew into Aramaic, the language of the Babylonians. Ezra taught that they had violated God's law by marrying "strange [foreign] wives," and he put them under covenant to "separate [themselves] from the people of the land, and from the strange wives."[10] Beginning with Ezra, the Jews began to place more emphasis on the law than on the ancient covenant that God had established with Abraham.

HELLENIZATION OF THE JEWS

Alexander was born in 356 BC. He was tutored by Aristotle at the age of thirteen, and at the age of twenty he inherited the throne of his father, Philip of Macedon. Within twelve years, Alexander had conquered the Persian Empire and Egypt and had established the city of Alexandria in Egypt, which became the chief cultural and intellectual center of the ancient world. Alexander died at the age of thirty-two and was succeeded by Ptolemy I, who founded the Ptolemaic dynasty in Egypt, and Seleucus I, founder of the Seleucid Empire in Syria. Ptolemy ruled over a large population of Jews who lived on Elephantine, an island in the Nile River in Egypt. Ptolemy II commissioned a Greek translation of the Hebrew Bible, since most of the Egyptian Jews had lost their ability to read and speak Hebrew. This translation became known as the Septuagint.[11]

Ptolemy took control of Palestine in 301 BC. In 198 BC, Antiochus III, a descendent of Seleucus, conquered the Ptolemys of Egypt to gain control of Palestine. Antiochus IV became the king of the Seleucid

Empire in 175 BC, and Greek ideas and institutions began to be imposed on the people of Palestine. Antiochus IV prohibited Sabbath observance, reading or teaching Mosaic law, the performance of circumcision, and the observance of Mosaic dietary laws. His most grievous act was to sacrifice unclean animals (pigs) on the altar of the temple. Thousands of people were killed when they resisted these changes.[12]

A Jew named Mattathias and his five sons, one of whom was named Judas Maccabaeus, rebelled against Antiochus IV, which resulted in the Maccabean war. Followers of Maccabaeus were known as Hasideans ("pious ones") and succeeded in expelling the Seleucids and retaking control of Jerusalem in 164 BC. They rededicated the temple that had been defiled by Antiochus IV. This event started the Hebrew celebration known as the Feast of Hanukkah ("Dedication"). The Maccabeans drove out the occupying Greek forces and established an independent nation in 142 BC.[13]

Two decades after Judas Maccabaeus defeated the Seleucid army, Simon Maccabaeus led the establishment of the Hasmonaean Kingdom (Hebrew: Hashmonai) in ancient Judea, and this dynasty ruled from 140 BC to 37 BC. The family name of the Hasmonaean dynasty originates with the ancestor of the house, Asamoneus or Asmoneus,[14] who is said to have been the grandfather of Mattathias but about whom nothing more is known. The origin of the Hasmonaean dynasty is recorded in the books of 1 and 2 Maccabees. These books are not part of the Hebrew Bible and are considered deuterocanonical by most Protestant Christians, but they are included in the Catholic and Eastern Orthodox canon. They include historical and religious material from the Septuagint; this material was codified by the Catholics and Eastern Orthodox churches.

The Hasmonaeans ruled as both high priests and kings of Judah from 135 BC until Herod the Great, a descendent of a Jewish convert in Idumaea, south of Judea, married into the Hasmonaean dynasty and ruled Judea from 37 BC to 4 BC.[15]

Hellenism is the name given to the influence of ancient Greek culture on other cultures. Following the widespread conquest of Alexander the Great, Greek culture and influence spread to the conquered nations, including Palestine. This culture was foreign to that of the Jews, who believed in one real God and rejected the mythological gods of the Greeks. The Jews believed that their God revealed his will to prophets, was all powerful, and had led their ancestors from Egypt through the Red Sea, whereas the Greeks based their reasoning on logic and scientific observations and viewed their polytheistic religion as philosophical instead of real. The Greeks saw logic and reasoning as the ultimate test of truth or falsehood. The populace of the Greeks and Romans still worshipped the local gods, but the cultured Greeks and Romans used religion to inspire and control the masses. They believed in humanism much more than the pantheon of symbolic gods worshipped by the masses.

When the Greeks conquered another country, they often sought to identify the gods of that culture with their own pantheon. However, the Seleucid king Antiochus IV inspired a Jewish revolt by trying to force the Jews to associate the god Yahweh with Zeus. The climax of this revolt resulted from his prohibition of circumcision and his desecration of the Jewish temple by sacrificing swine on its altars. As Greek rulers took control of foreign territories, they established Greek cities and gave land to Greek soldiers and citizens who lived among the local populations, spreading their culture through daily contact with their captives. Because the Greek language was required to participate in trade, Greek became the universal language of Alexander's conquered territories and the locals began to lose their ability to speak their native tongues, as the Hebrews had done during the Babylonian captivity and the resulting Diaspora. Greek became the language of the empire, which continued even after it was conquered by Rome.

Examples of great Greek cities relevant to the New Testament include Alexandria, built by the Ptolemys in Egypt; Antioch, built by the Seleucids on the coast of Syria; the Decapolis, a string of ten Greek towns between Galilee and Syria; and Caesaria Maritima, built on the coast of Palestine and named after the emperor.

JUDEAN REACTIONS TO HELLENIZATION

Hellenization had various effects on different classes of Jewish society. Josephus identified four separate sects of Judeans, and each reacted differently to their Greek captors.

Zealots. The Zealots, led by the Maccabaeus brothers, resisted Hellenization by organizing the overthrow of the Seleucid kings and established Jewish independence in 164 BC, as recorded in the apocryphal books of 1 and 2 Maccabees.

Sadducees. The Sadducees were wealthy priests who embraced Hellenization while trying to preserve the traditional interpretation of scriptures. Plato taught that the body was inherently evil but the spirit was pure and longed to be released from the evil body. This influenced the Sadducees, who did not believe in the existence of angels and bodily resurrection. The Sadducees did not believe that God took an interest or an active role in human affairs. They rejected the doctrines of divine punishment or reward and the afterlife. To them, death was final. The Sadducees were the priests who controlled the temple, and the high priest was a Sadducee.

Pharisees. The Pharisees were working-class people who were learned in the law but were not priests. They were critical of the Sadducees and the way the temple was run. They were respected by the "common" Jews as authorities on scripture. They resisted Hellenization but were submissive to their Roman captors, who ensured peace through the Pax Romana, which prohibited any nation in the empire from warring against another. The Pharisees followed an "oral" Torah, an unwritten code of law passed down orally from generation to generation in addition to the law that was divinely inspired and found in the written books of Moses. Their oral tradition was much stricter than the written law of Moses. It included such restrictions as how far one could walk on the Sabbath.

The Pharisees were the only sect to survive the revolt against the Romans in AD 66–70, and they were the foundation of Rabbinic Judaism. They accepted the doctrines of bodily resurrection and angels. Although the gospel authors are particularly critical of the Pharisees, Jesus's teachings are more like those of the Pharisees than those of any other Jewish sect existing at the time. However, they came to worship the law instead of the lawgiver.

Essenes. The Essenes were so thoroughly opposed to the Hellenizing of Judea that they abandoned Jerusalem and formed a strictly observant and monastic community in the desert near the Dead Sea, at Khirbet Qumran. They led a celibate life, although they also operated several satellite communities where members were allowed to have families so that the community could continue. They saw themselves as the true temple priesthood in exile. They were an apocalyptic community, awaiting the end time when God would judge them as the one sect that had remained true. They were also Messianic, expecting at least two messiahs to appear preceding the end times: one was to be a descendant of Aaron—a priestly messiah who would cleanse the temple in Jerusalem; the other was to be a Davidic messiah, who would lead the war against foreign oppression.

During Herod the Great's reign, the Jews maintained their own customary governing institutions. They considered the high priest of the temple to be their real leader, and the temple itself was seen as the central institution of the Jewish government. The high priest was appointed by Herod but always had to be drawn from the priestly class, or Sadducees. The Jews also had their own judicial system, headed by the Sanhedrin, or high court. The Sanhedrin had seventy-one members, drawn from the leadership of the two major sects, the Pharisees and the Sadducees. Being the larger group, it was the Pharisees that had majority representation in the court. They were also the more popular sect among the common Jews, so the Sadducees, and even the high priest, usually could not defy their rulings. It is likely, though, that the Sanhedrin, even its Pharisaic element, came from the wealthy, aristocratic segment of Jewish society and so was generally interested in maintaining the status quo.

ROMAN DOMINATION OF PALESTINE

A Jewish civil war broke out in 67 BC when two Hasmonaean brothers, Hyrcanus II and Aristobulus II, fought for control of Judea. They both appealed to the Roman general Pompey, who eventually seized control of Judea for Rome in 63 BC.[16]

Herod's father, Antipater, was appointed procurator, or governor, of Judea in 47 BC by Julius Caesar.[17]

CONCLUSIONS

The Old Testament chronicles the descendants of Adam and Eve as taught by prophets of the creator God, Jehovah, to worship the only true god and forsake the idolatry of those who worshipped false gods. Jehovah instituted animal sacrifice in similitude of a messiah who would be sacrificed for the sins of the people. He established his covenant with Abraham and his descendants to "have no other Gods before me," but the children of Israel broke the covenants of Abraham and rejected Jehovah as their king in favor of worldly kings like the pagan nations around them. While in captivity in Babylon, the children of

Israel clung to their customs but began to lose their Hebrew language and began speaking Aramaic, the language of their captors. Without their temple, they were unable to offer sacrifices, but after their return to Jerusalem under the sponsorship of Cyrus of Persia, they rebuilt Solomon's Temple and returned to strict adherence to the law of Moses. Then when they were conquered by Alexander, their Greek rulers tried to force the Greek gods upon them, even sacrificing pigs on the altars of the temple, which led to the Maccabean revolt, culminating in victory over their Greek rulers, and the rededication of the temple, now commemorated in the celebration of Hanukkah. In spite of their strong cultural heritage, they were variously influenced by their Greek rulers, some of them compromising and others rejecting Hellenization. By 67 BC, the Romans had conquered the Greeks ruling Palestine, installing Herod's father as governor of Judea.

The Old Testament clearly proclaims that the heavens and the earth were created by God (or Gods) and that men and women were made in the image of God. It also shows that God revealed his will to men on earth through prophets. This ancient scripture traces the history of the twelve tribes of Israel and outlines a form of sacrificial worship symbolic of the sacrifice to be made by the Messiah for the atonement of sins, so that men and women may return to live with God, their Heavenly Father.

NOTES

1. *Old Testament Student Manual: 1 Kings to Malachi, Religion 302 Student Manual* (Salt Lake City: The Church of Jesus Christ of Latter-day Saints, 1981), 114–15.
2. 2 Esdras 13:41–46, quoted in *Old Testament Student Manual: 1 Kings to Malachi, Religion 302 Student Manual* (Salt Lake City: The Church of Jesus Christ of Latter-day Saints, 1981), 114–15.
3. *Old Testament Student Manual: 1 Kings to Malachi, Religion 302 Student Manual*, 215–16.
4. Flavius Josephus, *Jewish Antiquities,* 10, 7, 2., quoted in *Old Testament Student Manual: 1 Kings to Malachi, Religion 302 Student Manual*, 216.
5. Flavius Josephus, *Jewish Antiquities*, 10, 8, 2., quoted in *Old Testament Student Manual: 1 Kings to Malachi, Religion 302 Student Manual*, 216.
6. Orr, James, M.A., D.D., ed., *International Bible Encyclopedia*, 1915, s.v. "captivity."
7. *Wikipedia*, s.vv. "Babylonian Captivity," http://en.wikipedia.org/wiki/

Babylonian_captivity.

8. S. Kent Brown and Richard Neitzel Holzapfel, *The Lost 500 Years* (Salt Lake City: Deseret Book, 2006), 15.
9. Flavius Josephus, *Jewish Antiquities* 9.5.7.
10. Brown and Holzapfel, *Lost 500 Years*, 26.
11. Ibid., 32–33.
12. Ibid., 42.
13. Ibid., 44–45.
14. Josephus Flavius, *Antiquities of the Jews* 1; 2; 3.
15. Brown and Holzapfel, *Lost 500 Years*, 54.
16. Ibid., 59–60.
17. Ibid., 65.

CHAPTER 2

BIBLICAL MANUSCRIPTS OF THE OLD TESTAMENT

ANCIENT SCRIPTURES

Search the scriptures; for in them ye think ye have eternal life: and they are they which testify of me.

John 5:39

BIBLE SCHOLARS BELIEVE THAT THE COLLECTION OF THE WRITTEN record of the Old Testament, as we have it today, began at the time of the prophet Hezekiah (about 730 BC to 686 BC) or later.[1] The Old Testament manuscripts extant today represent several different languages, due to the Persian, Babylonian, Greek, and Roman occupation of Jerusalem from 721 BC through the New Testament period. Below we will examine the origin and context of each of these Old Testament manuscripts.

THE SEPTUAGINT

"Septuagint" is the translation of the Jewish scriptures from Hebrew into Greek. When Alexander the Great completed his world conquests in 327 BC, Greek became the universal language of all nations ruled by the Greek empire, and many of the Jews who were scattered throughout the known world began to lose the ability to read the scriptures in Hebrew. Between 300 and 200 BC, it is believed that seventy to seventy-two Jewish scholars were commissioned during the reign of

Ptolemy Philadelphus to carry out the task of this translation. The term *Septuagint* means "seventy" in Latin, and this Old Testament book is so named because of these seventy Jewish scholars in Alexandria, Egypt, who completed the translation.[2]

The Septuagint was widely used among Hellenistic Jews. This Greek translation became the scriptures cited by the Christian Apostles and missionaries. Because the Christians were using the Septuagint to convert Jews to Christianity, "some Greek-speaking Jews eventually decided to re-translate the Hebrew Old Testament and to abandon the Septuagint, which, in their eyes, had become a Christian book."[3] The first attempt, made by Aquila in AD 130, was "slavishly literal to Hebrew expressions,"[4] making it "almost unusable" to Greek readers. About fifty years later, Theodotian made another Greek translation. When Old Testament passages quoted in the New Testament differ from our modern Old Testament, it is often because of the variant versions of the Septuagint at the time.[5]

THE MASORETIC TEXT

The Masoretic text, which is written in Hebrew, is "the basis for all translations of the Old Testament into other languages, including the King James Version." The contents of this manuscript were compiled and edited in about AD 90 by a group of survivors of the Jewish war that ended with the destruction of Jerusalem (AD 66–70). Rabbi Yohannan ben Zakkai led a group of Pharisees in a small town named Jamnia, between Jerusalem and Tel Aviv, to compose a manuscript that consolidated various differing manuscripts into one on which they all could agree. Finalization of this text, including the addition of punctuation and vowels to the Hebrew text, was left to the later Masoretes, groups of Hebrew scribes and scholars living in the holy lands and Babylon, in the sixth and seventh centuries AD. It was the Masoretic text that defined the canon of the Old Testament books.[6]

The oldest extant manuscripts containing substantial parts of the Masoretic text date from approximately the ninth century.

THE SAMARITAN PENTATEUCH

The Samaritan Pentateuch is believed to be based on "a very old set of documents" that some scholars estimate "reaches back to the days of the divided Israelite monarchy, before the Assyrians came to

Samaria and conquered the city in 722 B.C."[7] In about 100 BC, the Samaritans decided to make their scriptures more easily understood by the common people, changing expressions that were unique to antiquity. They also decided to limit the Pentateuch to the first five books of Moses, Genesis through Deuteronomy. The Jews returning from exile in Babylon treated the Samaritans as little better than Gentiles, and rivalry continued between these groups of Jewish communities. The Samaritans rejected books such as 1 Kings and Jeremiah, "which spoke of Jerusalem as the worship center of the nation," believing that Joshua built the first altar in the promised land on Mount Ebal, which is in Samaria. They also adjusted their scripture to defend their modest temple on Mount Gerizim "as the true center of worship."[8]

THE BOOKS OF THE HEBREW BIBLE

The Hebrew Bible is composed of the Torah, or the first five books of Moses, the prophets, and the writings, whereas the Protestant Bible is divided into history, poetry, and prophecy, as shown in the following table. The Septuagint, the Greek translation of the Hebrew Bible, is included in the table for reference, showing the apocryphal books in relation to the applicable categories in the Hebrew Bible.

A COMPARISON OF BIBLES

The Hebrew Bible (39 Books)	The Protestant Bible (39 Books)	The Septuagint (57 Books) *Apocryphal
Torah	**History**	**Law and History**
Genesis	Genesis	Genesis
Exodus	Exodus	Exodus
Leviticus	Leviticus	Leviticus
Numbers	Numbers	Numbers
Deuteronomy	Deuteronomy	Deuteronomy
	Joshua	Joshua
	Judges	Judges
	Ruth	Ruth
Prophets	1–2 Samuel	1–4 Kingdoms (Samuel & Kings)
Former Prophets	1–2 Kings	1–2 Paralipomena (Chronicles)
Joshua	1–2 Chronicles	*1 Esdras
Judges	Ezra	*2 Esdras (Ezra–Nehemiah)
1–2 Samuel	Nehemiah	Esther
1–2 Kings	Esther	*Judith
	Poetry	*Tobit
	Job	*1–4 Maccabees
Later Prophets	Psalms	Poetic and Prophetic Books
Isaiah	Proverbs	Psalms
Jeremiah	Ecclesiastes	*Odes
Ezekiel	Song of Solomon	*Prayer of Manasseh
		Proverbs
The Twelve (Minor Prophets)	**Prophecy**	**Poetic and Prophetic Books**
Hosea	Isaiah	Ecclesiastes
Joel	Jeremiah	Song of Solomon
Amos	Lamentations	Job
Obadiah	Ezekiel	*Wisdom of Solomon

Jonah	Daniel	*Ecclesiasticus (or Sirach)
Micah	Hosea	*Psalms of Solomon
Nahum	Joel	Hosea
Habakuk	Amos	Amos
Zephaniah	Obadiah	Micah
Haggai	Jonah	Joel
Zechariah	Micah	Obadiah
Malachi	Nahum	Jonah
	Habakkuk	Nahum
Writings	Zephaniah	Habakkuk
Psalms	Haggai	Zephaniah
Job	Zechariah	Haggai
Proverbs	Malachi	Zechariah
Ruth		Malachi
Song of Solomon		Isaiah
Ecclesiastes		Jeremiah
Lamentations		*Baruch
Esther		*Letter of Jeremiah
Daniel		Lamentations
Ezra-Nehemiah		Ezekiel
1–2 Chronicles		Daniel
		*Prayer of Azariah
		*Song of the Three Jews
		*Susanna
		*Bel the Dragon

Table from Brown and Holzapfel, *The Lost 500 Years*, 82.

THE VULGATE

Jerome's famous Latin translation of the Old Testament in AD 384, known as the Vulgate, included the books known as the Apocrypha. These books had been excluded from the Hebrew Bible when the Hebrew canon of scriptures was closed with the publication of the Masoretic text in AD 90, but they had been included in the Septuagint.[9]

THE OLD TESTAMENT APOCRYPHA

The books of the Apocrypha are of Jewish origin and were in use in the period at the end of the Old Testament and the beginning of the New Testament. The original Hebrew manuscripts were lost, and the Apocryphal books were available only in Greek and Latin until the discovery of some of them written in Hebrew and Aramaic among the Dead Sea Scrolls. They were included in the Greek Septuagint and were sometimes published between the Old and New Testaments in early Bibles.[10] Martin Luther included them in his 1534 translation of the Bible into German with the following comment: "The Apocrypha—that is, books which are not held equal to the Holy Scriptures, and yet are profitable and good to read."[11]

The books generally identified as Old Testament Apocrypha are

- 1 Esdras (3 Ezra)
- 2 Esdras (4 Ezra)
- Tobit
- Judith
- Additions to Esther
- Additions to Daniel
- Wisdom of Solomon
- Wisdom of Jesus the son of Sirach, or Ecclesiasticus (also known as Ben Sira)
- Baruch (and the epistle of Jeremiah usually incorporated within it)
- Song of the Three Children
- History of Susanna
- History of Bel and the Dragon
- Prayer of Manasses
- 1 Maccabees
- 2 Maccabees[12]

LOST BOOKS OF THE BIBLE

Jewish-Related Lost Books

- The Book of Jasher is mentioned in Joshua 10:13 and 2 Samuel 1:18.
- The Book of the Wars of the Lord—*Referenced at Numbers 21:14*

- The Book of the Annals of the Kings of Israel is mentioned in 1 Kings 16:20 regarding King Zimri. This appears to be a different book than any of those included in the Bible.
- The Books of the Annals of the Kings of Israel and Books of the Annals of the Kings of Judah are mentioned in the Books of Kings (1 Kings 14:19, 29). They are said to tell of events during the reigns of Kings Jeroboam of Israel and Rehoboam of Judah, respectively. Some believe that the information of these books was later compiled into Kings, but others differ, citing the above passages from Kings, which state they contain "other events."
- Books of Chronicles are mentioned on several occasions in the Book of Esther and also in Nehemiah 12:23. Some scholars believe that the book was ahistorical; it is, however, also noticed that the author was familiar with the customs at the Persian court, where the book is set. While the chronicles mentioned in Esther are thought by some scholars to be fictional, there is no doubt that the Kings of Persia did keep annals.
- The Book of Shemaiah the prophet, and of Iddo the Seer is mentioned in the book of 2 Chronicles (12:14–15). Iddo was a seer who lived during the reigns of Solomon, Rehoboam, and Abijah. His deeds were recorded in this book, which has been completely lost to history, excepting its title.
- The Covenant Code—*Referenced at Exodus 24:7*
- The Manner of the Kingdom—*Referenced at 1 Samuel 10:25*
- The Acts of Solomon—*Referenced at 1 Kings 11:41*
- The Annals of King David—*Referenced at 1 Chronicles 27:24*
- The Book of Samuel the Seer—*Referenced at 1 Chronicles 29:29*
- The Book of Nathan the Prophet—*Referenced at 1 Chronicles 29:29*
- The Book of Gad the Seer—*Referenced at 1 Chronicles 29:29*
- The History of Nathan the Prophet—*Referenced at 2 Chronicles 9:29*
- The Prophecy of Ahijah—*Referenced at 2 Chronicles 9:29*
- The Visions of Iddo the Seer—*Referenced at 2 Chronicles 9:29*
- The Book of Shemaiah the Prophet—*Referenced at 2 Chronicles 12:15*
- Iddo Genealogies—*Referenced at 2 Chronicles 12:15*

- The Story of the Prophet Iddo—*Referenced at 2 Chronicles 13:22*
- The Book of the Kings of Judah and Israel—*Referenced at 2 Chronicles 16:11, 2 Chronicles 27:7, and 2 Chronicles 32:32*
- The Book of Jehu—*Referenced at 2 Chronicles 20:34*
- The Story of the Book of Kings—*Referenced at 2 Chronicles 24:27*
- The Acts of Uziah—*Referenced at 2 Chronicles 26:22*
- The Vision of Isaiah—*Referenced at 2 Chronicles 32:32*
- The Acts of the Kings of Israel—*Referenced at 2 Chronicles 33:18*
- The Sayings of the Seers—*Referenced at 2 Chronicles 33:19*
- The Laments for Josiah—*Referenced at 2 Chronicles 35:25*
- The Chronicles of King Ahasuerus—*Referenced at Esther 2:23 and Esther 6:1*
- The Chronicles of the Kings of Media and Persia—*Referenced at Esther 10:2*

Christian-Related Lost Books

A line from the Book of Enoch is quoted in the Epistle of Jude (1:14–15) almost verbatim. The work is believed by most scholars to be pseudepigraphal, but the author of Jude seems to have believed it was Enoch's own words.

- The Epistle to Corinth—*Referenced at 1 Corinthians 5:9*
- The Earlier Epistle to the Ephesians—*Referenced at Ephesians 3:3–4*
- The Epistle from Laodicea to the Colossians—*Referenced at Colossians 4:16*
- The Earlier Epistle of John—*Referenced at 3 John 1:9*
- Missing Epistle of Jude—*Referenced at Jude 1:3*

PSEUDEPIGRAPHA

The Greek term *pseudepigrapha* means "falsely attributed writings."[13] Beyond the Old Testament Apocrypha, which designates Hebrew books excluded from the Masoretic Hebrew canon of the Old Testament but included in the Greek Septuagint, the term *pseudepigrapha* can be applied to a wide collection of writings attributed to Old and

New Testament sources. Because the authorship of these documents cannot be accurately determined, the validity of any religious doctrines they contain may be questionable. However, they offer additional historical insights to this period between the Old and New Testaments.

CONCLUSIONS

The Hebrew Bible was a collection of separate books, consisting initially of the Torah, or first five books of Moses, and was expanded to include revelations from Jehovah to many other prophets. It was written first in Hebrew and was then translated into Greek as the Septuagint by 200 BC, after Alexander spread the Hellenistic culture throughout his vast empire. The Samaritans had their own form of the Torah, called the Pentateuch, which was revised to the language of the day in about 100 BC. In about AD 400, Jerome completed his translation of the Old Testament into Latin from the Hebrew and from the Septuagint. The Hebrew Bible was canonized in about AD 90 by a group of Pharisee rabbis and later modified by adding vowels to the Hebrew text in the sixth to seventh century AD by a group of Jewish scribes and scholars known as the Masoretes. This became known as the Masoretic Text, which became the basis for all modern translations of the Old Testament. The Persian, Greek, and Roman domination of Judah from 721 BC until the birth of Jesus Christ had an influence on the translation of the Old Testament scriptures. Although these ancient scriptures went through many translations, we will show in a later chapter that the Dead Sea Scrolls, which date to about 170 BC, are believed to have been copied from earlier manuscripts, and they show remarkable consistency to our modern-day translations and give added confidence that the basic religious doctrines have been properly preserved though the centuries.

Many books of scripture or history referenced in the Bible are still lost to us today. What revelations from the Lord did they contain, or what clarifications of other revelations are we missing? Surely not all the revelations of God to his prophets have been preserved from generation to generation. This fact emphasizes the need for continuing revelation from God to prophets on the earth today, as we continue our search for truth.

NOTES

1. Kerry Muhlestein, ed., *How the New Testament Came to Be* (Provo, UT: Brigham Young University, 2006), 49.
2. Geoffrey W. Bromley, ed., *The International Standard Bible Encyclopedia*, (Grand Rapids, MI: Eerdmans, 1988), 4:402.
3. S. Kent Brown and Richard Neitzel Holzapfel, *The Lost 500 Years* (Salt Lake City: Deseret Book, 2006), 83.
4. Ibid.
5. Ibid.
6. Ibid., 77–78.
7. Ibid., 78.
8. Ibid., 79.
9. Ibid., 94.
10. Ibid.
11. Ibid., 95.
12. Ibid., 93.
13. Ibid., 97.

CHAPTER 3

THE DEAD SEA SCROLLS

THE DISCOVERY

> *And thou shalt be brought down, and shalt speak out of the ground, and thy speech shall be low out of the dust, and thy voice shall be, as of one that hath a familiar spirit, out of the ground, and thy speech shall whisper out of the dust.*
>
> *Isaiah 29:4*

ONE OF THE MOST EXCITING ARCHAEOLOGICAL DISCOVERIES OF our generation was made in 1947 when two young Bedouin goat herders found several earthen jars in a cave near the northwestern corner of the Dead Sea. The lids of some of the jars were sealed with wax to preserve the ancient scrolls that had been hidden in these jars over 1,900 years earlier. Some of the scrolls were wrapped in fabric covered with pitch to keep them dry. Hugh J. Schonfield writes in *Secrets of the Dead Sea Scrolls,* "Since the Dead Sea Scrolls were preserved in earthenware jars in caves, we must surely consider in the light of what is related of Jeremiah whether the deposit was not made of set purpose, and was not simply an expedient to save the books from destruction at the hands of the Romans in the War of AD 67–73 as scholars have maintained. I would suggest that the documents were concealed deliberately so that in the words of *Daniel*, they could 'be closed up and sealed until the Time of the end.'"[1]

R. H. Charles, in *The Apocrypha and Pseudepigrapha of the Old Testament*, states:

> From the Assumption of Moses, a pseudepigraphal apocalypse, we learn of books that are to come forth at the "end of days."
>
> "And receive thou the writing that thou mayst know how to preserve the books which I shall deliver unto thee, and thou shalt set these in order and anoint them with oil of cedar and put them away in earthen vessels in the place which He made from the beginning of the creation of the world, that His name should be called upon until the day of repentance in the visitation wherewith the Lord will visit them in the consumption of the end of days."[2]

The importance of this discovery was not understood by these desert tribesmen, but eventually some of the scrolls fell into the hands of scholars who recognized their priceless value. The scrolls contained the oldest known copies of many books of the Old Testament, some of which are over one thousand years older than our oldest manuscripts.[3] They also included the writings of a separate society that had rejected the authority of the rulers of the temple in Jerusalem and tried to preserve the purity of their ancient Hebrew religious worship by secluding themselves in a community near the caves where the scrolls were found.

Between 1947 and 1956, hundreds of caves near the Dead Sea were explored. Eleven caves revealed over eight hundred scrolls and fragments of scrolls, of which over two hundred were books of the Old Testament.[4] Most of the scrolls were made of animal skins, some were papyrus, and one was made of copper. Most were written in Hebrew, but some were in Aramaic and some in Greek. Every book of the Old Testament except for the Book of Esther was discovered in its entirety or represented among the thousands of fragments.[5] Multiple copies of many of the Old Testament books were found, although most are extremely fragmented. The Isaiah Scroll, which includes all sixty-six chapters of Isaiah, was preserved in its entirety and was twenty-four feet long.[6] In addition to the Old Testament books, many of the scrolls described a communal society of Jews who lived near the caves in a religious center named Qumran.

QUMRAN EXCAVATION

Khirbet Qumran was excavated and partially restored between 1951 and 1956 and revealed a complex that had been built around

150 BC and was inhabited until AD 68.[7] An earthen jar found at the Qumran excavation was identical to one of the jars found in Cave 1, which conclusively tied the inhabitants of Qumran to the scrolls found hidden in the nearby caves.[8] What makes this discovery so unique in the history of archaeological excavation is that it is extremely rare to find a complete library documenting the history of a society buried next to the ruins of their habitation. Normally archaeologists have to interpret their findings based on pottery, artifacts, and sometimes art or cave drawings, but rarely do they find a written history of the ancient inhabitants of the ruins being excavated.

THE ESSENES

Scholars believe that the inhabitants of Qumran were members of a religious group known as the Essenes. According to the Apocryphal books of 1 and 2 Maccabees, the Hellenization of the Holy Land began in the third century BC. "In 172 B.C., Onias III, the legitimate high priest, was murdered in Jerusalem. Onias was . . . descended from Zadok (King David's high priest . . .)," and all legitimate high priests in the temple of Jerusalem were descendents of Zadok. Onias was replaced by the Syrian rulers of the region with an intensely Hellenized Jew, not of the line of Zadok.[9]

Jewish rabbis began to apply logic and reasoning for interpretation of the scriptures, based on Greek influence, instead of seeking revelation from God as did the ancient prophets. They believed that "the holy spirit departed from Israel" after the last biblical prophets, and the Jews began to rely on the wisdom of the rabbis. Dr. Andrew Skinner, LDS scholar, points out that

> the influence of the holy spirit was emphasized among both Christians and Qumran covenanters. By contrast, as Professor [Shemaryahu] Talmon points out, rabbinic Judaism, which developed alongside these other two branches of Judaism, progressively moved away from prophets and "the spirit," and developed a rationalist stance. According to rabbinic tradition, after the demise of the last biblical prophets—Haggai, Zechariah, and Malachi—"the holy spirit departed from Israel," and from then on Israel was enjoined to incline their ear and "listen to the instructions of the [rabbinic] Sages."[10]

Eventually, some Jews rejected what they believed was the

"pollution of their ancestral religion"[11] by illegitimate holders of the high priesthood, and chose to seclude themselves in a desert commune, where they could preserve their religious heritage under the leadership of their prophet leader, known in the Dead Sea Scrolls as the Teacher of Righteousness.

Excavation of the Khirbet Qumran complex, built of stone, revealed a seventy-five-foot-long dining room, where the communal meal was observed each day. The adjoining pantry held over one thousand bowls, plates, and other dishes. Water was provided to the complex by a gravity flow aqueduct from the cliffs nearby to fill cisterns, ritual baths, and a pool.[12] Among the many scrolls found in the nearby caves was the Rule of the Community, or Manual of Discipline, which described the religious order and the requirements for purification by bathing in fresh water before entering the "Holy Temple," or sacred area, to partake of the communal meal.[13] One of the rooms in the Qumran complex has been called the "scriptorium," or writing room, because of inkwells found in desks in this room.[14]

Qumran was a communal society of righteous Jews who believed that the rabbinical Jews of the temple in Jerusalem were apostate from the teachings of the prophets. The society was made up exclusively of celibate males who wore white linen garments to symbolize purity and who ate ritual communal meals.[15] They were a covenant group devoted to perfect observance of the law of Moses, and they "regarded themselves as true Israel, surrounded by spiritual traitors and false brethren in a corrupt world."[16]

After twenty years at Qumran, God sent them the Teacher of Righteousness, who "claim[ed] that God specifically revealed to him all the mysteries of the prophets."[17] "After the passing of the Teacher of Righteousness, the [society was governed by a] quorum of three priests . . . with a quorum of twelve laymen."[18] The names or identities of this society listed in the scrolls include: the Community, the Counsel, the Congregation, the Men of Essa, Assembly of God, the Council of Truth, the Sons of the Eternal Council, the Sons of Zadok, the Elect of God, the Seers, the Pious, the Silent Ones, the Performers of the Law, the Physicians, the Puritans, the Retired Ones, the Brethren, the Servants of God, the Stout Ones, the Strong Race, the Mysterious Ones, the Holiness Sect, the Prophesiers, the Saints, the Bathers, the Daily Baptists, the Observers of the Laws of Purity, and the Apron Wearers.[19]

QUMRAN THEOLOGY

The theology of the Qumran society included common ownership of property (consecration of all earthly goods to the society), belief in predestination, belief in the afterlife but not physical resurrection, ritual bathing and cleansing, a required repentance for admission to the community, and baptism by immersion. Members of this society emphasized belief in the Holy Spirit and looked for the coming of two messiahs—one spiritual and one political.

Their religious beliefs were much like those of Christians, 150 years before the birth of Christ, which caused some concerns among modern theologians, who presumed that some of the theology of Jesus Christ may have been copied from this earlier civilization. Others, who believe that Jesus Christ was Jehovah of the Old Testament, believe that the Qumran leaders received their doctrines from the ancient prophets and were merely trying to preserve them until the coming of the Messiah. Although the Qumran complex was inhabited until the destruction of the Jews by the Romans in AD 68, there is no evidence that the inhabitants of Qumran recognized Jesus Christ as the Messiah, and there is no mention of Christ in the scrolls found at Qumran.

Although the Teacher of Righteousness "claim[ed] that God specifically revealed to him all the mysteries of the prophets," it is clear that the Essenes at Qumran did not have the fulness of the gospel and the plan of salvation as restored by revelation to the Prophet Joseph Smith.

Dana M. Pike, LDS scholar, writes,

> I feel strongly that Latter-day Saints can appreciate and understand the passages in the Dead Sea Scrolls that relate to the plan of salvation, but we must also appreciate that a clear or comprehensive understanding of this plan is not evidenced at Qumran. Though there are concepts that I have described as corrupted echoes of true doctrines, there are simply too many key points of the plan of salvation absent from the preserved texts. Doctrines such as the fall, the infinite atonement of the Savior, clear indications of a universal, physical resurrection, and eternal ordinances requiring the holy Melchizedek Priesthood are not attested. The Dead Sea Scrolls cannot teach Latter-day Saints anything about the plan of salvation that has not already been revealed by the Lord through his authorized servants. However, our study of the scrolls can help us to understand the beliefs of the Jewish inhabitants of Qumran and, because of the

contrasts such study can help us more fully appreciate the gospel truths restored in the latter days.[20]

CONTENTS OF THE SCROLLS

The scrolls have been dated from 327 BC–AD 73 based on carbon dating of the linen wrappings, and from 135 BC–AD 68 based on coins found in the community center and scroll caves.[21] Besides the books of the Old Testament, the collection of scrolls includes the Temple Scroll; the War Scroll (Sons of Light versus Sons of Darkness); Thanksgiving Hymns; and commentaries on books of the Old Testament, including Habakkuk, Hosea, Isaiah, Micah, and Psalms. Also included in the collection are some Apocrypha, or Pseudepigraphal texts, including the Genesis Apocraphon (Book of Adam and Eve), the Testaments of the Twelve Patriarchs, the Book of Jubilees, the Book of Enoch, Tobit, Sirach, and the Zadokite Text. The greatest significance of the contents of the scrolls is the discovery of one complete copy of the book of Isaiah, the Great Isaiah Scroll, which is nearly identical to the Book of Isaiah in our Bible today.

> The Isaiah Scroll (Manuscript A) is one of the first seven scrolls discovered in 1947 in a cave near Qumran, on the northwestern shores of the Dead Sea. Of the 220 biblical scrolls found in the area, the complete Great Isaiah Scroll is one of the best preserved and the only one containing an entire biblical book. Dating from approximately 120 BCE, it is also one of the oldest Dead Sea Scrolls, some one thousand years older than the oldest manuscripts of the Bible known to us before the Scrolls' discovery.[22]

Finding a copy of the book of Isaiah and his Messianic prophecies, which predate the birth of Jesus of Nazareth, proves that these prophecies were not revised after the ministry of Jesus to "predict" his ministry and his sacrifice after the fact.

The translation of the Dead Sea Scrolls was painstakingly slow because only a select group of scholars was allowed access to them, but this policy was changed in 1993 when the Israel Antiquities Authority decided to release all official photographs of the scrolls and scroll fragments on microfiche. In 1992, an electronic database was developed by Brigham Young University in conjunction with the Foundation for Ancient Research and Mormon Studies (FARMS), and this database became the source for the book *Discoveries in the Judean Desert*, published by the Oxford Press.[23]

The Dead Sea Scrolls provide Bible scholars with the opportunity to compare variant readings and discover errors in translation in the text of the Bible. The fact that many of the Old Testament books were found in multiple copies of scrolls aided studies of these variations. Numerous modern translations of the Old Testament have been revised based on these variant translations from the Dead Sea Scrolls. The discovery of the Dead Sea Scrolls was equivalent to finding a time capsule dating almost two thousand years ago and giving us a view of history that would otherwise have been lost to the world forever.

CONCLUSIONS

The Dead Sea Scrolls, dating to 150 BC or earlier, provide manuscripts of the Old Testament books that are one thousand years older than the oldest existing manuscripts in 1947 (which dated to AD 895), and they give scholars a means to correct minor variations in the scriptures due to scribal errors and omissions. They validate the Messianic prophecies of Isaiah as predating the birth of Jesus Christ. They hint of doctrines taught by Jesus Christ because they are based on revelations from Jehovah to ancient prophets—doctrines that were lost to the rabbinical Jews of the temple in Jerusalem.

In addition to the Old Testament scriptures, documents found with the Dead Sea Scrolls fill a huge knowledge gap about the religious sect known as the Essenes and their commune at Khirbet Qumran.

NOTES

1. Hugh J. Schonfield, *Secrets of the Dead Sea Scrolls: Studies Towards Their Solution* (New York: Barnes, 1960), 11.
2. R. H. Charles, *The Apocrypha and Pseudepigrapha of the Old Testament* (Oxford University: Clarendon Press, 1913), 2:415, quoted by Vernon W. Mattson Jr., *The Dead Sea Scrolls and Other Important Discoveries* (Tampa, FL: Buried Records Publications, 1979), 28
3. Donald W. Parry, "The Contribution of the Dead Sea Scrolls," in *LDS Perspectives on the Dead Sea Scrolls*, ed. Donald W. Parry and Dana M. Pike (Provo, UT: FARMS, 1997), 47.
4. Ibid., 48.
5. Ibid., 50.
6. Ibid., 48.

7. Andrew C. Skinner, "The Ancient People of Qumran," *LDS Perspectives*, 8.
8. Ibid., 10.
9. Ibid., 17–18.
10. Ibid., 33.
11. Ibid., 18.
12. Ibid., 8.
13. Ibid., 4.
14. Ibid., 9.
15. Ibid., 26–27.
16. Ibid., 30.
17. Ibid., 16–17.
18. Ibid., 32.
19. Vernon W. Mattson Jr., *The Dead Sea Scrolls and Other Important Discoveries* (Tampa, FL: Buried Records Publications, 1979), 20.
20. Dana M. Pike, "Is the Plan of Salvation Attested in the Dead Sea Scrolls?," in *LDS Perspectives on the Dead Sea Scrolls* (Provo, UT: FARMS, 1997), 90.
21. Mattson, *The Dead Sea Scrolls*, 28.
22. Communicated by the Foreign Press Officer, The Israel Museum, Jerusalem, 23 June 2008.
23. Donald W. Parry and Dana M. Pike, eds., introduction to *LDS Perspectives on the Dead Sea Scrolls* (Provo, UT: FARMS, 1997), x–xii.

CHAPTER 4

DOCTRINES TAUGHT IN THE OLD TESTAMENT

LOST OR HIDDEN MESSAGES IN THE OLD TESTAMENT

And truth is knowledge of things as they are, and as they were, and as they are to come.

Doctrine and Covenants 93:24

THIS CHAPTER EXPLORES HIDDEN MESSAGES IN THE BIBLE THAT have been lost to the understanding of the modern world and that have been brought to light by revelation to a modern prophet, Joseph Smith. Many scriptures in the Bible, whose meanings have been obscured by the loss of continuing revelation, are discussed from the LDS perspective without an attempt to prove their revealed messages. Most of these interpretations represent LDS doctrines, but those that are the opinion of the author will be identified as such.

GOD SPOKE TO PROPHETS

One of the most fundamental principles of the Bible, in both the Old and the New Testaments, is the concept that God revealed his will to prophets and commanded them to preach to the people. Sometimes those prophets were allowed to see into the future, in which case they were also known as seers and revelators, revealing things to come as shown to them by God.

Many modern Bible scholars, who do not really believe in prophecy, have attributed the writings of Isaiah to multiple authors because of the prophecies about future events that occurred after Isaiah's lifetime. For the same reasons, these scholars typically date the synoptic gospels (Matthew, Mark, and Luke) to AD 70 or later because they contain the Olivet Discourse, Jesus's sermon in which he foretold the destruction of Jerusalem and its temple, which happened in about AD 69.[1]

However, as shown in chapter 3, the dating of the Isaiah Scrolls to centuries before the coming of Jesus Christ shows that the Messianic prophecies of Isaiah were not fabricated after the birth and resurrection of Christ.

For those who lack faith in the Lord's ability to allow prophets to see into the future, a careful examination of the first chapter of the book of Ezekiel might help. This chapter shows (in the opinion of this author) that the ancient prophet Ezekiel beheld a vision, which some have interpreted to be that of jet airplanes taking off and landing, and Ezekiel did his best to describe this bizarre scene in the language of his day, which clearly shows that God can reveal future events to his prophets. This interpretation is not my own, but it is not official doctrine of The Church of Jesus Christ of Latter-day Saints. However, as an aerospace engineer, it is easy for me to visualize Ezekiel's description of this vision, which must have been almost incredible to him.

Ezekiel 1:4–28

> And I looked, and, behold, a whirlwind came out of the north, a great cloud, and a fire infolding itself, and a brightness was about it, and out of the midst thereof as the colour of amber, out of the midst of the fire.
>
> Also out of the midst thereof came the likeness of four living creatures [four airplanes]. And this was their appearance; they had the likeness of a man [a man's head visible through the cockpit window].
>
> And every one had four faces [cockpit windows?], and every one had four wings.
>
> And their feet were straight feet; and the sole of their feet was like the sole of a calf's foot [two tires on each landing strut]: and they sparkled like the colour of burnished brass [wheel rims].
>
> And they had the hands of a man under their wings on their four sides [landing gears]; and they four had their faces and their wings.

Their wings were joined one to another; they turned not when they went; they went every one straight forward [just like jet airplanes].

As for the likeness of their faces, they four had the face of a man, and the face of a lion, on the right side: and they four had the face of an ox on the left side; they four also had the face of an eagle [possibly decals, or Ezekiel's best guess at describing these future vehicles].

Thus were their faces: and their wings were stretched upward [slight tilt upward]; two wings of every one were joined one to another [tail wings], and two covered their bodies [main wings].

And they went every one straight forward: whither the spirit [energy] was to go, they went; and they turned not when they went.

As for the likeness of the living creatures, their appearance was like burning coals of fire [jet exhaust flames], and like the appearance of lamps: it went up and down among the living creatures; and the fire was bright, and out of the fire went forth lightning.

And the living creatures ran and returned as the appearance of a flash of lightning.

Now as I beheld the living creatures, behold one wheel upon the earth by the living creatures, with his four faces.

The appearance of the wheels and their work was like unto the colour of a beryl: and they four had one likeness [they all looked the same]: and their appearance and their work was as it were a wheel in the middle of a wheel [wheel inside the tire].

When they went, they went upon their four sides: and they turned not when they went [flew straight, unlike birds].

As for their rings, they were so high that they were dreadful; and their rings were full of eyes round about them four [possibly lights on the wings].

And when the living creatures went, the wheels went by them: and when the living creatures were lifted up from the earth, the wheels were lifted up [landing gears retracted upon takeoff].

Whithersoever the spirit [energy] was to go, they went, thither was their spirit to go; and the wheels were lifted up over against them: for the spirit of the living creature was in the wheels [the only part seen to move was the retracting landing gear, indicating the spirit or life energy of the creatures].

When those went [wheels lifted up], these went [jet planes took off]; and when those stood [wheels came down], these stood [jet planes landed]; and when those were lifted up from the earth [jets took off], the wheels were lifted up over against them: for the spirit of the living creature was in the wheels.

> And the likeness of the firmament upon the heads of the living creature [pilot] was as the colour of the terrible crystal [cockpit glass], stretched forth over their heads above.
>
> And under the firmament were their wings straight, the one toward the other: every one had two, which covered on this side, and every one had two, which covered on that side, their bodies [fuselage].
>
> And when they went, I heard the noise of their wings [jet flight sounds], like the noise of great waters, as the voice of the Almighty, the voice of speech, as the noise of an host: when they stood [jet engines still running], they let down their wings.
>
> And there was a voice from the firmament that was over their heads, when they stood, and had let down their wings.
>
> And above the firmament that was over their heads was the likeness of a throne [Ezekiel's vision turned to the throne of God, even greater that the vision of jet airplanes], as the appearance of a sapphire stone: and upon the likeness of the throne was the likeness as the appearance of a man above upon it.
>
> And I saw as the colour of amber, as the appearance of fire round about within it, from the appearance of his loins even upward, and from the appearance of his loins even downward, I saw as it were the appearance of fire, and it had brightness round about.
>
> As the appearance of the bow that is in the cloud in the day of rain, so was the appearance of the brightness round about. This was the appearance of the likeness of the glory of the Lord. And when I saw it, I fell upon my face, and I heard a voice of one that spake.

This interpretation, when explained to me, gave me faith that prophets could have visions of future events, for, to me, this vision was Ezekiel's best effort to describe a squadron of modern jet airplanes taking off and landing. But this indescribable vision of the accomplishments of modern man pales in comparison to the vision of the glory of the Lord on his throne in heaven, which humbled Ezekiel to bow before the Lord.

Although Jehovah spoke to dozens of prophets throughout the Old Testament, the children of Israel frequently rejected the prophets and reverted to idol worship; so much of what was revealed may have been lost to that generation and needed to be restored by another prophet in a later generation. Thus, the need continues for new prophets to each generation.

THE ATONEMENT TAUGHT THROUGH SACRIFICES

Another fundamental principle taught throughout the Old Testament was that a Messiah would come and offer himself as a sacrifice for the sins of all mankind. From the beginning of biblical history, God required his children to offer sacrifices to Him. The sacrifice was to be the firstborn lamb or goat and was to be perfect, without blemish. This was symbolic of the sacrifice of the perfect firstborn Son of God, who would sacrifice himself to atone for the sins of all people. This important law of sacrifice was introduced to Adam and Eve and their sons by an angel of the Lord (see Moses 4:4–8),[2] and it continued for thousands of years among the Hebrews in an exact manner. The book of Leviticus describes five types of sacrifices to be made by priests of the tribe of the Levites, descendants of Aaron:[3]

1. The burnt offering (see Leviticus 1; 6:8–13)
2. The meat offering (see Leviticus 2; 6:14–18)
3. The peace offering (see Leviticus 3; 7:11–21)
4. The sin offering (see Leviticus 4:1–5:13; 6:24–30)
5. The trespass offering (see Leviticus 5:14–6:7; 7:1–10)

In addition to the sacrifices, the ancient Jews celebrated five festivals each year:[4]

1. Passover, or Feast of Unleavened Bread
2. Pentecost, or Weeks, fifty days after Passover
3. New Year (Ro'sh ha-Shannah)
4. The Day of Atonement (Yom Kippur), or Day of Fasting
5. Tabernacles

The celebration of the Feast of Hanukkah ("Dedication"), began after 142 BC to celebrate the dedication of the temple after the Maccabees drove out the Seleucid rulers (see chapter 1, Hellenization of the Jews).

The Passover feast was a sacred meal that commemorated the Lord's deliverance of the children of Israel from the angel of death, which killed all the firstborn in Egypt during the time of the plagues. The details of this meal are recorded in Exodus 12. An unblemished lamb was to be slaughtered, and the blood of the lamb was to be placed on the doorposts of the house, where people could see it. "The flesh of the lamb was to be roasted and eaten with unleavened bread and bitter herbs. Care was to be taken that no bones were broken in the lamb, and any of the flesh that remained was to be completely burnt as an offering to the Lord,"[5] symbolizing the total sacrifice that the Messiah would make.

The symbolism is even stronger in the rituals celebrated on the Day of Atonement. On that day, the high priest brought a bullock to the altar as a sin offering, a ram as a burnt offering for himself and his house, and two male goats and a ram for the children of Israel. "He cast lots over the two goats, designating one as a sin offering to the Lord and the other as the 'scapegoat.'"[6]

"The priest killed the bullock and the goat for the sin offerings and entered the Holy of Holies, stepping into the presence of the Lord. There he offered incense before the Lord and sprinkled the blood of the bullock and goat on the mercy seat, signifying the power of the Lord to cover over, or forgive, the sins of the high priest, his family, and all of the Israelites." The "scapegoat" was then brought forth, "and upon its head the high priest confessed all the sins of Israel, symbolizing for the people that, through repentance and the blood of the Atonement, their sins could be removed." The priests then "took the scapegoat into the wilderness, where they released it so it would wander off, carrying everyone's sins away."[7]

It is unclear how much the Jews understood the significance of the symbolism of these sacrifices, but looking back on them from the hindsight of the New Testament, the significance is now hard to miss. The eating of the flesh of the lamb symbolized making the Lord a part of their lives, just as partaking of the sacrament—which symbolizes the body and blood of Christ in Catholic, Protestant, and LDS churches today—represents the acceptance of the sacrifice of the Savior. Instead of eating the bread of the last supper, the ancient Hebrews ate the meat of the sacrificial lamb, which represented the body and blood of the Messiah, who was to be offered for their sins. They released the scapegoat to symbolically carry away their sins, representing the Atonement whereby the Messiah would suffer for the sins of those who repent.

THE ATONEMENT TAUGHT THROUGH THE ARK OF THE COVENANT AND THE MERCY SEAT

After Jehovah gave the ten commandments to Moses on two stone tablets, he commanded Moses to build an ark, or box, of shittim wood, overlaid with pure gold, to house the "testimony," or commandments of the law. On the lid of the ark, and therefore above the law that the ark held, Moses was commanded to construct the mercy seat of shittim wood overlaid with pure gold. The ark was placed in the Holy of Holies of the Tabernacle, and once each year on Yum Kippur, the Jewish Day of Atonement, the high priest would enter the Holy of Holies and sprinkle the blood of the sacrificial lamb upon the mercy seat to signify that the sacrificial blood of the Lamb of God would provide atonement for the sins of the high priest and all the people. The type, or symbol, of the blood of Jesus Christ, who was Jehovah of the Old Testament, was shown in this sacred ordinance to be above the law, or greater than the law, in bringing salvation to the children of God. It was not the law or commandments that would bring about the atonement but the sacrificial blood of the Lamb of God. Once again, the symbolism seems to have been lost on the people, who later failed to understand the significance of the ordinances that they performed and observed so strictly.[8]

THE RESURRECTION

Although a belief in resurrection was certainly not universal among the Jews at the time of Jesus's ministry, this belief was professed by the Pharisees. Hellenization of Jewish religion had caused the Sadducees to reject the doctrine, but the Pharisees professed this belief, based on a number of Old Testament prophecies:

> The Lord killeth, and maketh alive: he bringeth down to the grave, and bringeth up. (1 Samuel 2:6)

> If a man die, shall he live again? All the days of my appointed time will I wait, till my change come. (Job 14:14)

> For I know that my redeemer liveth, and that he shall stand at the latter day upon the earth: And though after my skin worms destroy this body, yet in my flesh shall I see God. (Job 19:25–26)

> He will swallow up death in victory; and the Lord God will wipe away tears from off all faces; and the rebuke of his people shall he take away from off all the earth: for the Lord hath spoken it. (Isaiah 25:8)

> Thy dead men shall live, together with my dead body shall they arise. Awake and sing, ye that dwell in dust: for thy dew is as the dew of herbs, and the earth shall cast out the dead. (Isaiah 26:19)

> Therefore prophesy and say unto them, Thus saith the Lord God; Behold, O my people, I will open your graves, and cause you to come up out of your graves, and bring you into the land of Israel.
> And ye shall know that I am the Lord, when I have opened your graves, O my people, and brought you up out of your graves,
> And shall put my spirit in you, and ye shall live, and I shall place you in your own land: then shall ye know that I the Lord have spoken it, and performed it, saith the Lord. (Ezekiel 37:12–14)

> I will ransom them from the power of the grave; I will redeem them from death: O death, I will be thy plagues; O grave, I will be thy destruction: repentance shall be hid from mine eyes. (Hosea 13:14)

MAN WAS CREATED IN THE LIKENESS AND IMAGE OF GOD

> And God said, Let us make man in our image, after our likeness: and let them have dominion over the fish of the sea, and over the fowl of the air, and over the cattle, and over all the earth, and over every creeping thing that creepeth upon the earth.
> So God created man in his own image, in the image of God created he him; male and female created he them. (Genesis 1:26–27)

This scripture indicates that a plurality of gods participated in the creation—"Let us make man in our image"—and implies that if men and women are created in the image of God, then God must have a body resembling that of men and women. Further, it shows that as well as a Heavenly Father, we also have a Heavenly Mother ("male and female created he them"). The Hebrew name of Elohim, which is found in the Hebrew Bible, is a plural name indicating a plurality of gods.

The plurality of gods is explained in John 1, which identifies Jesus as the Word, who was in the beginning with God, and who was a God who created all things that were made. If Jesus was in the beginning with God, then God was his Heavenly Father. Jesus was Jehovah, the Spirit God of the Old Testament, who was the God of this earth, was born in the flesh to the virgin Mary, and spent his earthly life doing only what his Heavenly Father commanded him to do. Thus, Jesus and his Heavenly Father, to whom he prayed during his earthly ministry, were Elohim, or the Gods who together created the heavens and the earth, according to Genesis and John 1.

WHO IS GOD AND WHAT IS HIS NATURE?

This is one of the most fundamental questions men and women ask in trying to determine their relationship to God, and the one that creates the most confusion about religion.

The Nicene Creed

In AD 325, the Emperor Constantine called a council of bishops at Nicaea to settle a dispute about the nature of God. Arius (a presbyter of Alexandria who was the founder of Arianism) argued that the Son was created from the nonexistent and was of a different substance than the Father. Athanasius of Alexandria, the champion of orthodoxy, stressed the oneness of God while maintaining that there were three distinct Persons within the Godhead. He maintained that the Son was the same substance as the Father (and hence, was fully divine). Athanasius argued for the eternally personal existence of the Son. A mediating position was set forth by Eusebius of Caesarea, who argued that the Son was of a similar substance with the Father. After considerable debate, Athanasius won out, and Christ was recognized by the council as being on a level with the Father as an uncreated Being. The dispute was finally settled by a vote of the bishops present, and the document that resulted became known as the Nicene Creed:

> I believe in one God the Father Almighty; Maker of heaven and earth, and of all things visible and invisible.
>
> And in one Lord Jesus Christ, the only-begotten Son of God, begotten of the Father before all worlds [God of God], Light of Light, very God of very God, begotten, not made, being of one substance [essence] with the Father; by whom all things were made; who, for us men and for our salvation, came down from heaven, and was incarnate by the Holy Ghost of the Virgin Mary, and was made man; and was crucified also for us under Pontius Pilate; He suffered and was buried; and the third day He rose again, according to the Scriptures; and ascended into heaven, and sitteth on the right hand

> of the Father; and He shall come again, with glory, to judge both the quick and the dead; whose kingdom shall have no end.
>
> *And [I believe] in the Holy Ghost, the Lord and Giver of Life; who proceedeth from the Father [and the Son]; who with the Father and the Son together is worshiped and glorified; who spake by the prophets. And [I believe] in one Holy Catholic and Apostolic Church. I acknowledge one Baptism for the remission of sins; and I look for the resurrection of the dead, and the life of the world to come. Amen.

*This paragraph was added in AD 381.

The Athanasian Creed

A later variation of the Nicene Creed became known as the Athanasian Creed, which added more confusion by introducing the doctrine of the trinity, which is not mentioned in the Bible.

> We worship one God in trinity, and trinity in unity, neither confounding the persons nor dividing the substance. For the person of the Father is one; of the Son, another; of the Holy Spirit, another. But the divinity of the Father and of the Son and of the Holy Spirit is one, the glory equal, the majesty equal. Such as is the Father, such also is the Son, and such the Holy Spirit. The Father is uncreated, the Son is uncreated, the Holy Spirit is uncreated. The Father is infinite, the Son is infinite, the Holy Spirit is infinite. The Father is eternal, the Son is eternal, the Holy Spirit is eternal. And yet there are not three eternal Beings, but one eternal Being. So also there are not three uncreated Beings, nor three infinite Beings, but one uncreated and one infinite Being. In like manner, the Father is omnipotent, the Son is omnipotent, and the Holy Spirit is omnipotent. And yet there are not three omnipotent Beings, but one omnipotent Being. Thus the Father is God, the Son is God, and the Holy Spirit is God. And yet there are not three Gods, but one God only. The Father is Lord, the Son is Lord, and the Holy Spirit is Lord. And yet there are not three Lords, but one Lord only. For as we are compelled by Christian truth to confess each person distinctively to be both God and Lord, we are prohibited by the Catholic religion to say that there are three Gods or Lords. The Father is made by none, nor created, nor begotten. The Son is from the Father alone, not made, not created, but begotten. The Holy Spirit is not created by the Father and the Son, nor begotten, but proceeds. Therefore, there is one Father, not three

Fathers; one Son, not three Sons; one Holy Spirit, not three Holy Spirits. And in this Trinity there is nothing prior or posterior, nothing greater or less, but all three persons are coeternal and coequal to themselves. So that through all, as was said above, both unity in trinity and trinity in unity is to be adored. Whoever would be saved, let him thus think concerning the Trinity.

The Westminster Confession of Faith

In 1643, the English Parliament commissioned the Westminster Assembly to develop a creed for the Church of England. This assembly met daily from 1643 to 1649 and produced the Westminster Confession of Faith:

> I. There is but one only living and true God, who is infinite in being and perfection, a most pure spirit, invisible, without body, parts, or passions, immutable, immense, eternal, incomprehensible, almighty, most wise, most holy, most free, most absolute, working all things according to the counsel of His own immutable and most righteous will, for His own glory; most loving, gracious, merciful, long-suffering, abundant in goodness and truth, forgiving iniquity, transgression, and sin; the rewarder of them that diligently seek Him; and withal most just and terrible in His judgments, hating all sin, and who will by no means clear the guilty.
>
> II. God hath all life, glory, goodness, blessedness, in and of Himself; and is alone in and unto Himself all-sufficient, not standing in need of any creatures which He hath made, nor deriving any glory from them, but only manifesting His own glory in, by, unto, and upon them: He is the alone fountain of all being, of whom, through whom, and to whom, are all things; and hath most sovereign dominion over them, to do by them, for them, and upon them, whatsoever Himself pleaseth. In His sight all things are open and manifest; His knowledge is infinite, infallible, and independent upon the creature, so as nothing is to Him contingent or uncertain. He is most holy in all His counsels, in all His works, and in all His commands. To Him is due from angels and men, and every other creature, whatsoever worship, service, or obedience He is pleased to require of them.
>
> In the unity of the Godhead there be three Persons of one substance, power, and eternity; God the Father, God the Son, and God the Holy Ghost. The Father is of none, neither begotten nor proceeding; the Son is eternally begotten of the Father; the Holy Ghost eternally proceeding from the Father and the Son.

Many faiths today profess God to be without body, parts, or passions, so large that he fills the whole universe but so small he can dwell in your heart.

But what does the Bible actually tell us about God? In Genesis, God said, "Let *us* create man in *our* image, after our likeness" (Genesis 1:26, emphasis added). But Jesus spoke of one God, saying, "I and my Father are one" (John 10:31). He also taught of the three members of the godhead when he said, "Go ye therefore, and teach all nations, baptizing them in the name of the Father, and of the Son, and of the Holy Ghost" (Matthew 28:19). This issue is so important that we cannot rely on only the Old Testament or the New Testament, but we must use both plus modern revelation to discern the true nature of God.

The Old Testament uses various names for God, which are sometimes used interchangeably, as if the scribes who copied the texts were unsure of the differences. The names used for God are Elohim, Yhwh, and Jehovah.

The Hebrew word *Eloha* means "God," and its plural *Elohim* means "Gods." The name *Elohim* does not appear in the King James Version of the Bible, but it is the third word in the Hebrew text of Genesis and occurs frequently throughout the Hebrew Bible.

Latter-day Saints believe that Elohim is the name for Heavenly Father and that Jehovah was the name of his firstborn spirit Son, who created the earth with his Heavenly Father. They also believe that Jehovah—the Old Testament God of Abraham, Isaac, and Jacob—was born to the virgin Mary as the baby Jesus.

John 1:1–5, 10–17

> In the beginning was the Word, and the Word was with God, and the Word was God.
>
> The same was in the beginning with God.
>
> All things were made by him; and without him was not any thing made that was made.
>
> In him was life; and the life was the light of men.
>
> And the light shineth in darkness; and the darkness comprehended it not.
>
> He was in the world, and the world was made by him, and the world knew him not.
>
> He came unto his own, and his own received him not.
>
> But as many as received him, to them gave he power to become the sons of God, even to them that believe on his name:

> Which were born, not of blood, nor of the will of the flesh, nor of the will of man, but of God.
>
> And the Word was made flesh, and dwelt among us, (and we beheld his glory, the glory as of the only begotten of the Father,) full of grace and truth.
>
> John bare witness of him, and cried, saying, This was he of whom I spake, He that cometh after me is preferred before me: for he was before me.
>
> And of his fullness have all we received, and grace for grace.
>
> For the law was given by Moses, but grace and truth came by Jesus Christ.

When Jesus taught his disciples, he prayed to his Father in Heaven and taught them to do the same, which clearly indicates that he and Heavenly Father are two distinct individuals. So we are left with the question of why he on other occasions commented that he and his Father were one. This seeming difficulty can be explained by noting another instance when Jesus spoke of "being one," this time with a group of persons, and compared this oneness to that between himself and his Father. In the great intercessory prayer, Jesus prayed that he and his disciples would be one, as he and his Heavenly Father are one. Since the disciples were obviously separate beings, Jesus was not praying that he and they could be one flesh but rather that they could be one—or unified—in purpose. In a similar manner, Jesus and Heavenly Father were already unified in purpose, because, as Jesus said, he did only what his Father commanded him to do.

John 17:1–6, 20–21

> These words spake Jesus, and lifted up his eyes to heaven, and said, Father, the hour is come; glorify thy Son, that thy Son also may glorify thee:
>
> As thou hast given him power over all flesh, that he should give eternal life to as many as thou hast given him.
>
> And this is life eternal, that they might know thee the only true God, and Jesus Christ, whom thou hast sent.
>
> I have glorified thee on the earth: I have finished the work which thou gavest me to do.
>
> And now, O Father, glorify thou me with thine own self with the glory which I had with thee before the world was.
>
> I have manifested thy name unto the men which thou gavest me

> out of the world: thine they were, and thou gavest them me; and they have kept thy word.
>
> Neither pray I for these alone, but for them also which shall believe on me through their word;
>
> That they all may be one; as thou, Father, art in me, and I in thee, that they also may be one in us: that the world may believe that thou hast sent me.

Some Protestant denominations have confused the nature of the Godhead, calling it a Trinity that is somehow mystical in that God (Heavenly Father), Jesus Christ, and the Holy Ghost are different manifestations of the same being. If this were the case, then Jesus in the intercessory prayer would have been praying to himself. If the Westminster Creed's statement that God is without body, parts, or passions, were true, then Jesus Christ's resurrection would have no significance. These sincere seekers of truth obviously had difficulty understanding the true nature of God by relying on the Bible alone.

But God certainly didn't intend for his nature to be such a mystery. In recent history, God has cleared up these misconceptions in an unmistakable manner. When Joseph Smith, the Mormon prophet, was a fourteen-year-old boy, he went to a grove of trees near his father's farm to pray about which church to join. In response to his prayer, God himself and his Son Jesus Christ appeared and spoke with him. Describing this experience, Joseph Smith said,

> I saw a pillar of light exactly over my head, above the brightness of the sun, which descended gradually until it fell upon me. When the light rested upon me I saw two Personages, whose brightness and glory defy all description, standing above me in the air. One of them spake unto me, calling me by name and said, pointing to the other—*This is My Beloved Son. Hear Him!*

As a result of this vision, Joseph learned that Heavenly Father and Jesus Christ are separate and distinct individuals, both glorified and perfected in immortal, physical, resurrected bodies. We then are literal children of our Heavenly Father, as the scriptures teach, and as such are heirs to his kingdom, based on the Atonement of his Only Begotten Son.

The Son of Man

Another name for the Savior in the scriptures is "The Son of Man." But if he was born of the virgin Mary with God (Heavenly Father) as his father, why then is he called the Son of Man?

This question was answered by the Lord in a revelation to Moses, which was also given to the Prophet Joseph Smith:

Moses 6:57

> Wherefore teach it unto your children, that all men, everywhere, must repent, or they can in nowise inherit the kingdom of God, for no unclean thing can dwell there, or dwell in his presence; for, in the language of Adam, Man of Holiness is his name, and the name of his Only Begotten is the Son of Man, even Jesus Christ, a righteous Judge, who shall come in the meridian of time.

The ancient Hebrews were very careful not to blaspheme the name of God by frequent repetition of his name, so instead of calling the Messiah Son of Man of Holiness, the name was shortened to the Son of Man. (See Moses 6:57 above.)

WE LIVED AS SPIRITS IN HEAVEN BEFORE OUR BIRTH ON EARTH

The Lord revealed to the prophet Job that we lived with him in heaven before the creation of the earth:

Job 38:4–7

> Where wast thou when I laid the foundations of the earth? Declare, if thou hast understanding.
>
> Who hath laid the measures thereof, if thou knowest? Or who hath stretched the line upon it?
>
> Whereupon are the foundations thereof fastened? Or who laid the corner stone thereof;
>
> When the morning stars sang together, and all the sons of God shouted for joy?

How could all the sons of God shout for joy unless they lived as spirits before they were born in the flesh and before the cornerstone of the earth was laid? Why would God ask Job where he was when he, God, laid the foundations of the earth, if Job did not exist then as a spirit before his earthly birth? It is clear in this brief account that God was teaching Job about his premortal existence as a spirit son of God with all of the other "morning stars" waiting for their turn to be born in the flesh to experience their mortal life.

The same principle was expressed by the disciples of Jesus regarding a man who was born blind:

John 9:1–3

> And as Jesus passed by, he saw a man which was blind from his birth.
>
> And his disciples asked him, saying, Master, who did sin, this man, or his parents, that he was born blind?
>
> Jesus answered, Neither hath this man sinned, nor his parents: but that the works of God should be made manifest in him.

The disciples obviously understood the premortal existence of spirits and questioned if this man's sins in the pre-earth life caused him to be born blind. There is no reasonable explanation (other than reincarnation) of how a man could have sinned before he was born to cause himself to be born blind, unless he lived as a spirit before his birth. Since we know that the Jews did not believe in reincarnation, they must have understood the principle of the premortal existence of spirits in order to ask this question.

Jehovah also taught this principle to the prophet Jeremiah:

Jeremiah 1:4–5

> Then the word of the Lord came unto me, saying,
>
> Before I formed thee in the belly I knew thee; and before thou camest forth out of the womb I sanctified thee, and I ordained thee a prophet unto the nations.

This revelation to Jeremiah indicates that in a pre-earth spiritual existence, the spirit of Jeremiah was foreordained to be a prophet in his earthly existence. This principle differs from predestination, in that Jeremiah still had his freedom to choose whether he would follow the Lord in this life.

CONCLUSIONS

The Old Testament clearly proclaims that the heavens and the earth were created by God (or gods) and that men and women were made in the image of God. It also shows that God revealed his will to men on earth through prophets. The ancient scripture traces the history of the twelve tribes of Israel and outlines a form of sacrificial worship symbolic of the sacrifice to be made by the Messiah for the Atonement of sins so that men and women may return to live with God, their Heavenly Father. It prophesies of the resurrection, and it is clear that the sect of the Pharisees described in the New Testament and by Josephus believed in the resurrection. The New Testament prophets reveal that Jesus Christ was Jehovah, the God of Abraham, Isaac, and Jacob and the creator of all things.

The Old Testament doctrines, which are sometimes obscured by lack of modern revelation, include multiple gods (Heavenly Father and Jehovah) as the creators and teach that man was created in the likeness and image of God. They teach that all men and women existed as spirits in heaven before the creation of the earth and shouted for joy when they learned the plan of salvation. The creation story in Genesis shows that God gave man and woman the freedom, or right, to exercise their choice of good or evil. Later scriptures teach that they must pay the price of sin unless they accept the Atonement of the Messiah. Isaiah prophesied of the conditions of the birth of the Messiah, and Ezekiel preached the principle of the resurrection. The Old Testament sacrificial ordinances were types and symbols of the sacrifice that Jesus Christ would make for the salvation of mankind when he came to earth as the Messiah to fulfill the plan of salvation.

NOTES

1. Kent P. Jackson, *How the New Testament Came to Be* (Provo, UT: Brigham Young University, 2006), 33.
2. *The Book of Moses, An extract from the translation of the Bible as revealed to Joseph Smith the Prophet, June 1830–February 1831*, published by The Church of Jesus Christ of Latter-Day Saints as one of the books of the Pearl of Great Price, which is bound into the triple combination with the Book of Mormon and the Doctrine and Covenants. It was received by revelation from the Lord Jesus Christ to the Prophet Joseph Smith Jr. in conjunction with inspired revisions to the Bible to correct errant translations and add missing scriptures. It was first published in 1851.
3. S. Kent Brown and Richard Neitzel Holzapfel, *The Lost 500 Years* (Salt Lake City: Deseret Book, 2006), 152.
4. Ibid., 154.

5. Ibid.
6. Ibid., 155.
7. Ibid., 155–56.
8. Old Testament Student Manual, 174.

CHAPTER 5

THE CLAY TABLETS OF EBLA

> *That these made war with Bera king of Sodom, and with Birsha king of Gomorrah, Shinab king of Admah, and Shemeber king of Zeboiim, and the king of Bela, which is Zoar.*
>
> *Genesis 14:2*

ANOTHER EXCITING DISCOVERY OF AN ENTIRE ARCHIVE OF BURIED records that parallels the significance of the Dead Sea Scrolls is the excavation of the clay tablets of Ebla. Archaeologist Paolo Matthiae of the University of Rome began excavating a mound known as Tell Mardikah in northern Syria in 1968, where he unearthed a statue dedicated to the goddess Eshtar bearing the name of Ibbit-Lim, a King of Ebla.

The inscription on the statue, written in the Akkadian language, was translated to read:

> For the goddess Eshtar, a basin did Ibbit-Lim, son of Igrish-Hepa, king of the people of Ebla, bring [into the temple]. He whose name Eshtar caused to shine in Ebla, even Ibbit-Lim, [had sculpted] a statue for his life and for the life of his children.[1]

Although the existence of Ebla was known from Egyptian and Akkadian inscriptions, its location remained a mystery until this discovery by Matthiae. He continued his excavations of Tell Mardikah until 1974 when he discovered a treasure trove of ancient records on clay tablets that had been fired to preserve them.

Bermant and Weitzman record:

> Working in the remains of what had been the royal palace, he [Matthiea] stumbled upon an archive of thousand upon thousand of clay tablets, some neatly stacked on their edges for easy retrieval, some cracked, some crumbling into dust, but together comprising one of the most remarkable archaeological finds of modern times.[2]

These authors quote Professor Matthiae with this description of his exciting discovery:

> The tablets cover a period of a thousand years before Abraham, and a thousand years, even in the fourth millennium before Christ, was a very, very long time. They tell us much, but what they don't tell us—what they can't tell us—is whether the Bible is true or not. They have nothing to do with the Bible, at least not directly, and what we have here is not a biblical expedition. If we have tablets with legends similar to those in the Bible it means only that such legends existed round here long before the Bible.[3]

Over 20,000 clay tablets, written in cuneiform, were found in an archive room of a buried palace, resulting in excellent preservation of these ancient documents. About 80 percent of the tablets were written in the Sumerian language, but 20 percent were in an unknown language that scholars dubbed Eblaite.[4] Translation of these documents was made possible by discovery in the archive of the oldest known dictionary, which consisted of a bilingual list of Sumerian and Eblaite words.[5]

The tablets have been dated to about 2275 BC by carbon-dating the wood from the palace. Although they are not the oldest known writings, they constitute the oldest extensive archive ever discovered. Translation of the tablets reveals that Ebla was a city of 260,000 citizens of Semite origin.[6] Only a small number of these tablets have been completely translated, but thousands have been "catalogued and classified under their economic, administrative, historical, literary and lexical headings."[7] They describe the extensive business transactions of a thriving influential empire of a previously unknown culture predating Abraham.[8]

The majority of these documents are extensive trade records, including ledgers, daybooks, and inventories, but they also reveal exorbitant tributes of tons of silver and hundreds of pounds of gold,[9] received from conquered neighbors, which gives credence to the Biblical account of six hundred threescore talents of gold that Solomon received in one year (1 Kings 10:14). The tablets also include Eblaite laws assessing a fine for seduction of an unmarried virgin and death for rape.[10] These discoveries refute arguments by some historians who doubted that Moses could have written the law of Moses in his lifetime, presuming that Moses predated written languages.

The most significant findings in the Ebla tablets in relation to the Bible are the listings of ancient cities mentioned in the Bible. The five cities of the plain, Sodom, Gommorah, Admah, Zeboiim, and Bela which is Zoar, were found on one tablet in the exact order listed in Genesis 14:2. Also, one of the kings was listed with the same name given in Genesis, and Damascus is listed first on the same tablet.[11]

Genesis 14:2

> *That these* made war with Bera king of Sodom, and with Birsha king of Gomorrah, Shinab king of Admah, and Shemeber king of Zeboiim, and the king of Bela, which is Zoar.

Some Bible scholars have presumed that the tales of Sodom and Gomorrah were fables and not even real cities, since they had never been located, but the Ebla tablets establish them as real cities. Multiple excavations of the sites of Bab edh-Dhra and Numeira on the Jordanian side of the Red Sea have led some modern archaeologists to conclude that they are excellent candidates for the ancient cities of Sodom and Gomorrah. Both cities were destroyed by fire at about the same time, which some archaeologists date to 2350 BC, but according to the Ebla tablets, both were still viable cities when this clay tablet was inscribed, listing them before 2275 BC.

The Bible says that the Lord rained fire and brimstone on the cities of the plain:

Genesis 19:24–25

> Then the Lord rained upon Sodom and upon Gomorrah brimstone and fire from the Lord out of heaven;
>
> And he overthrew those cities, and all the plain, and all the inhabitants of the cities, and that which grew upon the ground.

Brimstone is defined in the dictionary as sulfur, and evidence of sulfuric ash has been found at the sites of Bab edh-Dhra and Numeira.

Other cities found listed in the Ebla tablets include Salem,[12] (which later became Jeru-Salem), and Ur of Haran.[13] Ur and Haran are both mentioned in Genesis 11:31

> And Terah took Abram his son, and Lot the son of Haran his son's son, and Sarai his daughter in law, his son Abram's wife; and they went forth with them from Ur of the Chaldees, to go into the land of Canaan; and they came unto Haran, and dwelt there.

The tablets also include the use of several personal names, which shows that they were common around 2300 BC, including: Abramu [Abraham], Ishmail [Ishmael], and Ishril [Israel].[14]

Three versions of a text described as an Eblaite creation hymn have been found. They have been translated by Pettinato as

Lord of heaven and earth:
The earth was not, you created it,
The light of day was not, you created it,
The morning light you had not [yet] made exist.[15]

CONCLUSIONS

The clay tablets discovered at the archaeological site known as Ebla in Syria are public records of an ancient city dating to 2500 BC. These records confirm many early cities and names found in the early Old Testament record and help support the validity of the scriptures we have today, including the creation story.

NOTES

1. Chaim Bermant and Michael Weitzman, *Ebla, A Revelation in Archaeology* (New York: Times Books, a division of the New York Times, 1979), 144.
2. Ibid., 4.
3. Ibid., 2.

4. Vernon Mattson Jr., *The Dead Sea Scrolls and Other Important Discoveries* (Tampa, FL: Buried Records Productions, 1979), 47.
5. Chaim Bermant and Michael Weitzman, *Ebla*, 158.
6. Ibid., 153.
7. Ibid., 151.
8. Ibid., 2.
9. Ibid., 160.
10. Ibid., 160.
11. Ibid., 187.
12. Ibid., 195.
13. Ibid., 190.
14. Ibid., 184.
15. Craig Davis Jr., *Dating the Old Testament* (New York: RJ Communications, 2007), 93.

SECTION 2

THE NEW TESTAMENT AND HISTORICAL EVIDENCE OF JESUS

CHAPTER 6

THE MINISTRY OF CHRIST AND THE ESTABLISHMENT OF HIS CHURCH

And he gave some, apostles; and some, prophets; and some, evangelists; and some, pastors and teachers;

For the perfecting of the saints, for the work of the ministry, for the edifying of the body of Christ:

Till we all come in the unity of the faith, and of the knowledge of the Son of God, unto a perfect man, unto the measure of the stature of the fullness of Christ.

Ephesians 4:11–13

DURING THE FINAL THREE YEARS OF JESUS CHRIST'S MORTAL LIFE, he organized a church that he endowed with his priesthood authority. After performing the ordinance of washing his apostles' feet, as described in John chapter 13, Jesus continued to instruct the apostles. He said, "Ye have not chosen me, but I have chosen you, and ordained you, that ye should go and bring forth fruit, and that your fruit should remain: that whatsoever ye shall ask of the Father in my name, he may give it you" (John 15:16).

In the light of modern revelation, this scripture indicates that Jesus conferred his priesthood authority upon the apostles through ordination (by laying his hands on them and ordaining them to the priesthood office of apostle). Later, using this priesthood power, they healed the sick and caused the lame to walk. The office of apostle was to be a prophet, a missionary, and a special witness to the ministry and teachings of the Lord Jesus Christ.

THE MELCHIZEDEK PRIESTHOOD

The office of apostle belonged to the Melchizedek, or higher, priesthood, of which Jesus Christ was the great high priest, as noted in Hebrews 4:14; 5:10; and Psalm 110:4.

> Seeing then that we have a great high priest, that is passed into the heavens, Jesus the Son of God, let us hold fast our profession. (Hebrews 4:14)

> Though he were a Son, yet learned he obedience by the things which he suffered;
>
> And being made perfect, he became the author of eternal salvation unto all them that obey him;
>
> Called of God an high priest after the order of Melchisedec. (Hebrews 5:8–10)

> The Lord said unto my Lord, Sit thou at my right hand, until I make thine enemies thy footstool.
>
> The Lord shall send the rod of thy strength out of Zion: rule thou in the midst of thine enemies.
>
> Thy people shall be willing in the day of thy power, in the beauties of holiness from the womb of the morning: thou hast the dew of thy youth.
>
> The Lord hath sworn, and will not repent, Thou art a priest for ever after the order of Melchizedek. (Psalm 110:1–4)

Melchizedek was the king of Salem (which later became Jerusalem), the high priest to whom Abraham paid his tithes, as noted in Genesis 14:

> And Melchizedek king of Salem brought forth bread and wine: and he was the priest of the most high God.
>
> And he blessed him, and said, Blessed be Abram of the most high God, possessor of heaven and earth:
>
> And blessed be the most high God, which hath delivered thine enemies into thy hand. And he gave him tithes of all. (Genesis 14:18–20)

The Lord revealed the history of the Melchizedek Priesthood to

Joseph Smith to enable the restoration of the original Church with the same priesthood held anciently, as noted in Doctrine and Covenants 107:1–6:

> There are, in the church, two priesthoods, namely, the Melchizedek and Aaronic, including the Levitical Priesthood.
>
> Why the first is called the Melchizedek Priesthood is because Melchizedek was such a great high priest.
>
> Before his day it was called *the Holy Priesthood, after the Order of the Son of God.*
>
> But out of respect or reverence to the name of the Supreme Being, to avoid the too frequent repetition of his name, they, the church, in ancient days, called that priesthood after Melchizedek, or the Melchizedek Priesthood.
>
> All other authorities or offices in the church are appendages to this priesthood.
>
> But there are two divisions or grand heads—one is the Melchizedek Priesthood, and the other is the Aaronic or Levitical Priesthood.

The office of elder is another office of the Melchizedek Priesthood. The Old Testament is filled with references to "the Elders of Israel," which was a ruling council for the Jews. Paul also ordained elders in the Christian Church, as noted in Acts 14:21–23:

> And when they had preached the gospel to that city, and had taught many, they returned again to Lystra, and to Iconium, and Antioch,
>
> Confirming the souls of the disciples, and exhorting them to continue in the faith, and that we must through much tribulation enter into the kingdom of God.
>
> And when they had ordained them elders in every church, and had prayed with fasting, they commended them to the Lord, on whom they believed.

Here again, the office of elder in the Melchizedek Priesthood was conferred by ordination from an apostle or another elder who had the authority from an apostle, and hence from Jesus Christ, to perform the ordination. With the priesthood authority, elders were able to anoint the sick and bless them through their faith to be healed, as noted in James 5:14–15:

> Is any sick among you? let him call for the elders of the church; and

> let them pray over him, anointing him with oil in the name of the Lord: And the prayer of faith shall save the sick, and the Lord shall raise him up; and if he have committed sins, they shall be forgiven him.

THE AARONIC PRIESTHOOD

The Aaronic Priesthood is named after Aaron, the brother of Moses, who was of the tribe of Levi, whom the Lord called to this lesser priesthood to be a spokesman for Moses as noted in Exodus 4:10–16:

> And Moses said unto the Lord, O my Lord, I am not eloquent, neither heretofore, nor since thou hast spoken unto thy servant: but I am slow of speech, and of a slow tongue.
>
> And the Lord said unto him, Who hath made man's mouth? Or who maketh the dumb, or deaf, or the seeing, or the blind? Have not I the Lord?
>
> Now therefore go, and I will be with thy mouth, and teach thee what thou shalt say.
>
> And he said, O my Lord, send, I pray thee, by the hand of him whom thou wilt send.
>
> And the anger of the Lord was kindled against Moses, and he said, Is not Aaron the Levite thy brother? I know that he can speak well. And also, behold, he cometh forth to meet thee: and when he seeth thee, he will be glad in his heart.
>
> And thou shalt speak unto him, and put words in his mouth: and I will be with thy mouth, and with his mouth, and will teach you what ye shall do.
>
> And he shall be thy spokesman unto the people: and he shall be, even he shall be to thee instead of a mouth, and thou shalt be to him instead of God.

From that time forward, the descendents of Levi were assigned to officiate as priests after the Priesthood of Aaron, as noted in Numbers 3:5–10:

> And the Lord spake unto Moses, saying,
>
> Bring the tribe of Levi near, and present them before Aaron the priest, that they may minister unto him.
>
> And they shall keep his charge, and the charge of the whole congregation before the tabernacle of the congregation, to do the service of the tabernacle.
>
> And they shall keep all the instruments of the tabernacle of the

> congregation, and the charge of the children of Israel, to do the service of the tabernacle.
>
> And thou shalt give the Levites unto Aaron and to his sons: they are wholly given unto him out of the children of Israel.
>
> And thou shalt appoint Aaron and his sons, and they shall wait on their priest's office.

John the Baptist held the office of a priest in the Aaronic Priesthood and was the last legitimate holder of this priesthood at the time of the baptism of Jesus.

Jesus established other offices of the priesthood, as Paul reported in Ephesians 4:11–12:

> And he gave some, apostles; and some, prophets; and some, evangelists; and some, pastors and teachers;
>
> For the perfecting of the saints, for the work of the ministry, for the edifying of the body of Christ.

The pastors noted in Ephesians 4:11 correspond with priests of the Aaronic Priesthood. Other offices in the Aaronic Priesthood include bishop, priest, teacher, and deacon. Although bishops and deacons are not mentioned in Ephesians 4:11, Paul described their qualifications in 1 Timothy 3:1–13:

> This is a true saying, If a man desire the office of a bishop, he desireth a good work.
>
> A bishop then must be blameless, the husband of one wife, vigilant, sober, of good behaviour, given to hospitality, apt to teach;
>
> Not given to wine, no striker, not greedy of filthy lucre; but patient, not a brawler, not covetous;
>
> One that ruleth well his own house, having his children in subjection with all gravity;
>
> (For if a man know not how to rule his own house, how shall he take care of the church of God?)
>
> Not a novice, lest being lifted up with pride he fall into the condemnation of the devil.
>
> Moreover he must have a good report of them which are without; lest he fall into reproach and the snare of the devil.
>
> Likewise must the deacons be grave, not doubletongued, not given to much wine, not greedy of filthy lucre;
>
> Holding the mystery of the faith in a pure conscience.
>
> And let these also first be proved; then let them use the office of a deacon, being found blameless.

> Even so must their wives be grave, not slanderers, sober, faithful in all things.
>
> Let the deacons be the husbands of one wife, ruling their children and their own houses well.
>
> For they that have used the office of a deacon well purchase to themselves a good degree, and great boldness in the faith which is in Christ Jesus.

THE PRIESTHOOD OFFICE OF THE SEVENTY

As further evidence that the Lord organized a Church while he was still on the earth, we see that he called and sent seventy elders as missionaries and sent them two by two into every city where he planned to go, to prepare the people for his teachings, as noted in Luke 10:1–2:

> After these things the Lord appointed other seventy also, and sent them two and two before his face into every city and place, whither he himself would come.
>
> Therefore said he unto them, The harvest truly is great, but the labourers are few: pray ye therefore the Lord of the harvest, that he would send forth labourers into his harvest.
>
> Go your ways: behold, I send you forth as lambs among wolves.

From modern revelation to Joseph Smith, we know that the Seventy was an office of the Mechizedek Priesthood with a missionary calling—the calling described as evangelists in Ephesians 4:11.

THE EARLY CHURCH WAS ORGANIZED BY PRIESTHOOD OFFICES

Thus the early Church, established by Jesus through his apostles, consisted of the priesthood offices of apostles, prophets, high priests, elders, Seventies (or evangelists), bishops, priests, teachers, and deacons. The higher priesthood, or Melchizedek Priesthood, included the offices of apostles (who were also prophets), high priests, and elders. The lesser priesthood, or Aaronic Priesthood, included the office of bishop, priest, teacher, and deacon. The apostles and seventy were traveling General Authorities, reporting to Jesus, while the bishops, priests, teachers, and deacons were local authorities whose duty was to administer to a local congregation.

DOCTRINES TAUGHT BY JESUS AND THE APOSTLES IN THE NEW TESTAMENT

The Commandment to Love

Jesus taught that the greatest commandments were "Thou shalt love the Lord thy God with all thy heart, and with all thy soul, and with all thy mind. This is the first and great commandment. And the second is like unto it, Thou shalt love thy neighbour as thyself" (Matthew 22:37–39). The writings of the apostles tell that he healed the sick, caused the lame to walk, made the blind to see, and even raised the dead.

The Beatitudes

Matthew 5:3–16

> Blessed are the poor in spirit: for theirs is the kingdom of heaven.
>
> Blessed are they that mourn: for they shall be comforted.
>
> Blessed are the meek: for they shall inherit the earth.
>
> Blessed are they which do hunger and thirst after righteousness: for they shall be filled.
>
> Blessed are the merciful: for they shall obtain mercy.
>
> Blessed are the pure in heart: for they shall see God.
>
> Blessed are the peacemakers: for they shall be called the children of God.
>
> Blessed are they which are persecuted for righteousness' sake: for theirs is the kingdom of heaven.
>
> Blessed are ye, when men shall revile you, and persecute you, and shall say all manner of evil against you falsely, for my sake.
>
> Rejoice, and be exceeding glad: for great is your reward in heaven: for so persecuted they the prophets which were before you.
>
> Ye are the salt of the earth: but if the salt have lost his savour, wherewith shall it be salted? it is thenceforth good for nothing, but to be cast out, and to be trodden under foot of men.
>
> Ye are the light of the world. A city that is set on an hill cannot be hid.
>
> Neither do men light a candle, and put it under a bushel, but on a candlestick; and it giveth light unto all that are in the house.
>
> Let your light so shine before men, that they may see your good works, and glorify your Father which is in heaven.

Faith

Matthew 17:20

> And Jesus said unto them, Because of your unbelief: for verily I say unto you, If ye have faith as a grain of mustard seed, ye shall say unto this mountain, Remove hence to yonder place; and it shall remove; and nothing shall be impossible unto you.

Repentance

Matthew 4:17

> From that time Jesus began to preach, and to say, Repent: for the kingdom of heaven is at hand.

Baptism

John 3:5

> Jesus answered, Verily, verily, I say unto thee, Except a man be born of water and of the Spirit, he cannot enter into the kingdom of God.

Being born of water is baptism. Being born of the spirit is receiving the ordinance of the Gift of the Holy Ghost. Jesus taught that all must be baptized by the water and the spirit to enter into the kingdom of heaven.

Mark 16:15–16

> And he said unto them, Go ye into all the world, and preach the gospel to every creature.
>
> He that believeth and is baptized shall be saved; but he that believeth not shall be damned.

Matthew 28:19–20

> Go ye therefore, and teach all nations, baptizing them in the name of the Father, and of the Son, and of the Holy Ghost:
>
> Teaching them to observe all things whatsoever I have commanded you: and, lo, I am with you alway, even unto the end of the world.

The Gift of the Holy Ghost

The Gift of the Holy Ghost (being born of the spirit) is an ordinance, like baptism, that is necessary for salvation, and it can only be performed by one holding the proper priesthood authority.

John 14:26

> But the Comforter, which is the Holy Ghost, whom the Father will send in my name, he shall teach you all things, and bring all things to your remembrance, whatsoever I have said unto you.

When Paul found disciples who had been baptized but had not heard of the Holy Ghost, he realized that they had not been taught and baptized by the proper authority, since Jesus taught that a man must be born of water and the spirit, so he baptized them again and bestowed the Gift of the Holy Ghost by the laying on of his hands.

Acts 19:1–6

> And it came to pass, that, while Apollos was at Corinth, Paul having passed through the upper coasts came to Ephesus: and finding certain disciples,
>
> He said unto them, Have ye received the Holy Ghost since ye believed? And they said unto him, We have not so much as heard whether there be any Holy Ghost.
>
> And he said unto them, Unto what then were ye baptized? And they said, Unto John's baptism.
>
> Then said Paul, John verily baptized with the baptism of repentance, saying unto the people, that they should believe on him which should come after him, that is, on Christ Jesus.
>
> When they heard this, they were baptized in the name of the Lord Jesus.
>
> And when Paul had laid his hands upon them, the Holy Ghost came on them; and they spake with tongues, and prophesied.

When Philip had baptized Samaritans and the apostles heard of his conversions, they sent Peter and John to perform this ordinance perhaps because Philip may not have had this priesthood power, which belongs only to the Melchizedec Priesthood, and not the Aaronic Priesthood, which Philip may have held.

Acts 8:5, 14–17

> Then Philip went down to the city of Samaria, and preached Christ unto them.

> Now when the apostles which were at Jerusalem heard that Samaria had received the word of God, they sent unto them Peter and John:
>
> Who, when they were come down, prayed for them, that they might receive the Holy Ghost:
>
> (For as yet he was fallen upon none of them: only they were baptized in the name of the Lord Jesus.)
>
> Then laid they their hands on them, and they received the Holy Ghost.

Obedience

Matthew 7:21

> Not every one that saith unto me, Lord, Lord, shall enter into the kingdom of heaven; but he that doeth the will of my Father which is in heaven.

Humility

Matthew 18:3–5

> And said, Verily I say unto you, Except ye be converted, and become as little children, ye shall not enter into the kingdom of heaven.
>
> Whosoever therefore shall humble himself as this little child, the same is greatest in the kingdom of heaven.
>
> And whoso shall receive one such little child in my name receiveth me.

Jesus Is the Promised Messiah

Jesus affirmed that he was Jehovah of the Old Testament, for which he was accused of blasphemy and would have been stoned had he not vanished from his accusers:

John 8:56–59

> Your father Abraham rejoiced to see my day: and he saw it, and was glad.
>
> Then said the Jews unto him, Thou art not yet fifty years old, and hast thou seen Abraham?

> Jesus said unto them, Verily, verily, I say unto you, Before Abraham was, I am.
>
> Then took they up stones to cast at him: but Jesus hid himself, and went out of the temple, going through the midst of them, and so passed by.

The translation of the Hebrew name YHWH, or Jehovah, is "I Am."

> Jesus used the phrase "I am" in many statements to His disciples, in John's book. For example, He says to the Samaritan woman regarding the Messiah, "I that speak unto thee am he" (John 4:26). To others He said, "I am the true bread" (John 6:35), "I am the living bread" (John 6:51), "I am the light of the world" (John 8:12), "I am the door of the sheep" (John 10:7), "I am the resurrection and the life" (John 11:25), "Ye call me Master and Lord: and ye say well; for so I am" (John 13:13), "I am the way, the truth, and the life" (John 14:6), and "I am the vine, ye are the branches" (John 15:5).[1]

When Moses asked God what his name was, he replied along these same lines:

Exodus 3:13–14

> And Moses said unto God, Behold, when I come unto the children of Israel, and shall say unto them, The God of your fathers hath sent me unto you; and they shall say to me, What is his name? what shall I say unto them?
>
> And God said unto Moses, I AM THAT I AM: and he said, Thus shalt thou say unto the children of Israel, I AM hath sent me unto you.

To the woman at Jacob's well in Samaria, Jesus proclaimed himself to be the Messiah:

John 4:25–26

> The woman saith unto him, I know that Messias cometh, which is called Christ: when he is come, he will tell us all things.
>
> Jesus saith unto her, I that speak unto thee am he.

Unity with the Father

John 17:11

> And now I am no more in the world, but these are in the world, and I come to thee. Holy Father, keep through thine own name those whom thou hast given me, that they may be one, as we are.

Jesus wanted his disciples to be unified with each other and with him, as he and his Father are unified.

Jesus Is the Good Shepherd

John 10:11–14

> I am the good shepherd: the good shepherd giveth his life for the sheep.
>
> But he that is an hireling, and not the shepherd, whose own the sheep are not, seeth the wolf coming, and leaveth the sheep, and fleeth: and the wolf catcheth them, and scattereth the sheep.
>
> The hireling fleeth, because he is an hireling, and careth not for the sheep.
>
> I am the good shepherd, and know my sheep, and am known of mine.

Jesus has other sheep (besides the Jews) who will hear his voice.

John 10:16

> And other sheep I have, which are not of this fold: them also I must bring, and they shall hear my voice; and there shall be one fold, and one shepherd.

Many people interpret this to mean that he will someday preach to the Gentiles, but when? In Matthew 15:24, the Lord said in response to a plea from a woman of Canaan, "I am not sent but to the lost sheep of the house of Israel."

The Book of Mormon tells of a Hebrew Prophet named Lehi, who was directed by the Lord to take his family and flee Jerusalem before the Babylonian captivity. The Book of Mormon records this family's wandering in the wilderness near the Red Sea for years before they built a ship and were guided by the Lord to a new promised land, which is believed by many Book of Mormon scholars to be Central America. The Book of Mormon tells of Christ's visit to Lehi's posterity after his resurrection in Jerusalem. These descendents of Lehi would be the other sheep that Jesus spoke about, since he was commanded to teach only the children of the covenant, the children of Israel. His apostles were commanded to preach to the Gentiles, but Jesus was not sent to teach them.

Jesus Will Voluntarily Lay Down His Life for the Sheep according to a Commandment from His Father

John 10:15, 17–18

> As the Father knoweth me, even so know I the Father: and I lay down my life for the sheep.
>
> Therefore doth my Father love me, because I lay down my life, that I might take it again.
>
> No man taketh it from me, but I lay it down of myself. I have power to lay it down, and I have power to take it again. This commandment have I received of my Father.

Jesus Promises Great Rewards for Those Who Believe on Him and Follow His Father

John 14:1–3

> Let not your heart be troubled: ye believe in God, believe also in me.
>
> In my Father's house are many mansions: if it were not so, I would have told you. I go to prepare a place for you.
>
> And if I go and prepare a place for you, I will come again, and receive you unto myself; that where I am, there ye may be also.

John 3:14–15

> And as Moses lifted up the serpent in the wilderness, even so must the Son of man be lifted up:
>
> That whosoever believeth in him should not perish, but have eternal life.

John 10:27–30

> My sheep hear my voice, and I know them, and they follow me:
>
> And I give unto them eternal life; and they shall never perish, neither shall any man pluck them out of my hand.

> My Father, which gave them me, is greater than all; and no man is able to pluck them out of my Father's hand.
>
> I and my Father are one.

1 Corinthians 2:9–11

> But as it is written, Eye hath not seen, nor ear heard, neither have entered into the heart of man, the things which God hath prepared for them that love him.
>
> But God hath revealed them unto us by his Spirit: for the Spirit searcheth all things, yea, the deep things of God.
>
> For what man knoweth the things of a man, save the spirit of man which is in him? even so the things of God knoweth no man, but the Spirit of God.

Salvation by Grace

The scriptures speak of two different salvations. The first is the salvation from physical death, which Christ overcame by the resurrection. The second is the salvation from the spiritual death, which means being separated from the Father and the Son in eternity. Salvation from the physical death, or resurrection, is a free gift to all men and women who ever lived or will ever live.

1 Corinthians 15:20–22

> But now is Christ risen from the dead, and become the firstfruits of them that slept.
>
> For since by man came death, by man came also the resurrection of the dead.
>
> For as in Adam all die, even so in Christ shall all be made alive.

Salvation from the spiritual death requires faith in Jesus Christ and obedience to his commandments, including repentance when we have sinned, in order to be worthy of his atoning sacrifice.

In the parable of the sheep and the goats (Matthew 25:31–46), Jesus described those who would "inherit the kingdom prepared for you from the foundation of the world" (verse 34). They are those who feed the hungry, clothe the naked, give drink to the thirsty, and take in strangers. In other words, they love their neighbors as themselves.

The last prophet to write in the Book of Mormon, Moroni, gave this assessment of the grace of Christ.

Moroni 10:32–33

> Yea, come unto Christ, and be perfected in him, and deny yourselves of all ungodliness; and if ye shall deny yourselves of all ungodliness, and love God with all your might, mind and strength, then is his grace sufficient for you, that by his grace ye may be perfect in Christ; and if by the grace of God ye are perfect in Christ, ye can in nowise deny the power of God.
>
> And again, if ye by the grace of God are perfect in Christ, and deny not his power, then are ye sanctified in Christ by the grace of God, through the shedding of the blood of Christ, which is in the covenant of the Father unto the remission of your sins, that ye become holy, without spot.

The Atonement

Jesus clearly taught that he was to be sacrificed for the sins of all men, as prophesied by all of the Old Testament prophets, in fulfillment of the types and symbols of the animal sacrifices practiced by the faithful Israelites. At the Last Supper, he instituted the sacrament, or the blessing and eating of bread and wine as symbols of his body and blood. Just as the eating of the meat of the sacrificial lamb was symbolic of accepting the sacrifice of the Messiah, the eating of the sacrament bread was to symbolize making the teachings of Jesus Christ a part of our bodies and minds. Jesus described himself as the "bread of life" and the "living water," and he taught that anyone who would partake of this bread would never hunger again and anyone who would drink of this living water would never thirst again. Partaking of these emblems of his body and blood represents acceptance of his sacrifice through repentance and keeping his commandments. In return, the partaker is given salvation from physical and spiritual death, and therefore eternal life.

The Resurrection

Jesus frequently taught his apostles about his coming death and resurrection, but they did not seem to comprehend it.

After Peter, James, and John witnessed the glorified Lord Jesus Christ conversing with Moses and Elias on the mount of transfiguration, the Lord told them to tell no man until after his resurrection.

Mark 9:9–10

And as they came down from the mountain, he charged them that they should tell no man what things they had seen, till the Son of man were risen from the dead.

And they kept that saying with themselves, questioning one with another what the rising from the dead should mean.

John 10:17–18

Therefore doth my Father love me, because I lay down my life, that I might take it again.

No man taketh it from me, but I lay it down of myself. I have power to lay it down, and I have power to take it again. This commandment have I received of my Father.

John 3:14–18

And as Moses lifted up the serpent in the wilderness, even so must the Son of man be lifted up:

That whosoever believeth in him should not perish, but have eternal life.

For God so loved the world, that he gave his only begotten Son, that whosoever believeth in him should not perish, but have everlasting life.

For God sent not his Son into the world to condemn the world; but that the world through him might be saved.

He that believeth on him is not condemned: but he that believeth not is condemned already, because he hath not believed in the name of the only begotten Son of God.

We Lived as Spirits before We Were Born

John 9:1–3

And as Jesus passed by, he saw a man which was blind from his birth.

And his disciples asked him, saying, Master, who did sin, this man, or his parents, that he was born blind?

Jesus answered, Neither hath this man sinned, nor his parents: but that the works of God should be made manifest in him.

This scripture clearly indicates that the apostles understood the doctrine of the premortal existence of spirits of all men as proclaimed to Jeremiah (Jeremiah 1:5) and to Job (Job 38:4–7).

We Are Children of God and Become Gods in Eternal Life

The Jews accused Jesus of blasphemy because he said, "I and my father are one." In his defense, Jesus cited a scripture from Psalms that identifies the children of the Most High as gods:

John 10:34–39

> Jesus answered them, Is it not written in your law, I said, Ye are gods?
>
> If he called them gods, unto whom the word of God came, and the scripture cannot be broken;
>
> Say ye of him, whom the Father hath sanctified, and sent into the world, Thou blasphemest; because I said, I am the Son of God?
>
> If I do not the works of my Father, believe me not.
>
> But if I do, though ye believe not me, believe the works: that ye may know, and believe, that the Father is in me, and I in him.
>
> Therefore they sought again to take him: but he escaped out of their hand.

Psalm 82:1–8

> God standeth in the congregation of the mighty; he judgeth among the gods.
>
> How long will ye judge unjustly, and accept the persons of the wicked? Selah.
>
> Defend the poor and fatherless: do justice to the afflicted and needy.
>
> Deliver the poor and needy: rid them out of the hand of the wicked.
>
> They know not, neither will they understand; they walk on in darkness: all the foundations of the earth are out of course.
>
> I have said, Ye are gods; and all of you are children of the most High.
>
> But ye shall die like men, and fall like one of the princes.
>
> Arise, O God, judge the earth: for thou shalt inherit all nations.

There Are Three Kingdoms in Heaven

The apostle Paul compared the three kingdoms in heaven to the glory of the sun, the moon, and the stars, and he stated that our bodies in the resurrection will be glorified with these different glories.

1 Corinthians 15:39–42

> All flesh is not the same flesh: but there is one kind of flesh of men, another flesh of beasts, another of fishes, and another of birds.
>
> There are also celestial bodies, and bodies terrestrial: but the glory of the celestial is one, and the glory of the terrestrial is another.
>
> There is one glory of the sun, and another glory of the moon, and another glory of the stars: for one star differeth from another star in glory.
>
> So also is the resurrection of the dead. It is sown in corruption; it is raised in incorruption:

2 Corinthians 12:1–5

> It is not expedient for me doubtless to glory. I will come to visions and revelations of the Lord.
>
> I knew a man in Christ above fourteen years ago, (whether in the body, I cannot tell; or whether out of the body, I cannot tell: God knoweth;) such an one caught up to the third heaven.
>
> And I knew such a man, (whether in the body, or out of the body, I cannot tell: God knoweth;)
>
> How that he was caught up into paradise, and heard unspeakable words, which it is not lawful for a man to utter.
>
> Of such an one will I glory: yet of myself I will not glory, but in mine infirmities.

Salvation for the Dead

For centuries since the birth of the early Church, multitudes of different religious denominations have struggled with the injustice of some people being saved because they had the opportunity for baptism while myriads of others did not. Some sects say that one must be baptized or they will be dammed to eternal hell with no chance of recovery. But this is not the doctrine taught by Jesus and his apostles.

John 5:24–29

> Verily, verily, I say unto you, He that heareth my word, and

> believeth on him that sent me, hath everlasting life, and shall not come into condemnation; but is passed from death unto life.
>
> Verily, verily, I say unto you, The hour is coming, and now is, when the dead shall hear the voice of the Son of God: and they that hear shall live.
>
> For as the Father hath life in himself; so hath he given to the Son to have life in himself;
>
> And hath given him authority to execute judgment also, because he is the Son of man.
>
> Marvel not at this: for the hour is coming, in the which all that are in the graves shall hear his voice,
>
> And shall come forth; they that have done good, unto the resurrection of life; and they that have done evil, unto the resurrection of damnation.

Peter tells that Jesus visited the dead in the spirit prison between his death and resurrection for the purpose of inaugurating the preaching to the dead so that they too could be heirs of salvation.

1 Peter 3:18–20

> For Christ also hath once suffered for sins, the just for the unjust, that he might bring us to God, being put to death in the flesh, but quickened by the Spirit:
>
> By which also he went and preached unto the spirits in prison;
>
> Which sometime were disobedient, when once the longsuffering of God waited in the days of Noah, while the ark was a preparing, wherein few, that is, eight souls were saved by water.

1 Peter 4:6

> For for this cause was the gospel preached also to them that are dead, that they might be judged according to men in the flesh, but live according to God in the spirit.

Baptism for the Dead

If a man or woman must be born of water and the spirit (receive baptism and the gift of the Holy Ghost) to enter the kingdom of heaven, what would be the purpose for the Lord to visit the spirits in prison, since they had not received these essential saving ordinances? What about all of the righteous children of Israel who had lived the commandments of Jehovah from the beginning of the world but had not had the opportunity for baptism? Are they to be denied salvation?

The answer to that last question is definitively no. Jesus taught his apostles that the ordinance of baptism may be performed for the dead by proxies on earth. The concept is that the spirits in prison are to be taught by those from paradise who accepted the gospel and were baptized while on the earth. Jesus inaugurated the preaching of the gospel to the spirits in prison but then delegated this preaching to others to carry on.

The fact that apostles in the early Church were practicing the ordinance of baptism for the dead is documented by Paul as he struggled to get the Sadducees who had converted to the Church to believe in the resurrection.

1 Corinthians 15:29

> Else what shall they do which are baptized for the dead, if the dead rise not at all? why are they then baptized for the dead?

This scripture clearly teaches that baptism for the dead was practiced in the early Church, but this is the only mention of this practice or doctrine recorded in the New Testament as we have it today. However, some of the books of the New Testament Apocrypha, which were not included in the New Testament canon, do record this practice.

Hugh W. Nibley, in his article *Baptism for the Dead in Ancient Times*, after discussing the secrecy that the resurrected Lord imposed on the apostles regarding his teachings during the forty days following his resurrection, provides his assessment of these secret teachings to the apostles:

> In 1895 there was found in Egypt a Coptic papyrus purporting to contain an account of the teaching of Christ to his apostles after the resurrection. . . . The subject of this epistle was salvation for the dead, a doctrine which . . . was believed in the early church to have been the main theme of Christ's teaching after the resurrection.
>
> What lends weight to these considerations is the fact that it was the common belief in the early church that the subject of that last great discourse was nothing less than salvation for the dead: indeed, that was only to be expected, the Lord having just returned from his own mission to the spirit world. While it was a favorite device of the Gnostics to gain a following in the church by claiming to possess

written accounts of the secret teachings of Christ after the resurrection, the rest of the church was not backward in producing scriptures dealing with salvation for the dead and bearing such titles as "The testament which our Lord Jesus Christ made with his apostles after his resurrection from the dead and the instructions which he gave them," some of these texts being of great antiquity and held to be authentic by the strictest Christians. The mere existence of these works is indicative of the keen interest that the Saints still felt in a subject that the later church ignored. The fact that the Gnostics were able to gain an immense and immediate success in the church by spurious versions of these "last and highest revelations" shows that they were exploiting a genuine hunger that the central church could no longer satisfy. We shall deal with this problem later.

Speaking of 1 Corinthians 15:29, Tertullian expostulated:

> Now if some of them are "baptized for the dead," can we not assume that they have a reason for it? Certainly he [Paul] is maintaining that they practiced this in the belief that the ordinance would be a vicarious baptism and as such be advantageous to the flesh of others, which they assumed would be resurrected, for unless this referred to a physical resurrection there would be no point in carrying out a physical baptism.

At the beginning of the fifth century, Epiphanius reported:

> From Asia and Gaul has reached us the account [tradition] of a certain practice, namely that when any die without baptism among them, they baptize others in their place and in their name, so that, rising in the resurrection, they will not have to pay the penalty of having failed to receive baptism, but rather will become subject to the authority of the Creator of the World. For this reason this tradition which has reached us is said to be the very thing to which the apostle himself refers when he says, "If the dead rise not at all, what shall they do who are baptized for the dead?"

Who in the church performed the actual ordinance of baptizing for the dead? It was "those apostles and teachers" of the first generation, according to the Shepherd of Hermas, who "went down living into the water" in behalf of those who had died and in speaking of the whole affair as a thing of the past that source implies that the work was confined to those men and their generation. This is clearly borne out in our other accounts.[2]

HISTORICAL SOURCE ON THE LIFE OF JESUS

Josephus, a Jewish historian who was aligned with the Romans after the siege of Jerusalem in AD 70, wrote the following:

> Now there was about this time Jesus, a wise man, if it be lawful to call him a man; for he was a doer of wonderful works, a teacher of such men as receive the truth with pleasure. He drew over to him both many of the Jews and many of the Gentiles. He was [the] Christ. And when Pilate, at the suggestion of the principal men amongst us, had condemned him to the cross, (9) those that loved him at the first did not forsake him; for he appeared to them alive again the third day; (10) as the divine prophets had foretold these and ten thousand other wonderful things concerning him. And the tribe of Christians, so named from him, are not extinct at this day.[3]

CONCLUSIONS

Jesus, while he was yet on the earth, established a church organized by priesthood offices, consisting of the Melchizedek and Aaronic Priesthood holders who were ordained by the apostles who held this priesthood authority. He identified himself as the Great "I AM" of the Old Testament and as the King or Messiah of the Jews for which he was eventually crucified by the Romans. He healed the lame and the blind and raised several people from the dead. He fulfilled his Father's will by offering himself as a sacrifice to atone for the sins of all men and women. He became the first person ever to be resurrected, and he showed his immortal body to his apostles, who lived out their lives bearing testimony of his divinity and resurrection. He taught his apostles for forty days after his resurrection and directed them to go into all the world, baptizing in the name of the Father and the Son and the Holy Ghost.

In his ministry, he taught the two greatest commandments are to "love the Lord thy God with all thy heart, and with all thy soul, and with all thy mind, and with all thy strength" and to "love thy neighbour as thyself" (Mark 12:30–31). He taught the principles of faith in the Lord Jesus Christ, repentance for our transgressions, baptism, and receiving the gift of the Holy Ghost, which principles the apostles continued to teach after his ascension. He substituted the sacrament of bread and wine for the animal sacrifices, since he fulfilled the ultimate sacrifice of God for man and was resurrected to give the gift of the resurrection to all men. He promised eternal life with him and his Father to those who would believe on him, be baptized in his name, obey his commandments, and repent when they sin.

The apostles were also prophets and were special witnesses to the ministry, crucifixion, and resurrection of Jesus Christ. The gospel, or good news message, that the apostles preached was that Jesus of Nazareth was the long-predicted Messiah, who was the sacrificial lamb of God who died for the sins of all the world and was resurrected so that everyone will be resurrected. Under great persecution, they gave their lives for their testimonies, which have remained powerful and convincing to hundreds of millions two thousand years later.

NOTES

1. David H. Yarn Jr., "Some Metaphysical Reflections on the Gospel of John," *BYU Studies* 3, no. 1 (1960): 1.
2. Hugh W. Nibley, *Baptism for the Dead in Ancient Times, Mormonism and Early Christianity*, vol. 4 of *The Collected Works of Hugh Nibley* (Salt Lake City: Deseret Book and FARMS, 1987), 100–67.
3. Josephus, *Antiquities of the Jews* 18.3.3. Note 9 reads: A.D. 33, April 3. Note 10 reads: April 5.

CHAPTER 7

THE MINISTRY OF THE APOSTLES

> *And he said unto them, Go ye into all the world, and preach the gospel to every creature.*
>
> *Mark 16:15*

THE CALLING OF THE TWELVE AND THEIR NAMES ARE GIVEN IN Mark 3:14–19.

> And he ordained twelve, that they should be with him, and that he might send them forth to preach,
>
> And to have power to heal sicknesses, and to cast out devils:
>
> And Simon he surnamed Peter;
>
> And James the son of Zebedee, and John the brother of James; and he surnamed them Boanerges, which is, The sons of thunder:
>
> And Andrew, and Philip, and Bartholomew, and Matthew, and Thomas, and James the son of Alphaeus, and Thaddaeus, and Simon the Canaanite,
>
> And Judas Iscariot, which also betrayed him.

It is clear from the scriptures that Peter was the lead apostle and that Peter, James, and John were favored apostles who were present with Jesus at the raising of the daughter of Jairus (Mark 5:37), on the mount of transfiguration (John 17:1–2), and at Gethsemane (Matthew 26:37). Eusebius (c. AD 275–339), Bishop of Caesarea in Palestine, wrote, "Peter, James, and John, after the ascension of the Savior, as those set at the head by the Savior, did not set themselves to establishing their relative degrees of authority, but chose James the Just to be Bishop of Jerusalem."[1] Thus, acting as the First Presidency of the apostles of the Church, Peter, James, and John ordained James the Just, the brother of Jesus, to be bishop of Jerusalem.[2] At the time, Jerusalem, not Rome, was the headquarters of the Church. There is no historical information that proves that Peter was ever a bishop of Rome. The office of bishop was a local office over a fixed geographical area, and Peter was the president, an apostle, and a general authority of the whole Church.[3]

THE GNOSIS, OR SECRET TEACHINGS OF JESUS TO THE APOSTLES

Many of Jesus's teachings to the masses and to his apostles during his ministry are recorded in the New Testament. After his resurrection, the risen Lord taught the apostles for an additional forty days before he again ascended into heaven, as noted in Acts 1:1–4:

> The former treatise have I made, O Theophilus, of all that Jesus began both to do and teach,
>
> Until the day in which he was taken up, after that he through the Holy Ghost had given commandments unto the apostles whom he had chosen:
>
> To whom also he shewed himself alive after his passion by many infallible proofs, being seen of them forty days, and speaking of the things pertaining to the kingdom of God:
>
> And, being assembled together with them, commanded them that they should not depart from Jerusalem, but wait for the promise of the Father, which, saith he, ye have heard of me.

Nowhere in the scriptures is there any record of Jesus's teachings to the apostles during the forty days after his resurrection and before his final ascension. Jesus was careful to teach the common people in parables to protect them from judgment for failing to live doctrines they were not ready to accept. He knew that the world was not ready for the higher principles of the gospel that he gave to the apostles, so he commanded them to keep these teachings to themselves.

Clement, the Bishop of Alexandria, speaks of the "gnosis," or secret knowledge given to the apostles by the resurrected Lord: "To James the Just and to John and Peter, the Lord gave the gnosis after his resurrection. . . . They gave it further to the other apostles, and the rest of the apostles in turn gave it to the seventy." But Hugh Nibley points out that "there is no account of its ever being passed on any further."[4] This secret knowledge that the Lord restricted to the leaders of the early Church became a source of speculation among groups of early Church members. Some of these people claimed to have this secret knowledge but actually invented their own doctrines based on Hellenistic influences. They became known as "Gnostics" and were considered heretics by the Early Church Fathers, or bishops of the second century. A great deal more will be said about the Gnostics in later chapters.

Hugh Nibley, in his article titled "Apocryphal Writings and Teachings of the Dead Sea Scrolls," wrote:

> Very nearly all of the early Christian documents (and there are over 200 of them) have to do with what the Lord taught the apostles after the resurrection. What was said in the forty days? The New Testament does not tell us. What did he tell the apostles? According to these documents, he gave them the ordinances of the temple—but only to the apostles, to be held in secret. They would last only two generations, he explains, then they would be taken away. So they were not to pass beyond the general authorities, but were given to them as a special blessing to make that dispensation complete. They would be restored later on (in our dispensation). The ordinances are described in great detail. You could almost go through the temple using just these documents, for so much is there. Now it is public property; anyone can use it. However, the authority remains in one church.
>
> That's why we're finding the libraries today—they were all buried on purpose. They were not to be read by just anyone; the records weren't to be sent abroad; the world wasn't to receive them. They were regarded as very secret. Because this was a very important part of the plan, it was easy for them to get lost. And after they were lost, people could pretend they had them. Hence the false Gnosticism, and all sorts of other phonies and quacks. There were at least eighty-eight different sects in the church, each claiming it had the secret teachings the Lord gave the apostles after the resurrection.
>
> That's what gnosis is: the knowledge of what the Lord taught the apostles after the resurrection.[5]

Nibley stated in this article that the forty-day documents have four things in common:

1. They were all secret. Because they were not handed down or included in the New Testament, it was easy for the Gnostics to fabricate doctrines which were supposedly taught by Jesus.
2. They paint a very gloomy picture. They indicate that the Lord told the apostles that the Church would not long survive in its original form. They speak of apostasy and a much later restoration, but that message was very unpopular, so it was suppressed. Some of this message from the Lord and his apostles is in the scriptures, but they are interpreted by modern gospel scholars to mean that the early apostles thought that the second coming and the end of the world was eminent, not that the end of the Church as they knew it would soon come to pass.
3. The Lord taught them strange doctrines that differed from the philosophies coming out of Alexandria. These doctrines most likely included temple ordinances and covenants that had been lost due to the disobedience of ancient Israel and their rejection of the prophets.
4. The Lord gave the apostles the ordinances of the temple. They were to be confined to the apostles, since the Lord told them that his true Church would not long survive before their martyrdom and the beginning of the great apostasy.[6]

THE MESSAGE OF THE RESURRECTION

The principal message the apostles preached about Christ's resurrection was that Jesus Christ, a man with human form but godlike powers, allowed himself to be crucified by men; died and was buried in a tomb; and then after three days was physically resurrected to a tangible, physical body that they were allowed to touch and handle. For the first time in human history, a man who walked the earth like all other men had overcome death and conquered mortality to become immortal, never to die again. Jesus had raised others from the dead—including the daughter of the ruler of the synagogue, the son of a widow, and Lazarus, who had lain in the grave four days, but all of these died again. The message of the apostles was that this Jesus, whom they knew to be a mortal man and whom they had served for the past three years, had risen from the grave with a physical, immortal body. He had appeared to them in a room whose doors and windows were bolted. He had bidden them to feel the prints of the nails in his hands and feet, and he had eaten a fish to show that he was not a spirit as they had supposed. After being taught by this resurrected Creator for forty days, they saw him ascend into heaven, attested by angels.

Their message was,

> If in this life only we have hope in Christ, we are of all men most miserable.
>
> But now is Christ risen from the dead, and become the first-fruits of them that slept.
>
> For since by man came death, by man came also the resurrection of the dead.
>
> For as in Adam all die, even so in Christ shall all be made alive. (1 Corinthians 15:19–22)

Because of the literal resurrection of Jesus Christ, all men and women will be resurrected. The power of this message from those who personally witnessed and handled the resurrected body of Jesus was sufficient to convert many of the Jews and even more of the Gentiles to believe in the reality of the resurrection. However, there were many more who did not believe, as indicated by Paul's message in 1 Corinthians 1:22–24:

> For the Jews require a sign, and the Greeks seek after wisdom:
>
> But we preach Christ crucified, unto the Jews a stumbling block, and unto the Greeks foolishness;
>
> But unto them which are called, both Jews and Greeks, Christ the power of God, and the wisdom of God.

According to Paul, the Jews required a sign. Following their return from exile in Babylon, Ezra had taught them to live the letter of the law, and soon they followed the law so strictly that they lost the spirit of revelation and depended entirely on rabbis as teachers instead. The signs they sought included circumcision and obedience to dietary laws. When they saw the apostles changing these to accommodate the gentile converts, the Jews viewed the changes as a stumbling block. LDS scholar Jenifer Lane, describing the differing perspectives of the Jews and the Greeks, wrote, "For many Jews, the logical conclusion of their assumptions was that God had already declared the terms of salvation through the Torah and that there was no need for any further revelation."[7]

Just as the Jews sought signs, Paul stated that the Greeks sought after wisdom. "For many Greeks, the logical conclusion of their assumptions was that God could not and would not take on a mortal body, suffer, and then be resurrected."[8] The crucifixion and resurrection of Jesus of Nazareth was foolishness to the Greeks.

Thus among both Jews and Gentiles there were many obstacles to the preaching of the gospel of Jesus Christ. In spite of this opposition, however, the apostles did their best to fulfill the Savior's command to "go ye into all the world, and preach the gospel to every creature" (Mark 16:15). They were successful in establishing branches of the Church all along the coast of the Mediterranean Sea, from Gaza to Corinth, and then on to Rome. It is even rumored that Thomas preached in India. Philip's tomb has recently been discovered in Turkey. Along with establishing branches, the apostles ordained bishops, who were local leaders chosen and acting under the direction of the apostles, and they ordained elders, priests, and teachers in each branch.

The apostles preached first to the Jews of the Diaspora, who had been scattered throughout the known world by the Assyrian and Babylonian captivities. After Peter received the revelation to take the gospel to the Gentiles (see Acts 10), he baptized a Roman Centurion named Cornelius and all of his family. Later the Apostle Paul became the minister to the Gentiles. He traveled throughout the Mediterranean Greek and coastal Asian cities on his three missionary journeys, and eventually he was imprisoned and martyred in Rome. Paul's missions are recorded in the Book of Acts, but there is little documented history of the missionary journeys of the other apostles. The expansion of the early Church into all the civilized world of the Mediterranean basin, however, attests to their success in spreading the gospel.

Almost everywhere the apostles went, they faced persecution, and not just from the Jews who didn't agree with their story of Christ's resurrection. They were persecuted by the Greeks for condemning the worship of idols and by the Romans for refusing to worship the Roman gods and the emperor of Rome as a god. Yet their eyewitness testimony of the ministry and resurrection of Jesus Christ resulted in many strong converts, as attested by some of these people's willingness to suffer martyrdom rather than deny their Savior. Most of the apostles themselves ended up giving their lives for their beliefs.

The ministry of the apostles lasted from the time of their calling in

AD 30 through about AD 69. Most of them died violent deaths as martyrs about the same time (AD 50–70). Apostolic succession had been established when the apostles prayed and chose Matthias to replace Judas as a member of the Twelve soon after Jesus's death and resurrection (see Acts 1:21–26), but with the numerous martyrdoms, the Quorum of the Twelve Apostles was not replenished, and the apostolic authority was lost from the earth. The table below lists the original twelve apostles and others who were later identified as such, including Matthias, Paul, and James, and what little is known about their apostolic missions and their martyrdoms and deaths.

The void caused by the loss of apostolic authority, divine revelation, and the authority to confer priesthood offices resulted in chaos and confusion within the early Church. It led to the apostasy predicted by Jesus and the apostles and eventually to the transformation of the doctrines Jesus had taught into a religion based not on continuing revelation from the Lord but on the precepts of men. It wasn't until AD 100 that a group of bishops known to the world today as the Early Church Fathers began to write to each other seeking council, lamenting the loss of apostolic leadership and revelation, espousing their interpretation of doctrines, and fighting heresies that were already rampant.

THE MISSIONS AND MARTYRDOM OF THE APOSTLES

Apostle	Missions	Death Date	Circumstances of Death	Source
Judas Iscariot	None	AD 34	Suicide	Matt. 27:5, Acts 1:18
James, son of Zebedee, elder brother of Apostle John		AD 44	Executed by the sword (beheaded) by order of King Herod Agrippa I	Acts 12:2
Peter, brother of Andrew	Rome	AD 67–68	Crucified upside down in Rome under persecution of Nero who blamed the Christians for the burning of Rome	Tradition
Andrew, brother of Peter	Scythia in Greece Asia Minor Thrace Patrae in Achaia	Unknown	Crucified by Romans in Edessa on an x-shaped cross (St. Andrew's Cross)	New Foxe's Book of Martyrs, 7
Phillip	Phyrgia	Unknown	Died in Heirapolis	New Foxe's Book of Martyrs, 6
Bartholemew		Unknown	Scourged, thrown into prison, then crucified	Tradition
Matthew	Jerusalem, Persians, Parthians, Medes	About AD 60 Served for 15 years in Jerusalem and was a scribe for Peter in Rome	Died as a martyr in Ethiopia, killed by a sword wound	Legend

Apostle	Missions	Death Date	Circumstances of Death	Source
Thomas	Parthia or Persia or India	Unknown	Buried in Edessa, martyred by a lance	Tradition
James son of Alpheus, also known as Thaddeus		At least 5 years after the death of Christ	Thrown from the Temple by Scribes and Pharasees, then stoned, and his brains dashed out with a fuller's club	Tradition
Simon the Cannanite	Unknown	Unknown	Unknown	Unknown
John the Beloved			Banished to the Isle of Patmos	
Paul	Corinth, Galatia, Ehphesia, Philippia, Colossia, Thessalonica, Imprisoned in Rome in AD 61.	AD 66	Beheaded in Rome under persecution of Nero who blamed the Christians for the burning of Rome	New Foxe's Book of Martyrs, 8.
Matthias	Elected to fill the place of Judas as an Apostle	Unknown	Stoned, then beheaded at Jerusalem	New Foxe's Book of Martyrs, 6
James, the brother of Jesus	Leader of the Church at Jerusalem	About AD 66	Ordered to be stoned by the high priest	Flavius Josephus, Jewish historian, from New Foxe's Book of Martyrs, 6

Other apostles identified in the scriptures to replace those who had died include:

- Paul (Romans 1:1; 11:13; 1 Corinthians 1:1; 9:1–2; 2 Corinthians 1:1; Gal. 1:1; Ephesians 1:1; Colossians1:1; 1 Timothy 1:1; 2:7; 2 Timothy 1:1, 11; Titus 1:1)
- James the Just, the Lord's brother (Galatians 1:19)
- Barnabas (Acts 14:4, 14)

CONCLUSIONS

While on the earth, Jesus ordained twelve apostles, who were called to be special witnesses of his teachings, miracles, and resurrection. Following his resurrection, he returned to the apostles and allowed them to handle his resurrected body and feel his wounds so that they could bear strong testimony of the reality of his resurrection. He taught them for forty days before his final ascension into heaven, but the nature of this instruction is not recorded in the New Testament. This secret knowledge given only to the apostles became known as "gnosis," and it included sacred ordinances reserved for the apostles and those who were worthy to make the covenants explained. Some of these ordinances are preserved in apocryphal documents. Since the contents of Jesus's teachings during those forty days were not known to the general public, others who pretended to have this sacred knowledge fabricated doctrines that were not taught by Jesus or the apostles, and they became known as the Gnostics, whom the Early Church Fathers described as heretics. The apostles spread the message of salvation through the known world and established churches by ordaining priesthood leaders in each city. The principal message of the apostles was the reality of the resurrection and the sacrifice offered by Jesus, the Lamb of God, for the salvation of all God's children upon the condition of repentance and baptism. This, they taught, was in fulfillment of the symbolic sacrifices the Hebrews had for centuries offered upon the altars of the Tabernacle and the temples. By AD 70, most of the apostles had died for their refusal to worship the pagan gods of the Romans or to deny their testimonies of Jesus to the Jewish leaders.

NOTES

1. Eusebius, *Historia Ecclesiastica*, 2.1.3, in PG 20:136, quoted by Hugh Nibley, *Apostles and Bishops in Early Christianity* (Salt Lake City and Provo, UT: Deseret Book and FARMS), 34.
2. Nibley, *Apostles and Bishops*, 49.
3. Ibid., 84.
4. Eusebius, *Historia Ecclesiastica* 2.1.4, in PG 20:136, quoted by Hugh Nibley, *Apostles and Bishops in Early Christianity,* 23.
5. Hugh W. Nibley, "Apocryphal Writings and Teachings of the Dead Sea Scrolls," in *Temple and Cosmos*, vol. 12 of *The Collected Works of Hugh Nibley* (Salt Lake City: Deseret Book and FARMS, 1992), 12:264–335.
6. Ibid.
7. Jennifer C. Lane, "Jews and Greeks: The Broader Context for Writing the New Testament," in *How the New Testament Came to Be* (Provo, UT: Brigham Young University, 2006), 72.
8. Ibid.

CHAPTER 8

THE WRITING AND CANONIZATION OF THE NEW TESTAMENT

THE NEW TESTAMENT TODAY CONSISTS OF TWENTY-SEVEN BOOKS: the four gospels; the book of Acts (which gives our only official history of the primitive church); the epistles or letters of the apostles Paul, Peter, James, John, and Jude; and the apocalyptic book of Revelation. But these books were not compiled and canonized until the middle of the third century—two hundred years after the conclusion of Christ's mortal ministry—and today, even though thousands of Greek manuscripts of these texts exist, most are fragmented and none are the "autograph," or original, copies. These facts have led some scholars to question the historicity of some of the books we now call scripture. This chapter examines the conditions, as far as they are known, of these writings in the early Church and how the four gospels and the epistles of Paul came to be recorded.

From the writings of the Early Church Fathers, we learn that various congregations may have had one or another of the gospels and some but certainly not all of the epistles of Paul and the other apostles. These Early Church Fathers quoted and paraphrased from some of the books that now make up our New Testament when they recorded their own histories between AD 80 and AD 140, proving that they had access to these records in written form. Richard D. Draper, an LDS gospel scholar, points out, "It is of note that these [records] seem to have been in place by the time the last of the apostles, John, left the scene and therefore witness that the Christians had a basic Christian Bible in place before the apostolic era ended."[1]

Now, almost two thousand years later, modern Bible scholars are casting doubt on the authorship and authenticity of some of the books of the New Testament, citing the numerous variations in the thousands of existing Greek manuscripts. As acclaimed gospel scholar Robert J. Matthews points out, "For most of the past century, a growing trend has developed among many biblical scholars casting doubt on the historical accuracy of the New Testament."[2] This chapter examines how the four gospels and the epistles of Paul came to be recorded. Subsequent chapters will discuss the predicted apostasy, the Early Church Fathers, and the influence of the Gnostics or heretics, as well as the impact of persecution and Hellenization on the doctrines of the early Church.

THE LANGUAGES OF JESUS AND THE APOSTLES

While the existing New Testament manuscripts are almost all written in Greek, this does not prove that the original documents of which these are copies were also written in that language. Aramaic, a Semitic language based on Hebrew that developed during the Jews' captivity in Babylon, was commonly spoken throughout Syria and Galilee in the first century AD. Greek was spoken in Palestine, near the area where Jesus grew up, and Jesus's use of the Greek word *cephas*, meaning rock, as a new name for Peter (see Matthew 16:18) indicates that he was familiar with the Greek language. Research documented in *Jesus Christ and the World of the New Testament* explains further that Jesus may well have spoken primarily Hebrew, at least in his younger years, before he learned Aramaic:

> The small, ancient cemetery of Nazareth, the hometown of Jesus, contains only Hebrew names and inscriptions, indicating that Nazareth may have remained a haven for Hebrew speakers in a largely Aramaic-speaking society. [Jesus read from a book of Isaiah in the Synagogue (most likely written in Hebrew).] Even if the inhabitants of Nazareth—as well as those of small remote villages like it—continued to speak Hebrew, Jesus and his disciples would still have had to speak in Aramaic to communicate with the general populace.[3]

According to this document, careful examination of the gospels indicates that the sayings of Jesus, even when translated into Greek, had "a strong Aramaic element," while the narrative accounts in the gospels seem to have been written originally in Greek. In several instances in the scriptures, the authors preserved the actual sayings of Jesus by using the

Aramaic word followed by the Greek translation. Although it is impossible to date the writing of the four gospels with any degree of certainty, most scholars concur that they were composed after AD 70. All of this information has led to the hypothesis that many different accounts of Jesus's sayings and doings were likely recorded in Aramaic and used as the source material for the writing of the gospels, which were then composed primarily in Greek.[4] Whatever such source materials may have existed, however, were lost during the Roman persecutions, when emperors Decius (AD 249–251) and Valerian (AD 253–260) ordered the burning of all Christian books.[5]

THE WRITING OF THE FOUR GOSPELS

When the apostles of the Lord began their ministry after the resurrection of Jesus, not a single New Testament document existed. Their only scriptures were the books of the Old Testament, most probably the Greek Septuagint, so their preaching was based on oral accounts of their own ministry with Jesus and of seeing the resurrected Lord and feeling the prints of the nails in his hands and in his feet. Richard Draper, in his article "The Earliest 'New Testament,'" states, "There is little evidence that written records existed among the early Christians before the sixth decade, but there is some. Eusebius reported that Mark recorded and disseminated Peter's memoirs not long after his death, [which is believed to have occurred in AD 67–68]."[6]

It is uncertain when exactly these oral traditions were first recorded, and their authenticity is further called into question by the fact that the original four Gospels were written anonymously and not titled. One possible explanation for this seeming peculiarity is that perhaps "the ancient authors did not want to draw attention to themselves" but wanted the focus to be on their testimonies of the Lord.[7] Another possibility is that the gospels were written by scribes rather than by the apostles who were eyewitnesses to the events they describe, and therefore the scribes chose to leave their names off their work. It was common for the apostles to have scribes to record their testimonies and write letters for them, since the literacy rate at the time of Jesus "was not more than 10–15 percent of the population," according to LDS scholar Lincoln H. Blumell.[8]

Because of the practice of using scribes, sometimes records were mistakenly attributed to the scribe rather than to the person who commissioned and directed the writing. Such was the case with the book known today as the gospel of Mark. The writer of this particular book is believed to be John Mark, the missionary companion of Paul and Barnabas and a scribe for Peter. Of him Papias, an early Christian from the second century, wrote:

> Mark became Peter's interpreter and wrote down accurately, but not in order, all that he [Peter] remembered of the things said and done by the Lord. *For he [Mark] had not heard the Lord or been one of his followers; but later, as I said, a follower of Peter.* Peter used to teach as the occasion demanded, without giving systematic arrangement to the Lord's sayings.[9]

In light of this information, it appears that "The Gospel According to Mark" would be better titled "The Gospel According to Peter." The Gospel of Luke was similarly penned by a scribe whose name it bears, this time a missionary companion of Paul. Thus, two of the four Gospels were written by and titled with the names of scribes to apostles, and the other two, Matthew and John, are attributed to the apostles themselves.[10]

A lack of original documents has called into question the authorship and dates of all four of the gospels as well as some of the other books attributed to the apostles because what exists today is at best copies of copies.[11] The copies of the manuscripts that survived have neither authors nor dates listed. Although there are over 5,700 variant Greek manuscripts of the books of the New Testament, only one, which contains a major portion of the Gospel of John, is dated earlier than the second century AD.[12] Some scholars argue that even if original documents were found, they would not have been written before AD 68, citing as evidence the fact that the gospels record Jesus prophesying of the destruction of Jerusalem and the temple, which occurred in that year. These scholars do not seem to believe in prophecy, and therefore they conclude that information regarding the event must have been written after the fact.[13] Further, they claim that this means the gospels could not have been written by the apostles, because the apostles died before this date.

It is important to remember that the men who physically recorded the events from the oral history of Jesus's life were not necessarily the true authors of the gospels. The authors were the apostles, who testified of the ministry of Jesus of Nazareth—his teachings, his miracles, his healings, and his suffering, crucifixion, death, and resurrection—but their testimonies were often recorded by their scribes. The translation into Greek from earlier Aramaic texts could possibly, therefore, have occurred after the deaths of the apostles themselves.

The Gospel According to Mark

Most New Testament scholars, by careful analysis of the texts of the four gospels, have concluded that the gospel of Mark was written before the other three. The authors of the books of Matthew and Luke evidently used text from Mark's gospel in the creation of their own, making some grammatical corrections and slightly rearranging the order of the stories and then adding other stories, probably from oral traditions. Because of the many similarities among these three gospels, Matthew, Mark, and Luke are called the synoptic Gospels, meaning that they have the same point of view. There do exist, however, a few almost identical passages in the gospels of Matthew and Luke that were not copied from Mark, leading scholars to postulate the existence of some yet-to-be-discovered additional source they identify as Q, an abbreviation for the German word *Quelle,* which means source.[14] For example, Matthew and Luke both record the story of the birth of Jesus, while Mark begins some thirty years later with the preaching of John the Baptist. Mark's gospel (believed to have been Mark's record of Peter's teachings) was directed to the Romans and focused on the daily activities of Christ.

The Gospel According to Luke

Whereas Mark's gospel begins with the preaching of John the Baptist and the baptism of Jesus, Luke's gospel begins with the birth of John the Baptist and recounts the virgin birth of the Christ child. Luke, a physician, was Paul's missionary companion and a biographer of many of his journeys, but Luke recorded more than the testimony of Paul alone. Paul may have passed on to him the oral history of Christ's ministry that he had received from Peter and the other apostles who were eyewitnesses to it, or Luke may have been in the presence of these men himself and heard their testimonies firsthand. Luke begins his gospel by explaining in these words why he felt compelled to write it:

> Forasmuch as many have taken in hand to set forth in order a declaration of those things which are most surely believed among us, Even as they delivered them unto us, which from the beginning were eyewitnesses, and ministers of the word; It seemed good to me also, having had perfect understanding of all things from the very first, to write unto thee in order, most excellent Theophilus, That thou mightest know the certainty of those things, wherein thou hast been instructed. (Luke 1:1–4)

Luke states that many others had already recorded the ministry of Jesus but that his gospel is based on testimonies of eyewitness accounts from the ministers of the word, or, in other words, the apostles. Luke also testifies that he has had a "perfect understanding of all things from the very first," which indicates that he heard these accounts from the eyewitnesses themselves, and that his purpose in writing is to set things "in order."[15] As the direct address to Theophilus indicates, Luke's gospel seems to be directed to the Greek-speaking gentile Christians to whom he ministered along with Paul. Luke includes stories about the women in the life of Jesus that are omitted from the other gospels.[16] Luke is also believed to have been the author of the Acts of the Apostles.

The Gospel According to Matthew

Tertullian, one of the Early Church Fathers (c. AD 155–230), described Matthew as the "most faithful chronicler of the Gospel."[17] LDS scholar Gaye Strathearn states: "Although modern scholars have debated the authorship of this Gospel, ancient Christian writings are unanimous in ascribing it to the tax collector named Matthew in Matthew 9:9."[18] In comments about Matthew as an editor, Strathearn writes: "He often used the Greek word *gegraptai* ("it is written") to introduce his scriptural quotations indicating that, on these occasions, he was not relying on oral versions."[19] Matthew's gospel seems to have drawn much of its source material from the Gospel of Mark, as evidenced by some grammatical corrections and textual identities. Matthew adds to Mark's account a detailed genealogy of Jesus, the stories of the wise men and the flight into Egypt, and the Sermon on the Mount. Matthew's gospel seems to be written for the conversion of the Jews, to whom he seems to direct his ministry by showing the genealogy of Jesus back to David and stressing the fulfillment of Old Testament prophecies about the Messiah. He emphasizes the eventual preaching of the gospel to the

Gentiles and the teaching that they will have more faith than the covenant people of Israel (see Matthew 8:11–12). Since Matthew is believed to have died in AD 60, seven years before Peter's execution in AD 67, and since scholars believe that the book of Matthew drew its source material from the book of Mark, disseminated by Peter's scribe Mark after Peter died in AD 67, it seems logical that the gospels of both Mark and Matthew were written by scribes under the direction of Peter and Matthew before they died. This assumption presumes the belief in the divinity of Jesus and his prophecy that the temple would be destroyed, which destruction by the Romans occurred in AD 68.

The Gospel According to John

The Gospel of John places "emphasis on who Jesus *was* rather than on what he *did* (as in the Gospel of Mark) or what he was *through birth* (as in the Gospels of Matthew and Luke)."[20]

It differs from the synoptic Gospels in that it was written from a different perspective. Instead of starting his Gospel with a historical account of the Savior's birth or baptism, as do the synoptic Gospels, John starts his Gospel with the introduction of Jesus as the Creator of the world: "In the beginning was the Word, and the Word was with God, and the Word was God" (John 1:1). "Some modern scholars believe that John wrote these words, at least in part, to counteract the Gnostic heresy that the spirit of God descended upon a mortal man (Jesus) at his baptism. John testified that Jesus Christ is real, both fully human and fully divine, not a phantom, as the Docetics falsely claim. John had seen, heard, touched, and broken bread with Him."[21]

John adds many more personal accounts of the ministry of Jesus not included in the other Gospels, including Jesus's conversation with Nicodemus, the story of the Samaritan woman at Jacob's well, the raising of Lazarus from the dead,[22] and the more complete account of the intercessory prayer after the Last Supper.

PAUL'S EPISTLES

The most prolific record we have from the early Church is Paul's collection of epistles that were written as he spread the gospel to the Gentiles after his own miraculous conversion from an ardent persecutor of Christians to one of the most valiant defenders of Jesus. Although Paul never knew Jesus during Jesus's mortal ministry, his early epistles probably predated the writing of the four Gospels, and most scholars therefore believe that they include the oldest written record of Jesus's ministry.

The dating of the epistles of Paul and the other apostles is difficult and a source of controversy among Bible scholars because none of them were dated by their authors. It is generally believed that Paul's two epistles to the Galatians were among his earliest, and in them Paul admonished the Saints in Galatia to be wary of those who contradict his teachings that the Gentiles do not need to follow the law of Moses. This places the date of these epistles sometime around the Jerusalem Conference of Apostles on the subject of circumcision, which was held in AD 49.[23] The books of 1 and 2 Thessalonians and 1 and 2 Corinthians are also believed to be among Paul's earlier epistles, believed to be written between AD 49 and 57.[24]

After Paul's conversion, he was taught by Peter and James, the brother of Jesus, and he declared that he received visions and revelations from the resurrected Lord. Jared W. Ludlow writes, "In many settings, Paul addressed the issue of God's election of a people through covenant. More specifically, he believed that the followers of Christ were now the elect people of God. Paul did not reject the Jews; in fact, he strongly wished for their acceptance of Jesus. But he nevertheless believed they must profess faith in Jesus in order to be among the elect."[25] Likewise, Paul taught that the priesthood was not limited to the tribe of Levi, as was the tradition among the Jews, but that all men of the house of Israel, and all of the gentile converts, could be ordained to the priesthood.

Most of Paul's epistles were directed to specific congregations where Paul had already preached and ordained local officers in the Church. The epistles were frequently directed at resolving specific problems or conflicts in these congregations, so they were not a comprehensive treatise on the principles of the gospel. The book of Romans is the nearest of all of Paul's epistles to a comprehensive summary of Christian theology, since he wrote this letter in advance of his planned visit to Rome.[26]

Lincoln H. Blumell, writing about scribes and ancient letters, states that even though Paul's epistles are generally accepted as authentic and are believed to have been "written in the mid-first century, we do not possess any of the autograph copies, and the earliest surviving collection we have is the Chester Beatty Papyrus (P46) that dates to about AD 200, which includes at best copies of copies of copies."[27] This lack of original documents, along with some grammatical and textual differences, has led modern Bible scholars to doubt that some of the writings of Paul and the other apostles were written by the ascribed apostles. The evidence that both Paul and Peter used scribes to write their epistles, however, counteracts this argument. It is quite possible that the apostles gave their trusted scribes license to express in their own words the dictated doctrines and principles.[28]

Paul's epistles, interestingly, almost always include a postscript—apparently in his own handwriting—certifying that they came from him and not an impostor. An example of such a postscript is found in 2 Thessalonians 3:17: "The salutation of Paul with mine own hand, which is the token in every epistle: so I write." This certification of authenticity was most likely necessitated by fraudulent letters circulated by others writing in the names of the apostles, as indicated by Paul's warning against such documents: "Now we beseech you, brethren, by the coming of our Lord Jesus Christ, and by our gathering together unto him, That ye be not soon shaken in mind, or be troubled, neither by spirit, nor by word, *nor by letter as from us*" (2 Thessalonians 2:1–2; emphasis added). Tertullian "discusses entire forged 'writings which wrongly go under Paul's name' and which circulated in his day."[29] Thomas Wayment, in his study of false gospels, cites additional evidence of a list of forged letters attributed to Paul in the earliest surviving list of canonical books. The author of the list added this note: "There is current also (an epistle) to the Laodiceans, another to the Alexandrians, forged in Paul's name for the sect of Marcion, and several others, which cannot be received in the catholic Church."[30]

GENERAL EPISTLES OF THE APOSTLES

Besides the epistles of Paul, the New Testament includes several general epistles, namely those of James, 1–2 Peter, 1–3 John, and Jude. Most of these epistles seem to be directed to the general audience of the entire Church, except for 1–3 John, which seem to be directed to a specific community with individual concerns. The author of James is believed to be James the brother of Jesus, who was not a follower of Jesus during his ministry but was converted afterward. "The epistle of Jude lists 'Jude, the servant of Jesus Christ, and brother of James.' Only one individual in the New Testament is referred to simply as 'James' without any further explanation—James, Jesus' younger brother. In the two lists of Jesus' siblings, a younger brother named Juda or Judas is mentioned (Mark 6:3; Matthew 13:55). Because the reference to James is certainly to be understood as James the brother of the Lord, then Jude in this instance must be Jesus' younger brother."[31]

CANONIZATION OF THE NEW TESTAMENT

The various books of the New Testament were not accepted as a closed canon until the fourth century.

> Early in the second century AD, Marcion, later deemed a heretic by the postapostolic church, listed the writings he felt were scriptural, including an edited version of the Gospel of Luke and many of the writings of Paul. By AD 185, the early Christian apologist Irenaeus had compiled his own list of authoritative Christian writings, including all four Gospels and all the epistles except for Hebrews, James, 2 Peter, 2–3 John, and Jude. Origen later accepted this canon, adding Hebrews to the list of accepted books. Finally, in AD 367, Athanasius of Alexandria recommended a list of the twenty-seven books currently in the New Testament (*Epistulae Festales* 39), a list that was confirmed by the Third Council of Carthage in AD 397.[32]

Since the epistles were not dated, the books of the New Testament were arranged according to type and size rather than date. Thus the four gospels were listed first, followed by the Acts of the Apostles. Then came the epistles of Paul, arranged from the longest to the shortest, and then the general epistles of the other apostles, again generally arranged from longest to shortest.[33]

VARIATIONS IN THE NEW TESTAMENT MANUSCRIPTS

As LDS scholar Carl W. Griffin points out, of the more than 5,700 Greek manuscripts of the New Testament now extant, "it would be difficult to find a sentence, even part of a sentence, for which the rendering is consistent in every single manuscript." However, Griffin also notes that "only a small fraction of these [variations] are significant, either in translating the text or for the doctrine they express."[34]

LDS scholar Carol F. Ellerston, in her study of New Testament manuscripts, shows that some of the variations were made intentionally, while others were inadvertent changes. Scribes who copied the manuscripts sometimes tried to fix grammar or confusing text, and they sometimes tried to clarify doctrines by adding words or phrases.[35] An example of probable intentional alteration can be found in the King James translation of Matthew 5:22, from the Sermon on the Mount:

> Ye have heard that it was said by them of old time, Thou shalt not kill; and whosoever shall kill shall be in danger of the judgment: But I say unto you, That whosoever is angry with his brother *without a cause* shall be in danger of the judgment: and whosoever shall say to his brother, Raca, shall be in danger of the council: but whosoever shall say, Thou fool, shall be in danger of hell fire. (Matthew 5:21–22; emphasis added)

According to scholars Daniel K. Judd and Allen W. Stoddard, "The earliest surviving manuscript of Matthew 5:22 . . . dated as early as AD 125–150 . . . does not include any form of the phrase 'without a cause.' . . . Textual evidence shows that the phrase 'without a cause' was first added to some New Testament texts by at least the third or fourth century."[36] Judd and Stoddard conclude that the change was likely the result of later copyists attempting to soften the doctrine rather than of earlier copyists accidentally omitting the phrase.

Another variation between various copies of the same manuscript occurs in Matthew 19:9. The King James version is translated thus:

> And I say unto you, Whosoever shall put away his wife, except it be for fornication, and shall marry another, committeth adultery: and whoso marrieth her which is put away doth commit adultery.

John Gee, in "The Corruption of Scripture in Early Christianity," cites two other manuscripts dating to the same time in the fourth century read thus:[37]

> Whosoever divorces his wife except for adultery and marries another commits adultery.

> Whosoever divorces his wife except by reason of sexual immorality makes her commit adultery and whosoever marries the divorced woman commits adultery.

The variations in translation or copying create an interesting problem in this case, because in each version different parties are guilty of adultery. In the King James Version

1. the first and second husbands commit adultery, but not the wife. In the second version
2. only the husband who initiates the divorce commits adultery, unless his wife first committed adultery. And in the third version
3. the husband who initiates the divorce is not guilty of adultery, but the divorced wife and her next husband are. It is not possible from the age of the manuscripts to determine which version is the true teaching of Jesus. However, based on simple justice, it would seem that version number 2 is the most just, since only the husband who is not justified in divorcing his faithful wife should be guilty of adultery.

Although there are tens of thousands of textual variants in the New Testament manuscripts, LDS scholar Carol F. Ellerston, in her study of New Testament manuscripts, concludes "that if all of the other Greek manuscripts were lost, almost the entire New Testament could be reconstructed from the writings of the Church Fathers. (The term *Church Fathers* refers to the prominent early Christian writers in the first few centuries after the Apostles). These quotations help place specific readings and types of texts in definite places and times."[38] In other words, the lack of original documents and the plentitude of variations among existing documents does not hinder our understanding of what happened while the Savior walked the earth: Christian scholars who lived many centuries ago and who had access to original information recorded enough facts to help modern researchers piece together the fragments into a clear picture of what Christ and his apostles did and taught.

CONCLUSIONS

The earliest Christian writings we have today are the epistles of Paul, who corroborates the message taught in the four Gospels, that Jesus of Nazareth was Jehovah, the God of the Old Testament, and the promised Messiah. The teachings of Jesus and his apostles are essentially preserved by these Gospel writers, whether the oral testimonies of the apostles were recorded with their own pens or by the pens of their scribes or others who heard their teachings. The writings of the Early Church Fathers also document the scriptures that they had in the early second century. The King James Version of the New Testament is clearly not perfect and does not include all the teachings of Jesus to his apostles, but it is sufficient to convey the essential message of Jesus for all men and women to have faith in him and his Heavenly Father, to repent and be baptized, to love God and one another, and to look forward to their literal resurrection from the dead, with hope of eternal life with Jesus and Heavenly Father.

NOTES

1. Richard D. Draper, "The Earliest 'New Testament,'" in *How the New Testament Came to Be* (Salt Lake City and Provo, UT: Deseret Book and BYU Religious Studies Center, 2006), 264.
2. Robert J. Matthews, *Joseph Smith and the New Testam*ent, in *How the New Testament Came to Be,* 309.
3. Richard Neitzel Holzapfel, Eric D. Huntsman, and Thomas A. Wayment, *Jesus Christ and the World of the New Testament*, (Salt Lake City, UT: Deseret Book Company, 2006), 52.
4. Holzapfel, Huntsman, Wayment, "The Language of Jesus," in *Jesus Christ and the World of the New Testament*, 53.
5. Holzapfel, Huntsman, Wayment, "The Greek Gospels," in *Jesus Christ and the World of the New Testament*, 54.
6. Draper, "The Earliest 'New Testament,'" 263.
7. Kent P. Jackson, "Asking Restoration Questions," in *How the New Testament Came to Be*, 30.
8. Lincoln H. Blumell, "Scribes and Ancient Letters," in *How the New Testament Came to Be*, 210.
9. Papias, quoted in Eusebius, *History of the Church*, 3.39.15–16, cited by Frank F. Judd Jr., "Who Really Wrote the Gospels," in *How the New Testament Came to Be*, 125. Emphasis by Judd.
10. Papias, quoted in Eusebius, *History of the Church*, 3.39.15–16, cited by Frank F. Judd Jr., "Who Really Wrote the Gospels?," in *How the New Testament Came to Be*, 125.
11. Daniel K. Judd and Allen W. Stoddard, "Without a Cause," in *How the New Testament Came to Be*, 161.
12. See Carol F. Ellertson, "New Testament Manuscripts," in *How the New Testament Came to Be,* 95–96.
13. Jackson, "Asking Restoration Questions," 33.
14. Thomas A. Wayment, "First Century Sources," in *How the New Testament Came to Be,* 114–15.
15. Ibid., 112–13.
16. Alexander B. Morrison, "Plain and Precious Things," in *How the New Testament Came to Be*, 4.

17. Tertullian, *On the Flesh of Christ*, in *The Anti-Nicene Fathers: Traditions of the Writings of the Fathers down to AD 325*, ed. Alexander Roberts and James Donaldson (Grand Rapids, MI: Eerdmans, 1980), 3:540, quoted by Gaye Strathearn in *How the New Testament Came to Be*, 141.
18. Gaye Strathearn, "Matthew as an Editor of the Life and Teachings of Jesus," in *How the New Testament Came to Be*, 141.
19. Ibid., 143.
20. Holzapfel, Huntsman, Wayment, *Jesus Christ and the World of the New Testament*, 49.
21. Alexander B. Morrison, "Plain and Precious Things," 5.
22. Ibid.
23. Eric D. Huntsman, "Paul's Letters," in *How the New Testament Came to Be*, 192.
24. Holzapfel, Huntsman, Wayment, *Jesus Christ and the World of the New Testament*, 212.
25. Jared W. Ludlow, "Paul's Use of Old Testament Scripture," in *How the New Testament Came to Be*, 231–32.
26. Huntsman, "Paul's Letters," 194.
27. Lincoln H. Blumell, "Scribes and Ancient Letters," in *How the New Testament Came to Be*, 215.
28. Blumell, "Scribes and Ancient Letters," in *How the New Testament Came to Be*, 221.
29. Tertullian, *De Baptismo*, 17 (ANF 3:677), quoted by John Gee, "The Corruption of Scripture in Early Christianity," in *Early Christians in Disarray*, ed. Noel B. Reynolds (Provo, UT: Brigham Young University Press, 2005), 174.
30. Thomas A. Wayment, "False Gospels: An Approach to Studying the New Testament Apocrypha," in *How the New Testament Came to Be*, 293.
31. Holzapfel, Huntsman, Wayment, *Jesus Christ and the World of the New Testament*, 274.
32. Ibid., 6.
33. Ibid., 4.
34. Carl W. Griffin and Frank F. Judd Jr., "Principles of Textual Criticism," in *How the New Testament Came to Be*, 86.
35. Carol F. Ellertson, "New Testament Manuscripts," in *How the New Testament Came to Be*, 102.
36. Judd and Stoddard, "Without a Cause," 160–61.
37. John Gee, "The Corruption of Scripture in Early Christianity," in *Early Christians in Disarray*, ed. Noel B. Reynolds (Provo, UT: Brigham Young University Press, 2005), 187.
38. Ellertson, "New Testament Manuscripts," 96.

CHAPTER 9

THE PREDICTED APOSTASY IN THE PRIMITIVE CHURCH

For I know this, that after my departing shall grievous wolves enter in among you, not sparing the flock. Also of your own selves shall men arise, speaking perverse things, to draw away disciples after them.

Acts 20:29–30

PROTESTANT CHRISTIAN SECTS UNIVERSALLY ACCEPT THE IDEA that the medieval Roman Catholic Church strayed far from Jesus's original teachings and organization and was thus in need of a reformation. For many years, scholars have assumed that this apostasy, or falling away from the original faith, resulted from one of three factors. These were (1) external persecution by the Jews and the Romans, (2) the Hellenization of Christianity due to the influence of Greek philosophy, and (3) the influence of Constantine, who chose bishops and appointed himself the head of the Church even though he was still a sun worshipper and was not baptized until near his death. Modern scholars, however, upon reexamining the writings of the Early Church Fathers and the recently translated Gnostic gospels found at Nag Hammadi in 1945, have concluded that the apostasy began in the earliest days of the early Church, even while the apostles were still alive.

SCRIPTURAL PREDICTIONS OF THE APOSTASY

It is clear from the writings of Paul that the Saints he instructed frequently strayed from his teachings, thus the many epistles to admonish them to repentance. Likewise, the Apostles Peter, James, Jude, and John all admonished the Saints to repent and to return to the faith and doctrines they had been taught. It is generally assumed that their admonitions were successful and that the early Church survived, only to later be brought down by tyrants like Nero, who burned Christians at the stake and fed them to lions in the Coliseum.

According to scholar Kent P. Jackson, the Greek word *apostasia* is inadequately translated as "falling away, but it actually means 'rebellion,' 'mutiny,' 'revolution.'"[1] Noel B. Reynolds states that "LDS scholars today conclude increasingly that the root causes of the apostasy were the abandonment or breaking of sacred covenants by the Christians themselves."[2] Cyprian, the Bishop of Carthage, wrote, "Even many bishops, who ought to be guides and patterns to the rest, neglecting the peculiar duties of their stations, gave themselves to secular pursuits:—They deserted their places of residence and their flocks: They traveled through distant provinces in quest of pleasure and gain; gave no assistance to the needy brethren; but were insatiable in their thirst of money:—They possessed estates by fraud and multiplied usury."[3]

We need only to look at the New Testament scriptures themselves to see numerous predictions by Jesus and the apostles of the early demise of the Church. This doctrine, however, was not popular among those who rebelled against apostolic authority and eventually led away many of the faithful. Their misdeeds were documented in the writings of the early Christian fathers, who diligently fought against these heretics and all others who were successful in sowing seeds of dissension among the faithful of the flock.

Jesus himself warned his followers about false prophets who would lead them astray: "For many shall come in my name, saying, I am Christ; and shall deceive many. . . . For there shall arise false Christs, and false prophets, and shall shew great signs and wonders; insomuch that, if it were possible, they shall deceive the very elect" (Matthew 24:5, 24). This teaching is also evident in Jesus's parable of the wheat and the tares. In this parable, the apostles sow good wheat, but after they are martyred and sleep, the false prophets inspired by Satan sow tares of false teachings among the wheat, or the very elect, choking out the truth in the hearts of many. Truth and false doctrines coexisted in the early Church for centuries, until the truth eventually became choked out and lost. It then needed to be resown, or restored, by a real sower.

In his second epistle to the Thessalonians, Paul warned the faithful that some would attempt to lead them astray by falsely preaching that the Second Coming of Christ was at hand. He warned individuals to avoid these false teachers, but he offered no hope for the preservation of the Church before the promised Second Coming, saying that "that day shall not come, except there come a falling away first, and that man of sin be revealed, the son of perdition" (2 Thessalonians 2:3). Peter issued a similar warning: "There shall be false teachers among you, who privily shall bring in damnable heresies, even denying the Lord that bought them, and bring upon themselves swift destruction. And many shall follow their pernicious ways; by reason of whom the way of truth shall be evil spoken of" (2 Peter 2:1–2). To the elders of the church at Ephesus, Paul said, "For I know this, that after my departing shall grievous wolves enter in among you, not sparing the flock. Also of your own selves shall men arise, speaking perverse things, to draw away disciples after them" (Acts 20:29–30).

Jesus warned the apostles that they themselves would suffer persecution and death at the hands of the Jews: "They shall put you out of the synagogues: yea, the time cometh, that whosoever killeth you will think that he doeth God service. And these things will they do unto you, because they have not known the Father, nor me" (John 16:2–3).

LDS scholar Hugh Nibley writes of the apostasy or falling away from the truth by describing Christ's prophecies to his apostles:

> (I) Jesus announced in no uncertain terms that his message would be rejected by all men, as the message of the prophets had been before, and that he would soon leave the world to die in its sins and seek after him in vain. The Light was soon to depart, leaving a great darkness "in which no man can work" while "the prince of this world" would remain, as usual, in possession of the field. (II) In their turn the disciples were to succeed no better than their Lord: "If they have called the master of the house Beelzebub, how much more shall they call them of his household?" Like him they were to be "hated of all men," going forth as sheep among wolves, "sent last as it were appointed unto death," with the promise that as soon as they completed their mission the end would come.

> (III) But what of the church? Those who accepted the teaching were to suffer exactly the same fate as the Lord and the apostles; they were advised to "take the prophets for an example of suffering affliction and patience," and to "think it not strange concerning the fiery trial which is to try" them, but rejoice rather to suffer as Christ did "in the flesh . . . that we may also be glorified together." After them too the prince of this world was waiting to take over; they too were to be lambs among wolves, rejected as were the Master and the disciples: "The world knoweth us not because it knew him not." Knowing that "whosoever will save his life must lose it," they openly disavowed any expectation of success, individual or collective, in this world. (IV) As for the doctrine, it was to receive the same rough treatment, soon falling into the hands of worldly men who would "pervert the gospel of Christ" from a thing the world found highly obnoxious to something it was willing to embrace, for such has always been the fate of God's revelations to men. [4]

Hugh Nibley, quoting Eusebius, Bishop of Ceaserea (c. AD 275–339), writes that "after he [Peter] and James were dead for at least twenty-four years, Eusebius specifically states that 'John the beloved returned from Patmos and continued to govern the churches.'"[5] According to Hugh Nibley, Eusebius "cites a very old source telling how, as long as an apostle remained alive, the spoilers and dissenters had to content themselves with lurking in dark corners, only to throw off all disguise and come out boldly into the open the moment the last apostle was dead."[6]

With the death of the apostles, by AD 100 the true church that Jesus had established was being usurped by impostors from within, who began to change and mold it to their perceptions without the benefit of revelation from the Holy Spirit or the resurrected Lord.

KNOWLEDGE LOST OR BLURRED AS A RESULT OF THE APOSTASY

The result was the loss of understanding of basic gospel teachings that had been revealed by God to the prophets from the beginning of man. These basic teachings are in the Bible but have become lost to the understanding of many people, due to the loss of prophets who can properly interpret their meanings. When these messages are understood collectively, the blur of confusion about Heavenly Father's plan, our relationship to him and his Son Jesus Christ, and our purpose here on earth becomes focused and clear for the first time.

Below are some examples of lost or hidden knowledge that is sometimes misunderstood:

- God the Father and Jesus Christ are separate, immortal, resurrected beings, and the Holy Ghost is a spirit who testifies of the Father and the Son.
- We are created in the express image of Heavenly Father, who has an immortal and glorified physical body.
- All men and women lived as spirits with God and Jesus in Heaven before the creation of the earth.
- There was a plan in heaven for the creation of the earth so that each of us could obtain a mortal body and learn by faith to keep the commandments.
- In the spirit world, before the creation, we were foreordained (not predestined) to perform important works in this life.
- One third of the spirits in heaven chose to follow Lucifer instead of Heavenly Father and the Savior, and they were cast down to the earth, never to receive mortal bodies.
- Agency, or the right to choose good or evil, is given by the Father to all of his children. This explains why bad things happen to good people.
- Jesus Christ was the creator of all things on this earth under the direction of his Heavenly Father.
- Jesus Christ was Jehovah of the Old Testament, the Spirit God of Abraham, Isaac, and Jacob, before being born in the flesh to the virgin Mary.
- Jesus told his apostles he had other sheep that he must visit, that they would hear his voice, and that there would be one fold and one shepherd. Some assumed he meant the Gentiles, but Jesus was not called to preach unto the Gentiles. The other sheep were descendants of the tribe of Israel who had migrated to the American continent. The Book of Mormon records Christ's visit to the descendants of the Jewish prophet Lehi in Central America after his resurrection in Jerusalem.
- Jesus visited the spirits in the spirit prison during the time between his crucifixion and his resurrection and preached to them to liberate the captives.
- The early apostles performed the ordinance of baptism for the dead in behalf of their ancestors.

- All men and women will be resurrected because of the resurrection of Christ, which makes salvation from physical death a free gift to all, through no works of their own.
- All men and women who accept Jesus Christ as their Savior, are baptized, and endure to the end in repentance and faith will receive the blessings of the Atonement, be forgiven of their sins, and be rewarded in the highest kingdom of heaven.
- Heaven consists of three different kingdoms, comparable to the glory of the sun, the moon, and the stars, and in the resurrection, our bodies will be glorified with different glories comparable to these three kingdoms.

THE PROMISED RESTORATION

As surely as the words of the Savior and the apostles prophesied of a falling away, or loss of the Church and its priesthood, they also foretold of a restoration of the gospel to the earth before the Second Coming of Christ. The Apostle Peter referred to this restoration of the gospel as "the times of refreshing" and "the times of restitution of all things" (Acts 3:19, 21), and he stated that it had been spoken of "by the mouth of all [God's] holy prophets since the world began" (v. 21).

APOSTLE PETER

Acts 3:20–21

> He shall send Jesus Christ,
>
> Whom the heaven must receive until the times of restitution of all things, which God hath spoken by the mouth of all his holy prophets since the world began.

Many of the prophets' teachings, however, were lost to the world because wicked people rejected the prophets. Others of these teachings were preserved, only to be altered or abbreviated by scribes over the ages. Their meanings have been twisted by those who, lacking the priesthood and the spirit of revelation, introduced different meanings, and the original simplicity of the gospel of Jesus was lost and distorted to the point that religion became a mass of confusion and frustration for many.

By the early 1500s, the Protestant reformers (Luther, Calvin, Tyndale, Wycliff, and Huff, to name a few) recognized the need for a reformation of the Church of Rome. None of them, however, claimed divine authority to institute these changes.

MARTIN LUTHER

"I have sought nothing beyond reforming the Church in conformity with the Holy Scriptures. The spiritual powers have been not only corrupted by sin, but absolutely destroyed; so that there is now nothing in them but a depraved reason and a will that is the enemy and opponent of God. I simply say that Christianity has ceased to exist among those who should have preserved it."[7]

JOHN WESLEY

John Wesley (1703–1791), the founder of Methodism, said,

> It does not appear that these extraordinary gifts of the Holy Ghost were common in the Church for more than two or three centuries. We seldom hear of them after the fatal period when the Emperor Constantine declared himself a Christian. . . . The real cause [of this] was, 'the love of many,' almost of all Christians, so called, was 'waxed cold.' The Christians had no more the Spirit of Christ than the other Heathens. The Son of Man, when he came to examine his Church, could hardly 'find faith upon earth.' This was the real cause why the extraordinary gifts of the Holy Ghost were no longer to be found in the Christian Church—because the Christians were turned Heathens again, and had only a dead form left.[8]

ROGER WILLIAMS

Roger Williams, pastor of the oldest Baptist church in America at Providence, Rhode Island, in 1638, refused to continue as pastor on the grounds that "there is no regularly constituted church on earth, nor any person authorized to administer any church ordinance; nor can there be until new apostles are sent by the Great Head of the Church, for whose coming I am seeking."[9]

THOMAS JEFFERSON

"The religion builders have so distorted the doctrines of Jesus, so muffled them in mysticisms, fancies and falsehoods, have caricatured them into forms so inconceivable, as to shock reasonable thinkers. . . .

Happy in the prospect of a restoration of primitive Christianity, I must leave to younger persons to encounter and lop off the false branches which have been engrafted into it by the mythologists of the middle and modern ages."[10]

Although these courageous pioneers blazed a trail for the eventual restoration of the gospel, their effort led only to an attempted reformation. The reformers were not prophets and did not claim to be. They did not have the priesthood authority of the apostles, as people like Roger Williams well knew.

The promised restoration was yet to occur in the spring of 1820, when the Lord called a new prophet to lead this restoration "of all things, which God hath spoken by the mouth of all his holy prophets since the world began" (Acts 3:21). This restoration will be described in a later chapter.

CONCLUSIONS

The rebellions against the teachings of Jesus and the apostles began while the apostles were yet on the earth. Their predictions of the end of the Church were later distorted and interpreted to mean the end of the world, and not the end of the Church. Most of the true teachings of Jesus were preserved in the books of the New Testament but were hidden from the common masses in the medieval church until the development of the printing press and the publication of the Bible in languages that the masses could read. But just as a falling away from the teachings of Jesus and the apostles was predicted, a restoration was also prophesied, so that the fulness of the gospel of Jesus Christ would be on the earth again to prepare for his Second Coming.

NOTES

1. Kent P. Jackson, "Asking Restoration Questions," in *How the New Testament Came to Be* (Salt Lake City and Provo, UT: Deseret Book and BYU Religious Studies Center, 2006), 35.
2. Noel B. Reynolds, "What Went Wrong with the Early Christians," in *Early Christians in Disarray* (Provo, UT: Brigham Young University Press, 2005), 4–5.
3. Milner, *Church History*, Cent. III, ch. 8, quoted by James E. Talmage, *The Great Apostasy*, (Salt Lake City, UT: Deseret Book Company, 1909), 86.
4. Hugh W. Nibley, "The Passing of the Primitive Church: Forty Variations

on an Unpopular Theme," from *Mormonism and Early Christianity,* vol. 4 in *The Collected Works of Hugh Nibley* (Salt Lake City: Deseret Book, 1987), 168–208.

5. Eusebius, *Historia Ecclesiastica*, 3.23.6 in *PG* 20:257, quoted by Hugh Nibley, *Apostles and Bishops in Early Christianity* (Salt Lake City and Provo, UT: Deseret Book and FARMS, 2005), 9–10.
6. Hugh Nibley, *Apostles and Bishops in Early Christianity* (Salt Lake City and Provo, UT: Deseret Book and FARMS, 2005), 9.
7. *In Galat.* (*1535*) *Weins IX, P.I. 293, 24-27, p. 50, Luther and his Times, p. 509, Martin Luther, 188*, as cited in *The Falling Away and Restoration of the Gospel of Jesus Christ Foretold*, Pamphlet, LDS Tracts.
8. John Wesley, "The More Excellent Way," *Wesley's Works*, vol. 7, sermon 89, pp. 26–27.
9. Roger Williams, quoted by William Cullen Bryant in *Picturesque America* (New York: D. Appleton, 1872–74), 502–3.
10. *Jefferson's Complete Works,* vol. 7. pp. 210 and 257, as cited in *The Falling Away and Restoration of the Gospel of Jesus Christ Foretold*, Pamphlet, LDS Tracts.

CHAPTER 10

THE PRIMITIVE CHURCH AFTER THE APOSTLES

THE MISSING DECADES

> *The burning question in the time of the apostolic fathers was, Who is in charge around here? No one, including the apostolic fathers themselves, knew the answer.*
>
> *Hugh Nibley*

HISTORY HAS PRESERVED VERY FEW RECORDS OF WHAT HAPPENED to the Primitive Church between AD 70 and AD 110. We have the stories of persecution and martyrdom brought on by Nero, who made the Christians scapegoats after he was accused of setting the fires that caused Rome to burn, and we have the letters written by the Early Church Fathers, but beyond these, much is left to speculation. We can imagine that there was much confusion in the Church as the news of the apostles' martyrdom spread through Christian communities. Without the apostles to lead the Church, the bishops they had ordained became the only authorized leaders. But soon the bishops began to be martyred as well, creating the dilemma of deciding how to call and ordain new bishops to replace them. The office of bishop became an appointment by the congregation instead of a calling received by revelation through the proper authority.

The grievous wolves that Paul had warned about began to usurp leadership of some congregations, inventing doctrines of their own that had not been taught by the apostles. An example of this is preserved by "a letter attributed to Clement, called Bishop of Rome (c. 90–100). As spokesman for the Roman church, Clement wrote to the Christian community at Corinth at a time of crisis: certain leaders of the Corinthian church had been divested of power. Clement says that 'a few rash and self-willed people' drove them out of office: 'those of no reputation [rose up] against those with reputation, the fools against the wise, the young against the old.'" Clement insisted that the rightful leaders be restored.[1]

THE EARLY CHURCH FATHERS

Until recently, most of the knowledge we had of the primitive Church came from the writings of the Early Church Fathers, the early bishops, and Christian writers from the second century AD. The discovery and translation of the Nag Hammadi codices, however, now adds new insights into this early period.

The book of Acts, which chronicles the missionary journeys of the apostles, concludes its account shortly before the execution of Peter and Paul in Rome, which, according to tradition, occurred in about AD 66. At the turn of the second century, the writings of the Early Church Fathers reveal that the apostles are gone and none have been chosen to replace them.[2] The pattern of apostolic succession, established with the calling of Matthias to replace Judas, was interrupted by the martyrdom of the apostles.

The apostles had ordained bishops during their mortal ministries in various congregations, but bishops of the early Church clearly understood that they were local authorities, having jurisdiction over their local congregations but not general authority for the whole Church, as did the apostles. They felt the void caused by the loss of apostolic authority and lamented the loss of revelation. Ignatius, the third Bishop of Antioch, wrote: "Shall I reach such a pitch of presumption . . . as to issue orders to you as if I were an apostle?"[3] Hugh Nibley writes, "Exactly like Ignatius, Polycarp, [Bishop of Smyrna], writing to the churches, must confess that he is in no wise to be considered on par with the apostles: "For neither I, nor any other such one, can come up to the wisdom of the blessed and glorious Paul. He, when among you, accurately and steadfastly taught the word of truth in the absence of those who were then alive. And when absent from you, he wrote a letter . . . which will build you up in that faith which has been given you."[4]

As the Early Church Fathers battled the heresies of the Gnostics and the persecution of the Romans, they lamented the lack of general Church authorities to whom to appeal for answers. Nibley reasons,

> The burning question in the time of the apostolic fathers was, Who is in charge around here? No one, including the apostolic fathers themselves, knew the answer. In their days, the churches were writing letters to each other to be read and considered and then handed on: the bishop of Smyrna writes to the bishop of Philippi; the bishop of Antioch does the same, also sending letters of advise and council to the churches at Tralles, Ephesus, Rome, Philadelphia, and Magnesis—explaining that he has no right to give orders but finds himself unable to keep silence in the face of the way things are going. . . . None of these advisors sets himself up as an authority or a superior and, what is more significant, none of them, though desperately pressed for leadership, knows of any higher authority to which he can recommend those whom he is instructing. The perfect equality of bishops is evident enough, but it is also repeatedly stated as a basic principle.[5]

The Romans destroyed Jerusalem in AD 68–70, by which time many of the Jews and remaining Christians had already fled the city. Nero was the emperor of Rome at the time of the martyrdom of Peter and Paul, and he was followed by Vespasian, Titus, Domitian, and Diocletian, all of whom continued persecution of the Christians and destroyed early Christian records. Although no autograph manuscripts of the books of the New Testament exist, it has been said that the four Gospels could almost be re-created from the writings of the early Church Fathers.[6] However, the various congregations of the Church scattered throughout the ancient world where the apostles organized the Church did not have all of the books of the New Testament, which was not canonized until the fourth century. Many local churches may have had only one of the four Gospels. Ireneaus, a Christian bishop of Lyon in Gaul (now France), writing in AD 180, is the first Christian author to list all four of the Gospels together.[7] However, some scholars now believe that there was a collection of core materials as early as AD 125. The four Gospels were all known, and the early Church writers all used them, with the exceptions of Clement of Rome and Polycarp.[8]

The following table lists the names and circumstances of these early Christian writers.

THE EARLY CHURCH FATHERS

Name	Habitat	Birth	Death	Role(s)
Clement I of Rome	Rome	unknown	c. 102	Pope Clement I, the bishop of Rome from roughly AD 88–98. His epistle, 1 Clement (c 96), was copied and widely read in the Early Church. Clement calls on the Christians of Corinth to maintain harmony and order. It is the earliest Christian epistle outside the New Testament. Tradition identifies him as the fourth pope of Rome and his epistle has been construed to assert Rome's papal primacy over its audience, the church in Corinth.
Justin	Rome	100	165	Justin Martyr (Justin the Martyr, also known as Justin of Caesarea) (100–165) was an early Christian apologist. His works represent the earliest surviving Christian apologies of notable size. Most of what is known about the life of Justin Martyr comes from his own writings. According to church tradition, Justin suffered martyrdom at Rome under Marcus Aurelius when Rusticus was prefect of the city (between 162 and 168).
Polycarp	Smyrna (now in Turkey)	c 69	c. 155	Polycarp of Smyrna (c 69–ca. 155) was a Christian bishop of Smyrna (now in Turkey). It is recorded that he had been a disciple of John. The options for this John are John the son of Zebedee traditionally viewed as the author of the Fourth Gospel, or John the Presbyter. Traditional advocates follow Eusebius in insisting that the apostolic connection of Polycarp was with John the Evangelist, and that this John, the author of the Gospel of John, was the same as the Apostle John. (Continued on next page.)

Name	Habitat	Birth	Death	Role(s)
				(Continued from previous page.) In c. 155, the Smyrnans demanded Polycarp's execution as a Christian, and he died a martyr. His story has it that the flames built to kill him refused to burn him, and that when he was stabbed to death, so much blood issued from his body that it quenched the flames around him. Polycarp is recognized as a saint in both the Roman Catholic and Eastern Orthodox churches.
Ignatius	Antioch	c. 35	c. 107	Saint Ignatius of Antioch (also known as Theophorus)(c. 35–107) was the third Bishop or Patriarch of Antioch and a student of Apostle John. En route to his martyrdom in Rome, Ignatius wrote a series of letters which have been preserved as an example of the theology of the earliest Christians.
Irenaeus	Gaul (now France)	130	202	Irenaeus was bishop of Lugdunum in Gaul, which is now Lyons, France. His writings were formative in the early development of Christian theology, and he is recognized as a saint by both the Eastern Orthodox Church and the Roman Catholic Church. He was a notable early Christian apologist. He was also a disciple of Polycarp, who was said to be a disciple of John the Evangelist. The Shepherd of Hermas (2nd century) was popular in the early church and even considered scriptural by some of the early Church fathers, such as Irenaeus. It was written in the city of Rome, in the language of Greek. The Shepherd had great authority in the 2nd and 3rd centuries. (Continued on next page.)

Name	Habitat	Birth	Death	Role(s)
				(Continued from previous page.) His best-known book, *Against Heresies* (c 180), enumerated heresies and attacked them. Irenaeus wrote that the only way for Christians to retain unity was to humbly accept one doctrinal authority—episcopal councils. Irenaeus proposed that all four gospels be accepted as canonical.
Tertullian	Carthage (now Tunisia)	155	230	Quintus Septimius Florens Tertullianus, anglicized as Tertullian, (ca. 155–230) who was converted to Christianity before 197, was a prolific writer of apologetic, theological, controversial, and ascetic works. He was the son of a Roman centurion. Tertullian denounced Christian doctrines he considered heretical, but later in life adopted views that themselves came to be regarded as heretical. He wrote three books in Greek and was the first great writer of Latin Christianity, thus sometimes known as the "Father of the Latin Church." He was evidently a lawyer in Rome. He is said to have introduced the Latin term "trinitas" with regard to the Divine (Trinity) to the Christian vocabulary.

Name	Habitat	Birth	Death	Role(s)
Clement of Alexandria	Alexandria (Egypt)	c. 150	c. 215	Clement of Alexandria (Titus Flavius Clemens) was the first member of the Church of Alexandria to be more than a name, and one of its most distinguished teachers. He united Greek philosophical traditions with Christian doctrine and valued gnosis that with communion for all people could be held by common Christians. He developed a Christian Platonism. Like Origen, he arose from Catechetical School of Alexandria and was well versed in pagan literature.
Origen	Alexandria (Egypt)	c. 185	254	Origen of Alexandria Origen, or Origen Adamantius was an early Christian scholar and theologian. According to tradition, he was an Egyptian who taught in Alexandria, reviving the Catechetical School, where Clement had taught. The patriarch of Alexandria at first supported Origen but later expelled him for being ordained without the patriarch's permission. He relocated to Caesarea Maritima and died there after being tortured during a persecution.
Cyprian	Carthage (now Tunisia)		258	Saint Cyprian (Thascius Caecilius Cyprianus) (died September 14, 258) was bishop of Carthage and an important early Christian writer. He was probably born at the beginning of the 3rd century in North Africa, perhaps at Carthage, where he received an excellent classical (pagan) education. After converting to Christianity, he became a bishop (in 249) and eventually died a martyr at Carthage.

Name	Habitat	Birth	Death	Role(s)
Athanasius of Alexandria	Alexandria, Egypt	c. 296	373	Athanasius of Alexandria was a theologian, Pope of Alexandria, and a noted Egyptian leader of the 4th century. He is remembered for his role in the conflict with Arianism and for his affirmation of the Trinity. At the First Council of Nicaea (in 325), Athanasius argued against the Arian doctrine that Christ is of a distinct substance from the Father.
Gregory of Nazianzus	Nazianzus in Cappadocia	329	389	Saint Gregory of Nazianzus set out to demonstrate that Christians could hold their own in conversations with learned Greek-speaking intellectuals and that Christian faith, while it was against many of the ideas of Plato and Aristotle (and other Greek Philosophers), was an almost scientific and distinctive movement with the healing of the soul of man and his union with God at its center—one best represented by monasticism. They made major contributions to the definition of the Trinity finalized at the First Council of Constantinople in 381 and the final version of the Nicene Creed which was formulated there.
Eusebius	Caesarea (Palestine)	c. 275	339	Eusebius of Caesarea (often called Eusebius Pamphili, Eusebius [the friend] of Pamphilus) was a bishop of Caesarea in Palaestina and is often referred to as the father of church history because of his work in recording the history of the early Christian church and forging unity among proto-orthodox advocates. An earlier version of church history by Hegesippus, that he referred to, has not survived.

Name	Habitat	Birth	Death	Role(s)
Augustine of Hippo	Rome	354	430	Aurelius Augustinus, Augustine of Hippo, or Saint Augustine (November 13, 354–August 28, 430), Bishop of Hippo, was a philosopher and theologian. Augustine, a Latin Father and Doctor of the Church, is one of the most important figures in the development of Western Christianity. Augustine was radically influenced by Platonism. He framed the concepts of original sin and just war as they are understood in the West. When Rome fell and the faith of many Christians was shaken, Augustine developed the concept of the Church as a spiritual City of God, distinct from the material City of Man. Augustine's work defined the start of the medieval worldview, an outlook that would later be firmly established by Pope Gregory the Great.
Jerome	Rome	ca. 347	420	Jerome (ca. 347–September 30, 420) is best known as the translator of the Bible from Greek and Hebrew into Latin. He also was a Christian apologist. Jerome's edition, the Vulgate, is still an important biblical text of the Roman Catholic Church. He is recognized by the Ropman Catholic Church as a Doctor of the Church.

This table was created from Wikipedia, s.v. "Church Fathers" (http://en.wikipedia.org/wiki/Church_Fathers) and s.v. "Eusebius of Caesarea" (http://en.wikipedia.org/wiki/Eusebius_Father_of_Ecclesiastical_History).

EUSEBIUS CITES SCHISMS AND HERESIES IN THE EARLY CHURCH

LDS Scholar James E. Talmage, writing in *The Great Apostasy*, notes:

> Eusebius, whose writings date from the early part of the fourth century, cites the writings of Hegesippus, who lived in the first quarter of the second century, as follows:
>
> "The same author [Hegesippus] also treats the beginning of the heresies that arose about this time, in the following words: 'But after James the Just had suffered martyrdom, as our Lord had for the same reason, Simeon, the son of Cleophas, our Lord's uncle, was appointed the second bishop [of Jerusalem] whom all proposed as the cousin of our Lord. Hence they called the Church as yet a virgin, for it was not yet corrupted by vain discourses. Thebuthis made a beginning, secretly to corrupt it on account of his not being made bishop. He was one of those seven sects among the Jewish people. Of these also was Simeon, whence sprang the sect of the Simonians; also Cleobius, from whence came the Cleobians; also Dositheus, the founder of the Dosithians. From these also sprung the Gortheonians, from Gorthoeus; and also Masbotheans from Masbotheus. Hence also the Meandrians, and Marcionists, and Caprocratians and Valentinians, and Basilidians, and the Saturnillians, every one introducing his own peculiar opinions, one differing from the other. From these sprung the false Christs and the false prophets and false apostles, who divided the unity of the Church by the introduction of corrupt doctrines against God and against his Christ."[9]

THE HERESIES OF GNOSTICISM

Many of the writings of the apostolic fathers were devoted to their fight against the false teachings of the Gnostics. Elaine Pagels's excellent book *The Gnostic Gospels*, based on recent translations of the Nag Hammadi codices, documents the beliefs of the Gnostics and the efforts of the apostolic fathers to refute them.

The term *gnosis* implies possession of knowledge. To some early Christians who followed the Gnostic tradition, it implied knowledge of the secret teachings of Jesus to his apostles during the forty days after his resurrection. It is believed that these teachings included the ordinances of the temple, which were reserved only for those who were spiritually prepared to receive them, such as the apostles and the Seventy.

Jesus taught, "Give not that which is holy unto the dogs, neither cast ye your pearls before swine, lest they trample them under their feet, and turn again and rend you" (Matthew 7:6). He also taught in parables so that those who were not spiritually ready to receive certain doctrines would not be condemned for not living them. Although many of these secret teachings are recorded in books of the New Testament Apocrypha that were rejected from the canon of the New Testament, many in the Gnostic communities of the early Church simply invented presumed teachings of Jesus to show that they had gained the gnosis by some metaphysical means, adding greatly to the confusion about the forty-day teachings of Jesus to his apostles.

THE JEWS REQUIRE A SIGN, THE GREEKS SEEK AFTER WISDOM

LDS scholar James E. Faulconer writes, "Partly under the influence of Greek philosophy, Jewish intellectuals thought of God as absolutely transcending the world. Thus, for Greeks and Jews, the central tenet of Christianity, that God had come to earth in a human body, suffered, died, and was resurrected to return to his Father, was sheer foolishness at best: an affront to human intelligence for the Greeks, blasphemy for the Jews."[10] This explains why the Apostle Paul wrote, "For the Jews require a sign, and the Greeks seek after wisdom: But we preach Christ crucified, unto the Jews a stumbling block, and unto the Greeks foolishness" (1 Corinthians 1:22–23).

Plato believed that the body was a hindrance to spiritual purification:

> The body introduces a turmoil and confusion and fear into the course of speculation, and hinders us from seeing the truth; and all experience shows that if we would have pure knowledge of anything we must be quit of the body, and the soul in herself must behold all things in themselves: then, I suppose, that we shall attain that which we desire, and of which we say that we are lovers, and that is wisdom.
>
> . . . The foolishness of the body will be cleared away and we shall be pure and hold converse with other pure souls, and know of ourselves the clear light everywhere; and this is surely the truth. For no impure thing is allowed to approach that which is pure . . . what is purification but the separation of the soul from the body . . . the release of the soul from the chains of the body?[11]

Jennifer Lane writes in *How the New Testament Came to Be*, "Since the body was antithetical to God's nature, the ideas of the incarnation and the Resurrection were against reason. . . . Plato upheld the idea of divine impassibility (God's inability to suffer or feel pain). . . . The idea that Jesus, being God, could 'serve as a slave and be sick and die' seems to him as 'wicked and impious.'"[12]

Faulconer states in *Early Christians in Disarray* that the Gnostics "tried to weaken the belief in Christ's embodiment. Some argued, for example, that he did not really have a body, but only seemed to."[13] Thus the Gnostic philosophy was greatly influenced by Platonic thought.

THE NAG HAMMADI LIBRARY

A new window has been opened into the teachings of the Gnostics, whom the apostolic fathers battled as heretics, with the publication and English translation of all of the texts of the Nag Hammadi Library. In 1945 an exciting archaeological discovery was made in Upper Egypt near the town of Nag Hammadi. While digging for fertilizer at the base of a large bolder, an Egyptian peasant discovered an earthenware jar that contained twelve papyrus codices plus eight leaves from a thirteenth, as well as fifty-two separate tractates, bound in leather. Due to duplications, there are forty-five separate titles. The writings are from a group of early Christians, now classified as Gnostics, who wrote in Coptic, which is a form of Egyptian written with a modified Greek alphabet. Elaine Pagels writes:

> The scholar Frederick Wisse has suggested that the monks who lived at the monastery of St. Pachomius, within the sight of the cliff where the texts were found, may have included the Nag Hammadi texts within their devotional library. But in 367, when Athanasius, the powerful Archbishop of Alexandria, sent an order to purge all "apocryphal books" with "heretical" tendencies, one (or several) of the monks may have hidden the precious manuscripts in the jar and buried it on the cliff on the Jabal al-Tarif, where Muhammad Ali found it 1,600 years later.[14]

The manuscripts have been dated to AD 350–400, but they may be copies of original documents dating to AD 120, "since Irenaeus, the orthodox Bishop of Lyons, writing c. 180, declares that the heretics 'boast that they possess more gospels than there really are,' and complains that in his time such writings already have won wide circulation—from Gaul through Rome, Greece, and Asia Minor."[15]

The Nag Hammadi Library includes the following titles:

The Prayer of the Apostle Paul
The Apocryphon of James
The Gospel of Truth
The Treatise on the Resurrection
The Tripartite Tractate
The Apocryphon of John
The Gospel of Thomas
The Gospel of Philip
The Hypostasis of the Archons
On the Origin of the World
The Exegesis of the Soul
The Book of Thomas the Contender
The Gospel of the Egyptians
Eugnostos the Blessed
The Dialog of the Savior
The Apocalypse of Paul
The First Apocalypse of James
The Second Apocalypse of James
The Apocalypse of Adam
The Acts of Peter and the Twelve Apostles
The Thunder, Perfect Mind
Authoritative Teaching
The Concept of Our Great Power
Plato, Republic
The Discourse on the Eighth and Ninth
The Prayer of Thanksgiving
Asclepius
The Paraphrase of Shem
The Second Treatise of the Great Seth
Apocalypse of Peter
The Teachings of Silvanus
The Three Steles of Seth
Zostrianos
The Letter of Peter to Philip
Melchizedek

The Thought of Norea
The Testimony of Truth
Marsanes
The Interpretation of Knowledge
A Valentinian Exposition with On the Anointing, On Baptism A and B, and On the Eucharist A and B
Allogenes
Hypsiphrone
The Sentences of Sextus
Fragments
Trimorphic Protennoia
The Gospel of Mary
The Act of Peter[16]

GNOSTICS USED DOCTRINAL DISPUTES AS A PRETEXT FOR USURPING AUTHORITY

Elaine Pagels views the doctrinal disputes raised by the Gnostics as a pretext for obtaining authority in the Church. The basic dispute is over the doctrine of the resurrection. After the death of the apostles, there were no more living witnesses to testify of his resurrection. Pagels states:

> Tertullian, a brilliantly talented writer (c. AD 190) speaking for the majority, defines the orthodox position: "as Christ rose bodily from the grave, so every believer should anticipate the resurrection of the flesh" . . . Yet some Christians—those he calls heretics—dissent. Without denying the resurrection, they reject the literal interpretation; some find it extremely revolting, repugnant, and impossible . . . Tertullian declares that anyone who denies the resurrection *of the flesh* is a heretic, not a Christian. [17]

The Gnostics, who were members of the Church led astray by false teachers, began to doubt the literal resurrection, believing instead in a spiritual resurrection. They doubted that Jesus was human at all and therefore taught that he did not actually suffer and die on the cross. Evidence of this false teaching is found in the second and third epistles of John, where the apostle warns his readers against such teachings:

> For many deceivers are entered into the world, who confess not that Jesus Christ is come in the flesh. This is a deceiver and an antichrist.

> Look to yourselves, that we lose not those things which we have wrought, but that we receive a full reward.
>
> Whosoever transgresseth, and abideth not in the doctrine of Christ, hath not God. He that abideth in the doctrine of Christ, he hath both the Father and the Son.
>
> If there come any unto you, and bring not this doctrine, receive him not into your house, neither bid him God speed:
>
> For he that biddeth him God speed is partaker of his evil deeds. (2 John 1:7–11)

In 3 John, the apostle identifies one of these deceivers by name and warns the church to shun him. This deceiver seems to have been a bishop, or one having authority, because he cast out of the church those who did receive the teachings of John and the other "brethren." John pledges to visit this congregation shortly.

> I wrote unto the church: but Diotrephes, who loveth to have the preeminence among them, receiveth us not.
>
> Wherefore, if I come, I will remember his deeds which he doeth, prating against us with malicious words: and not content therewith, neither doth he himself receive the brethren, and forbiddeth them that would, and casteth them out of the church.
>
> Beloved, follow not that which is evil, but that which is good. He that doeth good is of God: but he that doeth evil hath not seen God.
>
> Demetrius hath good report of all men, and of the truth itself: yea, and we also bear record; and ye know that our record is true.
>
> I had many things to write, but I will not with ink and pen write unto thee:
>
> But I trust I shall shortly see thee, and we shall speak face to face. Peace be to thee. Our friends salute thee. Greet the friends by name. (3 John 1:9–14)

Whether John was able to strengthen them or they were overcome by the deceiver is not known from the scriptures or any other source.[18]

Elaine Pagels states that the authority of the apostles derives from their "experience of the resurrected Christ," and that "orthodox Christians have accepted the view that the apostles alone held definitive religious authority, and that their only legitimate heirs are priests and bishops, who trace their ordination to that same apostolic succession." Pagels says the Gnostic view of the resurrection "symbolized how

Christ's presence could be experienced in the present. What mattered was not literal seeing, but spiritual vision. . . . The disciples themselves misunderstood what Jesus said: those who announced that their dead master had come back physically to life mistook a spiritual truth for an actual event. The Gnostic Gospels ridicule those who take the resurrection literally."[19]

The Gnostic Gospel of Philip states,

"Those who say that they will die first and then rise are in error," but they must "receive the resurrection while they live." [20]

Irenaeus shows that the Gnostics believe that they are superior to the apostles:

> They consider themselves "mature," so that no one can be compared with them in the greatness of their *gnosis*, not even if you mention Peter or Paul or any of the other apostles. . . . They imagine that they themselves have discovered more than the apostles, and that the apostles preached the gospel still under the influence of Jewish opinions, but they themselves are wiser and more intelligent than the apostles.[21]

Irenaeus accused the Gnostics as frauds, "trying to pass off as 'apostolic' what they themselves had invented. He declares that the followers of the gnostic teacher Valentinus, being 'utterly wreckless,'

> put forth their own compositions, while boasting that they have more gospels than there really are . . . They really have no gospel which is not full of blasphemy. For what they have published . . . is totally unlike what has been handed down to us from the apostles."[22]

The authors of the Gnostic gospels attributed their writings to various apostles, without having any claim to authenticity through associations with them. They "openly acknowledged that they derived their gnosis from their own experience."[23] Pagels states, "Like circles of artists today, Gnostics considered original creative invention to be the mark of anyone who becomes spiritually alive."[24]

Pagels shows that the Gnostics felt that "all who had received the gnosis . . . had gone beyond the church's teaching and had transcended the authority of its hierarchy."[25] The Gnostic *Testimony of Truth* declares that the Gnostic becomes a "disciple of his [own] mind," discovering that his own mind "is the father of the truth."[26]

A Gnostic Christian from Asia Minor named Marcion taught that there were two different Gods—1) the Old Testament God who was the creator, and 2) the Father, or God of Love, declared by Jesus. This doctrine of "dualism" proclaimed by the Marcionites states that "there is another God besides the creator."[27] The Gnostic teacher Valentinus did not subscribe publicly to the dualistic nature of God, which made it difficult for Irenaeus to screen out Gnostics of this sect. Irenaeus said of the Gnostics, "Such persons are, to outward appearances, sheep, for they seem to be like us, from what they say in public, repeating the same words [of confession] that we do; but inwardly they are wolves."[28]

Pagels shows that "Valentinus claims . . . he has received from Theudas, a disciple of Paul's, initiation into a secret doctrine of God. Paul himself taught this secret wisdom, he says, not to everyone, and not publicly, but only to a select few whom he considered to be spiritually mature. Valentinus offers, in turn, to initiate 'those who are mature' into his wisdom, since not everyone is able to comprehend it."[29]

In secret, Valentinus initiated "those who are mature" into his gnosis. "According to Valentinus, what Clement and Ignatius mistakenly ascribe to God actually applies only to the creator. Valentinus, following Plato, uses the Greek term for 'creator' (*demiurgos*), suggesting that he is a lesser divine being, who serves as the instrument of the higher powers. It is not God, he explains, but the demiurge who reigns as king and lord, who acts as a military commander, who gives the law and judges those who violate it—in short the 'God of Israel.'"[30]

Valentinus teaches the initiates to "reject the creator's authority and all his demands as foolishness. What Gnostics know is that the creator makes false claims to power ('I am God and there is no other') that derive from his own ignorance. Achieving gnosis involves coming to recognize the true source of divine power—namely, 'the depth' of all being."[31]

However, the Gnostics, claiming superiority to the apostles, and the bishops who derived their authority from them, began to hold secret meetings of the church without the knowledge or presence of the bishops.[32]

Irenaeus, Bishop of Lyons, defined the true gnosis:

> True gnosis is that which consists in the doctrine of the apostles, and the ancient constitution [systema] of the church throughout the whole world, and the character of the body of Christ according to the succession of bishops, by which they have handed down that which exists everywhere.[33]

Elaine Pagels's book *The Gnostic Gospels* is filled with many more examples of the Gnostic teachings taken from the recent translations of the Nag Hammadi Library and gives incredible insight to these heretical beliefs that caused such frustration among the Early Church Fathers. Without belaboring these issues, enough of Pagels's insightful assessment of these beliefs has been presented to show that the "grievous wolves" that Paul foresaw were, in fact, not sparing the flock and were sowing their tares amid the wheat of the unwary converts to Christianity, as foretold in Jesus's parable.

OTHER VIEWS OF GNOSTIC CORRUPTION OF THE GOSPEL

LDS scholar John Gee, in *The Corruption of Scripture in Early Christianity*, quotes Clement of Alexandria to show how Carpocrates, by deception, obtained the secret ordinances that the Lord taught to the apostles in the forty days following his resurrection, and how Carpocrates added to and corrupted those ordinances.

"A work attributed to Clement of Alexandria (ca. 150–215), head of the catechetical school at Alexandria, describes the corruption of the Gospel of Mark by Carpocrates":

> Now then, Mark, during Peter's stay in Rome, wrote down the acts of the Lord, nevertheless, not telling all, nor even hinting at the sacred ones (*tas mystikas*) but selecting those which he thought most useful for the growth of the investigator's faith. When Peter was martyred, Mark came to Alexandria; polishing both his own and Peter's notes, from which by transferring into his first book those things appropriate for those progressing in the testimony (*gnosis*), he compiled a more spiritual gospel for the use of those being perfected (*ton teleioumenon*). In no way, however, did he betray those things not discussed, nor did he write down the initiatory teaching (*hierophantiken didaskalian*) of the Lord. But adding to the previously written acts yet others, he still added certain sayings thereto, the explanation of which would be capable of initiating (*mystagogesein*) their hearers into the holy of holies (*adyton*) of the truth veiled seven times. Wherefore, he prepared it thus—neither corruptly nor unprecautiously—so I deem it. And when he died he left his compilation at the church which is in Alexandria, where it is kept very safe and secure to this day, being read only by those who are initiated into the great mysteries (*tous myoumenous ta megala mysteria*).[34]

"But Carpocrates who was taught by defiled demons who continuously plot the destruction for the children of men, having even used the arts of deception, thus enslaved a certain elder of the church in Alexandria so that he prepared a copy of the secret gospel (*tou mystikou euangeliou*). And he explained it according to his own blasphemous and carnal thought. But still he defiled it by mixing into the immaculate and holy words the most abominable lies. From this tincture he extracted the Carpocrationa doctrine."[35]

After citing this account, John Gee admits that it may be a forgery: "Ironically, it is not known whether this text itself is authentic or an ancient, medieval, or modern forgery."[36]

Thomas A. Wayment, in his study of false gospels states,

> A considerable body of New Testament apocryphal texts originates from a period when divergence between mainstream Christianity and its many branches was still quite recent, enough so to cause confusion between the various Christian communities. At the end of the first century, and particularly into the second and third centuries, a variety of Christianities—or groups professing divergent beliefs about Christ and His gospel—sought for converts among both Gentiles and other Christian communities. In their efforts to win converts, Christian communities were faced, much as they are today, with conflicting arguments based on the same Christian texts. To help differentiate themselves, some circles of Christians, particularly Gnostic and other marginalized Christian communities, forged documents to further their claims. Some examples of this type of writing survive today, including the recently published Gospel of Judas, a late-second-century forgery which appears to have been written in an effort to validate and promote Gnostic doctrines.[37]

Wayment describes the salient features of the Gnostic gospels as:

- a subtle correction of the Synoptic or Johannine accounts
- the elevation of a single person, usually an apostle
- preservation of the sayings of Jesus, almost always in new forms or contexts
- the preservation and transmission of secret teachings
- a suppression of the humanity of Jesus or his mortal traits as they appear in the scriptural gospels.[38]

Wayment discusses fictional texts, written for enjoyment, including "romances, legendary accounts, and fictional acts of the apostles to satisfy this need"[39] for fictional literature. He gives as examples the infancy narratives of Jesus and the Acts of Pilate. He also describes apocalyptic works "written during the second and third centuries, which promised the glorious return of the Savior and the ultimate vindication of the Saints. They became a popular form of expressing hope in the Second Coming, promising vindication to the oppressed."[40] He believes that these texts were "probably aimed at satisfying the needs of an oppressed people rather than preserving Christian traditions about Jesus' return in glory."[41] He gives as examples the Apocalypse of Peter, the Apocalypse of Paul, the Shepherd of Hermies, and the Ascension of Isaiah.

Wayment concludes: "It is safe to say, based on current research, that every apocryphal text that claims to preserve the teachings of a New Testament figure was forged. The same cannot be said of the canonical texts, which indicates that the early Church was quite successful at separating the wheat from the chaff. At the same time, however, the apocryphal literature can inform us about the development of the Church in the post-apostolic era."

Early Church leaders faced the threat of outsiders, posing as insiders, who attempted to redirect the affairs of the Church through the creation of forged gospels and letters. Without the aid of the apostles, those early Church leaders had to distinguish between forgeries and the genuine letters and gospels of Jesus's disciples.[42]

THE PERSECUTION OF THE CHRISTIANS

The true cause of the apostasy was rebellion by the early Christians from the covenants and ordinances given to them by the apostles, even during the lives of the apostles, which allowed the Gnostic wolves among them to sow seeds of false doctrine as a means of usurping authority once only granted by the apostles themselves. However, this rebellion was not universal at first, for the doctrine of the resurrection lived on in the hearts and minds of the faithful and was passed down to the second and third generations of early church leaders. While their belief in the resurrection was unshakeable, they admitted that they were not the recipients of the gifts of the Holy Ghost or of revelations like those received by the apostles.

Between the crucifixion of Jesus and the final martyrdom of the apostles, the Jewish leaders continued to persecute the Christians.

James E. Talmage writes in *The Great Apostasy:* "Not only did the Jews wage relentless persecution against those of their numbers who professed Christ, but they sought to stir up opposition on the part of the Romans, and to accomplish this end charged that the Christians were plotting treason against the Roman government."[43]

The same persecutions that resulted in the execution of the apostles by AD 70 continued to claim the lives of those Christians who were the most faithful. Normally the Romans were tolerant of other religions, but the Christians, in their efforts to spread the gospel, ridiculed those who worshipped idols as superstitious pagans, and they refused to worship the Roman gods and the Roman emperors who claimed to be gods themselves. The Romans concluded that the Christians were not only arrogant but also enemies to the public tranquility.[44]

In AD 64 a large fire consumed much of Rome, and some blamed Nero, who was a very unpopular dictator. To deflect suspicion from himself, Nero blamed the Christians, who professed a belief that the world would be destroyed by fire. James E. Talmage records the words of Tacitus, a Roman historian, who writes:

> With this view, he [Nero] inflicted the most exquisite tortures on those men who, under the vulgar appellation of Christians were already branded with deserved infamy. They derived their name and origin from Christ, who in the reign of Tiberius suffered death by the sentence of the procurator, Pontius Pilate. For a while this dire superstition was checked; but it again burst forth; and not only spread itself over Judea, the first seat of this mischievous sect, but was even introduced into Rome, the common asylum which receives and protects whatever is impure, whatever is atrocious. The confessions of those that were seized discovered a great multitude of their accomplices, and they were all convicted, not so much for the crime of setting fire to the city, as for their hatred of mankind. They died in torments, and their torments were embittered by insults and derision. Some were nailed on crosses; others sewn up in the skins of wild beasts and exposed to the fury of dogs; others, again, smeared over with combustible materials, were used as torches to illuminate the darkness of the night. The gardens of Nero were destined for the melancholy spectacle, which was accompanied with a horse-race, and honored with the presence of the emperor, who mingled with the populace in the dress and attitude of a charioteer. The guilt of the Christians deserved indeed the most exemplary punishments,

> but the public abhorrence was changed into commiseration, from the opinion that those unhappy wretches were sacrificed, not so much to the public welfare as to the cruelty of a jealous tyrant.[45]

Christians were accused of being magicians, astrologers, and atheists (because they refused to worship the Roman gods and the emperor). Roman governors, when accused Christians were brought before them, tried to persuade them to denounce Christ and recite prayers to the pagan gods and declare the divinity of the emperor, as the price for their freedom. Refusal to comply consigned them to death by many hideous and cruel means, usually to provide cheap entertainment for the Roman populace, as free substitutes for gladiators, who had to be paid.

Elaine Pagels recounts the trial of Justin (whom tradition calls "the martyr") in AD 165, by Rusticus, a prefect of the emperor, Marcus Aurelius:

> "Well, then," said the prefect Rusticus, "let us come to the point at issue, a necessary and pressing business. Agree to offer sacrifice to the gods." "No one of sound mind," said Justin, "turns from piety to impiety." The prefect, Rusticus then said, "If you do not obey, you will be punished without mercy." When they replied, "Do what you will; we are Christians, and we do not offer sacrifice to idols," Rusticus pronounced sentence: "Let those who have refused to offer sacrifice to the gods and to yield to the emperor's edict be led away to be scourged and beheaded in accordance with the law."[46]

Ignatius, Bishop of Antioch, in AD 107, who was was condemned to death by wild beasts in the Roman Coliseum, wrote the following to his fellow Christians:

> I write to all the Churches, and impress on them all, that I shall willingly die for God, unless ye hinder me. I beseech of you not to show an unseasonable good-will towards me. Suffer me to become food for the wild beasts, through whose instrumentality it will be granted me to attain to God. I am the wheat of God, and am ground by the teeth of the wild beasts, that I may be found the pure bread of God. Rather entice the wild beasts, that they may become my tomb, and may leave nothing of my body; so that when I have fallen asleep, I may not be found troublesome to any one. Then shall I be a true disciple of Jesus Christ, when the world shall not see so much as my body. Entreat the Lord for me, that by these instruments I may be found a sacrifice to God.[47]

However, throughout these years of intense persecutions of the orthodox Christians, the Gnostic Christians, for the most part, denounced martyrdom as foolishness. Many of the Gnostic sects did not believe in the humanity of Jesus, nor his suffering on the cross, and believed instead in a spiritual resurrection.

The Gnostic text named the *Second Treatise of the Great Seth*, found at Nag Hammadi, falsely relates Christ's teaching that

> it was another, their father, that drank the gall and the vinegar; it was not I. They struck me with the reed; it was another, Simon, who bore the cross on his shoulder. It was another upon whom they placed the crown of thorns. But I was rejoicing in the height over all of the wealth of the archons and the offspring of their error, of their empty glory. And I was laughing at their ignorance.[48]

The Gnostic *Testimony of Truth* ridicules Christian martyrs, saying that they do not know who Christ is:

> The foolish—thinking in their heart that if they confess, "We are Christians," in word only (but) not with power, while giving themselves over to ignorance, to a human death, not knowing where they are going, nor who Christ is, thinking that they will live, when they are (really) in error—hasten toward the principalities and authorities. They fall into their clutches because of the ignorance that is in them.[49]
>
> These are [empty] martyrs, since they bear witness only to themselves. And yet they are sick, and are not able to raise themselves. But when they are "perfected" with a (martyr's) death, this is the thought that they have witin them: "If we deliver ourselves over to death for the sake of the Name, we shall be saved." These matters are not settled in this way. . . . They do not have the Word which gives [life].[50]

In the midst of such cruel persecutions, the orthodox Christians held fast to the testimonies of the apostles, which had been handed down to them by oral traditions and written gospels, and suffered even more from these denials by the Gnostics, who often claimed to be more spiritual members of the church than the orthodox Saints. It is undoubtedly the testimonies of these brave martyrs that brought many converts to orthodox Christianity and ultimately resulted in the preservation of the writings of the apostles, if not the continuation of the original Church as established by Jesus Christ. Hugh Nibley says in

Apostles and Bishops in Early Christianity, "When the apostolic authority was withdrawn, when the rites and ordinances were taken away, they kept alive the memory of the Savior and the apostles."[51]

CONTINUED PERSECUTIONS BY ROMAN EMPERORS

Domitian

The second official persecution by a Roman emperor began in AD 93 during the reign of Domitian, who, according to tradition, heard a prediction from the family of Jesus that "there would arise one who would weaken if not overthrow the power of Rome. With this as his ostensible excuse, this wicked ruler waged terrible destruction on an innocent people."[52]

Trajan

The third official persecution of Christians by Rome came during the reign of the emperor Trajan, who ruled Rome from AD 98 to 117. Although he is considered by historians as one of the better Roman emperors, he allowed persecution of Christians for their refusal to sacrifice to Roman gods. A letter to Trajan from Pliney, governor of Pontus, asked for advice as to how to handle those accused of being Christians. Trajan directed that "Christians were not to be hunted or sought after vindictively, but if accused and brought before the judgment seat, and if they refused to renounce their faith, they were to be put to death."[53]

Marcus Aurelius

Under Marcus Aurelius, emperor from AD 161 to 180, persecution was most severe in Gaul (now France). Polycarp, Bishop of Smyrna, and Justin Martyr, Bishop of Rome, suffered martyrdom under the reign of Marcus Aurelius, again for refusal to worship the pagan gods of Rome.[54]

Justin, in Palestine (c. 135), wrote:

"It is clear that no one can terrify or subdue us who believe in Christ, throughout the whole world. For it is clear that though beheaded, and crucified, and thrown to wild beasts, in chains, in fire, and all other kinds of torture, we do not give up our confession; but the more such things happen, the more do others, in larger numbers, become believers."[55]

The ancient document The Martyrdom of Polycarp describes the trial of the Bishop of Smyrna who was arrested and challenged to deny Christ and avoid a sentence of death as a Christian.

> When then he was brought before him, the proconsul enquired whether he were the man. And on his confessing that he was, he tried to persuade him to a denial saying, 'Have respect to thine age,' and other things in accordance therewith, as it is their wont to say; 'Swear by the genius of Caesar; repent and say, Away with the atheists.' Then Polycarp with solemn countenance looked upon the whole multitude of lawless heathen that were in the stadium, and waved his hand to them; and groaning and looking up to heaven he said, 'Away with the atheists.' But when the magistrate pressed him hard and said, 'Swear the oath, and I will release thee; revile the Christ,' Polycarp said, 'Fourscore and six years have I been His servant, and He hath done me no wrong. How then can I blaspheme my King who saved me' But on his persisting again and saying, 'Swear by the genius of Caesar,' he answered, 'If thou supposest vainly that I will swear by the genius of Caesar, as thou sayest, and feignest that thou art ignorant who I am, hear thou plainly, I am a Christian.[56]

Polycarp was buried alive in the public arena.

Diocletian

Diocletian ruled from AD 284 to 305. Talmage noted that Diocletian attempted

> a total suppression of the Christian religion. To this end he ordered a general destruction of Christian books, and decreed the penalty of death against any and all who kept such works in their possession. . . . At the end of the decade of terror the Church was in a scattered and seemingly hopeless condition. Sacred records had been burnt; places of worship had been razed to the ground; thousands of Christians had been put to death; and every possible effort had been made to destroy the Church and abolish Christianity from the earth.[57]

Diocletian's efforts to eradicate Christianity were so intense that at the end of this decade of horrific terror, monuments were raised to proclaim success, "for having extinguished the name of Christians who brought the Republic to ruin, . . . for having everywhere abolished the superstition of Christ; . . . for having extended the worship of the gods."[58]

Historically, the church grew in numbers in times of bitter persecutions and became more fragmented in times of peace until Constantine adopted Christianity as the state religion in AD 325.

CONCLUSIONS

The Early Church Fathers preserved most of the teachings of the four Gospels and the apostles' epistles in letters between various bishops to congregations of the early Church, and their relentless battles against the Gnostic heretics established the orthodox Church based on the apostolic traditions. The recent discovery of the Nag Hammadi Library has validated the views of the Early Church Fathers regarding the heretical teachings of the Gnostics, which were clearly based on imagined experiences and fraudulent scriptures, written to solidify their authority and self-proclaimed spirituality. The vicious persecution of Christians by first the Jews and then the Romans, instead of stamping out the Christian movement, fueled the growth of the Church as onlookers saw the determination of the Christians to give their lives for their testimonies of Jesus Christ.

NOTES

1. Clemens Romanus, *I Clement 3.3*, quoted by Elaine Pagels, *The Gnostic Gospels* (New York: Random House, 1979), 34.
2. Kent P. Jackson, "Asking Restoration Questions," in *How the New Testament Came to Be* (Salt Lake City and Provo, UT: Deseret Book and BYU Religious Studies Center, 2006), 35.
3. Ignatius, *Epistola ad Philadelphipheneses*, 4, in PG 5:828, quoted by Hugh Nibley, *Apostles and Bishops in Early Christianity* (Salt Lake City, UT: Deseret Book Company, 2005), 25.
4. Polycarp, *Epistola ad Philippenses,* 3.2 in PG 5:1008, quoted by Hugh Nibley, *Apostles and Bishops in Early Christianity*, 28.
5. Hugh Nibley, *Apostles and Bishops in Early Christianity* (Salt Lake City and Provo, UT: Deseret Book and FARMS, 2005), 102.
6. Carol F. Ellertson, "New Testament Manuscripts," in *How the New Testament Came to Be*, 96.
7. Frank F. Judd, Jr., "Who Really Wrote the Gospels?," in *How the New Testament Came to Be*, 130.
8. Richard D. Draper, "The Earliest 'New Testament,'" in *How the New Testament Came to Be*, 266.
9. Eusebius, *Ecclesiastical History*, Book IV, ch 22, quoted by James E.

Talmage, *The Great Apostasy* (Salt Lake City, UT: Deseret Book Company, 1909), 93.

10. James E. Faulconer, "The Concept of Apostasy in the New Testament," in *Early Christians in Disarray*, ed. Noel B. Reynolds (Provo, UT: FARMS and Brigham Young University Press, 2005), 160.
11. Plato, *Phaedo,* 498-499, quoted in Jennifer C. Lane, "Jews and Greeks," in *How the New Testament Came to Be*, 65.
12. Lane, "Jews and Greeks," 66, 68.
13. Faulconer, "The Concept of Apostasy in the New Testament," 160.
14. Pagels, *The Gnostic Gospels*, 120–21.
15. Pagels, *The Gnostic Gospels*, xvi.
16. James M. Robinson, ed., *The Nag Hammadi Library in English,* 3rd ed. rev. (San Francisco: Harper Collins, 1988), xii–xiv.
17. Tertulian, *De Resurrectione Carnis*, 2, quoted by Elaine Pagels, *The Gnostic Gospels*, 4-5.
18. Richard Neitzel Holzapfel, Eric D. Huntsman, and Thomas A. Wayment, *Jesus Christ and the World of the New Testament* (Salt Lake City: Deseret Book, 2006), 277.
19. Elaine Pagels, *The Gnostic Gospels*, 10–12.
20. *Gospel of Philip*, 73.1–3, in NHL 144, and 57.19–20, in NHL 135, quoted by Elaine Pagels, *The Gnostic Gospels*, 12.
21. Irenaeus, AH, 1.13.6, quoted by Elaine Pagels, *The Gnostic Gospels*, 21.
22. Irenaeus, AH, 3.11.9, quoted by Elaine Pagels, *The Gnostic Gospels*, 17.
23. Elaine Pagels, *The Gnostic Gospels*, 18.
24. Ibid., 19.
25. Ibid., 25.
26. *Testimony of the Truth*, 43.26 in NHL 410, quoted by Pagels, *The Gnostic Gospels*, 131–32.
27. Elaine Pagels, *The Gnostic Gospels*, 29.
28. Irenaeus, AH, 3.16.6, quoted by Elaine Pagels, *The Gnostic Gospels*, 32.
29. Irenaeus, AH, 3.2.1-3.1, and Praefatio 2;3.15-.1-2, quoted by Elaine Pagels, *The Gnostic Gospels*, 36–37.
30. Elaine Pagels, *The Gnostic Gospels*, 37.
31. Elaine Pagels, *The Gnostic Gospels*, 37.
32. Ignatius, *Magnesins 6.1; Trallians 3.1; Ephesians 5.3*, quoted by Elaine Pagels, *The Gnostic Gospels*, 39–40.
33. Irenaeus, AH 4.33.8, quoted by Elaine Pagels, *The Gnostic Gospels*, 105.
34. *Clement of Alexandria and a Secret Gospel of Mark*, Cambridge, MA: Harvard University Press, 1973), 38, quoted by John Gee, "The Corruption of Scripture in Early Christianity," in *Early Christians in Disarray*, 168–69.

35. Clement of Alexandria, *Letter to Theodore*, 1.15–2.10, in Smith, *Clement of Alexandria and a Secret Gospel of Mark*, 448–51, plates I-II; cf. Hamblin, "Early Christian Initiation Ritual," 210–11, quoted by John Gee in *Early Christians in Disarray*, 168–69.
36. John Gee, "The Corruption of Scripture in Early Christianity," in *Early Christians in Disarray*, 169.
37. Thomas A. Wayment, "False Gospels: An Approach to Studying the New Testament Apocrapha," in *How the New Testament Came to Be* (Salt Lake City and Provo, UT: Deseret Book and BYU Religious Studies Center, 2006), 295.
38. Ibid., 296.
39. Ibid., 298.
40. Ibid., 299.
41. Ibid., 299–300.
42. Ibid., 300–301.
43. James E. Talmage, *The Great Apostasy* (Salt Lake City: Deseret Book, 1909), 59.
44. Ibid., 66.
45. Ibid., 68–69.
46. "The Martyrdom of Saints Justin, Chariton, Charito, Euelpistis, Heirax, Paeon, Liberian, and Their Community," Recencion B, 5, in The Acts of Christian Martyrs, ed. H. Mursurillo (Oxford, 1972), 53, quoted by Elaine Pagels, *The Gnostic Gospels,* 79–80.
47. Ignatius, Epistle to the Romans 4.1–2, translated by A. Roberts and J. Donaldson.
48. Second Treatise of the Great Seth, James M. Robinson, ed., The Nag Hammadi Library in English, 3rd ed. rev. (San Francisco: Harper Collins, 1988) VII 49, 10-70, 12. Translated by Roger A. Bullard and Joseph A. Gibbons, 365.
49. *Testimony of Truth*, James M. Robinson, ed., The Nag Hammadi Library in English, 3rd ed. rev. (San Francisco: Harper Collins, 1988), IX 29, 6-74, 30, Translated by Soren Giversen and Birger A Pearson, 450.
50. Ibid., 451.
51. Hugh Nibley, *Apostles and Bishops in Early Christianity,* 53.
52. James E. Talmage, *The Great Apostasy* (Desert Book Company, Salt Lake City, UT 1909), 69–70.
53. Ibid., 70–71.
54. Ibid., 71–72.
55. Justin, *Dialogue with Trypho*, 110.4, quoted by Elaine Pagels, *The Gnostic Gospels*, 83.
56. "Martyrdom of Saint Polycarp" 9–10, The Wesley Center Online: The

Martyrdom Of Polycart Or Letter of the Smyrnaeans, http://wesley.nnu.edu/sermons-essays-books/noncanonical-literature/the-martyrom-of-polycarp-or-letter-of-the-smyrnaeans.

57. Talmage, *The Great Apostasy,* 72–73.
58. Ibid., 75.

CHAPTER 11

THE CHURCH ESTABLISHED BY CONSTANTINE

This people draweth nigh unto me with their mouth, and honoureth me with their lips; but their heart is far from me.

But in vain they do worship me, teaching for doctrines the commandments of men.

Matthew 15:8–9

AFTER TWO CENTURIES OF CHRISTIANS BEING VICIOUSLY PERSEcuted by Roman emperors, Constantine won a decisive victory over Maxentius and was proclaimed Western Augustus, or ruler of the Western Empire. According to tradition, before that battle, he proclaimed that he was shown in a vision that he would conquer with the sign of Christ. His warriors were said to have worn the sign of the cross on their shields even though most of them were pagans. Following the battle in 313, he met Licinius, Emperor of the Eastern Empire, in Milan, and these two emperors issued the Edict of Milan, which banned persecution of Christians. Constantine's mother, later elevated to Sainthood as St. Helena, was a Christian, although his father, a Roman General and also a junior emperor, was not a Christian. In AD 320, Licinius violated the Edict of Milan and began another persecution of Christians in the Eastern Empire. Constantine marched against him during a civil war that he won in AD 324, when he became the emperor of the entire Roman Empire. In AD 330, Constantine rebuilt the city of Byzantium in the Eastern Empire and designated it as Nova

Roma (New Rome). This city was renamed Constantinople in AD 327, after Constantine's death.

Once Christianity became the official state religion of the Roman Empire, persecution of Christians ceased and persecution of the heretics was officially sanctioned. These heretic persecutions included the burning of Gnostic gospels, which may have inspired the preservation of the Nag Hammadi Library in an earthen jar in the desert. The office of bishop took on new power and authority under the protection of the Roman government. The bishop was not only the ecclesiastical authority of a city, but also its mayor or governor, with civil authority to execute justice according to the civil law.[1] "*Ekklesia* means public assembly, 'the ruling popular assembly of the Greek city state.'"[2] Instead of being called by revelation and ordained to the office of bishop as was the practice by the apostles in the early Church, now the office of bishop became one of political campaigns, wherein the bishop was chosen by "acclamation."[3] In other words, the candidate whose supporters shouted the loudest during a caucus of citizens in the public square became the next bishop. Some bishops were appointed to that position by Constantine himself, giving them both religious and civil authority. This practice introduced worldly ambition into the once sacred office of bishop as established by the Lord and his apostles, and clearly shows the lack of revelation in the selection of the one who should be the "Lord's anointed" leader.

James E. Talmage said in *The Great Apostasy*,

> The office of a bishop came to be more highly esteemed than the rank of a general. The emperor himself was the real head of the Church. It became unpopular and decidedly disadvantageous in a material sense to be known as a non-Christian. Pagan temples were transformed into churches, and heathen idols were demolished.[4]

By this time thousands of orthodox Christian leaders had been executed under the previous ten officially sanctioned persecutions, (the most recent under Diocletian), and most of the early manuscripts of the scriptures had been intentionally destroyed. Controversy regarding official Christian doctrines raged between bishops competing for power and authority in the newly sanctioned Church of Rome. Constantine, hoping to use the Church as a means of uniting the people under both civil and religious harmony, was dismayed by the bickering of the bishops. In order to resolve these disputes, he called the first ecumenical council of the post-apostolic church, in which he became the de facto head of the church, filling the void of central leadership (albeit not divine guidance) that had been left by the death of the apostles.

CONFUSION ABOUT THE NATURE OF GOD

With the invented doctrines of the Gnostic heretics, the influence of Greek philosophy, and the loss of the divine revelation to the apostles, confusion about the very nature of God was abundant. Clement of Alexandria (AD 150–215) was the first of the Christian fathers to promote the idea of an incorporeal God. But Noel B. Reynolds, in *What Went Wrong with Early Christians*, says that "in the first and second centuries, both Jews and Christians generally believed that God was embodied."[5] David L. Paulsen, in *The Doctrine of Divine Embodiment*, states that the Hebrew Bible, which was essentially the most common scripture available to the early Christians, described God as embodied. Genesis 1:26 states, "And God said, let us make man in our own image, after our likeness." There are also many scriptures that refer to the body parts of God: "I [Jacob] have seen God face to face" (Genesis 32:30), "the Lord spake to Moses face to face" (Exodus 33:11), and "I will take away my hand, and thou shalt see my back parts: but my face shall not be seen" (Exodus 33:23).[6] Stephen, while being martyred, saw "the heavens opened, and the Son of Man, standing on the right hand of God" (Acts 7:56).

Paulsen quotes Origen, as student of Clement of Alexandria, who "adopted the Platonistic metaphysics of his culture," by espousing "his incorporealistic concept of God. . . . How God himself is to be understood,—whether as corporal, and formed according to some shape, or of a different nature from bodies—[is] a point which is not clearly indicated in our thinking."[7]

THE ARIANS

Arius (ca. AD 320), a presbyter (elder) of the church in Alexandria, "took the traditional teachings that Jesus is subordinate to the Father, that God is an indivisible, eternally unchanging substance, and that God created everything outside of himself from nothing" concluded that "Jesus cannot be God in the strict sense and must have been created from nothing."[8]

Arius taught that God the Father and the Son did not exist together eternally. Further, Arius taught that Jesus was created by the Father out of nothing and that there was a time when the Son did not exist. The Arians believe that Jesus is or was a "creature," or a "created being."

The Arian controversy began in Alexandria in 318 and spread throughout the Christian churches, leading up to the Nicene Council called in the year 320 by the Roman emperor Constantine. Pope Alexander of Alexandria condemned this teaching by Arias, who fled to Palestine, where he gained acceptance. This philosophy was in direct contradiction to the orthodox teachings of the Apostolic Church Fathers, who by this time espoused the doctrine of the Trinity, or divine Sonship of the Logos (or Word). Most orthodox or mainstream Christian historians considered this philosophy of Arius to be heresy. The Nicene Creed, approved by all but three of the roughly 300 bishops at the Council, repudiates the doctrine of Arianism.[9]

TERTULLIAN'S VIEWS ON THE TRINITY

This teaching by the Arians was in opposition to the doctrine of the Trinity, which was espoused by Tertullian.

Speaking of Tertullian, *The History of the Church* by Walker, Norris, Lotz, and Handy, states:

> His most notable contribution to theology . . . was made in the track, *Against Praxeas,* in which he mounted an attack on a 'monarchian' teacher who had denied the substantive reality of the Logos [Word] as distinct from the Father (see II:8). In this work, Tertullian evolved the earliest systematic form of the doctrine of the Trinity, arguing that there is one divine 'substance' which is articulated, or 'administered' into three distinct but continuous 'persons': Father, Logos/Son, and Spirit. At the same time, he offered a reflective account of the incarnation, explaining that the person of Christ is a union of two distinct, unconfused 'substances,' divine and human, in a single 'person.' This terminology—hard to interpret by reason of the differences between the meanings of Tertullian's Latin terms and those of their modern English derivatives—became the basis of all later Latin and western trinitarian and Christological discourse.[10]

Tertullian writes in his treatise *Against Praxaes*:

> We, however, as we indeed always have done (and more especially since we have been better instructed by the Paraclete, who leads men indeed into all truth), believe that there is one only God,

> but under the following dispensation . . . that this one only God has also a Son, His Word, who proceeded from Himself, by whom all things were made, and without whom nothing was made. Him *we* believe to have been sent by the Father into the Virgin, and to have been born of her—being both Man and God, the Son of Man and the Son of God, and to have been called by the name of Jesus Christ; *we* believe Him to have suffered, died, and been buried, according to the Scriptures, and, after He had been raised again by the Father and taken back to heaven, to be sitting at the right hand of the Father, *and* that He will come to judge the quick and the dead; who sent also from heaven from the Father, according to His own promise, the Holy Ghost, the Paraclete, the sanctifier of the faith of those who believe in the Father, and in the Son, and in the Holy Ghost. That this rule of faith has come down to us from the beginning of the gospel, even before any of the older heretics, much more before Praxeas . . .
>
> As if in this way also one were not All, in that All are of One, by unity (that is) of substance; while the mystery of the dispensation is still guarded, which distributes the Unity into a Trinity, placing in their order the three *Persons*—the Father, the Son, and the Holy Ghost: three, however, not in condition, but in degree; not in substance, but in form; not in power, but in aspect; yet of one substance, and of one condition, and of one power, inasmuch as He is one God, from whom these degrees and forms and aspects are reckoned, under the name of the Father, and of the Son, and of the Holy Ghost.[11]
>
> Bear always in mind that this is the rule of faith which I profess; by it I testify that the Father, and the Son, and the Spirit are inseparable from each other, and so will you know in what sense this is said. Now, observe, my assertion is that the Father is one, and the Son one, and the Spirit one, and that They are distinct from Each Other. This statement is taken in a wrong sense by every uneducated as well as every perversely disposed person, as if it predicated a diversity, in such a sense as to imply a separation among the Father, and the Son, and the Spirit.[12]

Even though Tertullian professed a belief in the Trinity, which later was transformed into the Westminster Confession of Faith, ("There is but one only living and true God, who is infinite in being and perfection, a most pure spirit, invisible, without body, parts, or passions."), Tertullian still professed an unshakeable conviction in the corporeal nature of God and Jesus Christ. Davie L. Paulsen notes that:

> He argued that (1) God, like all that is, is embodied, (2) beings of spirit may take on more solid bodily form, (3) Christ in the Incarnation specifically took on flesh that was unqualifiedly human, (4) human flesh is a sacred and glorious substance, (5) the same fleshy body that falls in human death rises in the resurrection, and (6) Christ's resurrected body is an everlasting and crucial attribute of the Godhead.[13]

The simple and true explanation of the relationship between the Father, the Son, and the Holy Ghost is, as Jesus Christ clearly taught while on earth, that his will is only to do the will of his Father and that he is totally obedient to his Father in all things. Joseph Smith, the Prophet, learned through revelation from Christ that Jehovah was chosen by the Father during our premortal existence in the heavens before the creation of the earth, to become the creator of all things and to become the Savior to atone for the sins of all who ever live upon this earth, upon the condition of their repentance and faith in him. Heavenly Father totally delegated to Jehovah, who was born to the Virgin Mary, as the Christ named Jesus, all authority over this earth. The Father has never spoken to a man on earth except to introduce his Only Begotten Son. The Father and the Son are so united in purpose that the Son knows the mind and will of the Father and is authorized to speak for the Father, as if he were the Father. The Holy Ghost is a spirit personage, yet to be born in the flesh, who is likewise totally unified with the mind and will of the Father and the Son and is the communicator between mortals and the Father and the Son, who are one unified Godhead. The Father is God and the Son is also a god who represents the Father in every way but humbles himself before the Father and teaches us to pray to the Father in his (the Son's) name. The Father, the Son, and the Holy Ghost are one unified Godhead, consisting of three distinct, glorified, and immortal gods.

THE NICENE COUNCIL

The Arian versus Trinity controversy led Constantine to convene the First Council of Nice (AD 325). Barry R. Beckmore, writing about Christian Councils, writes, "At this time, nearly all Christian intellectuals assumed that God was a unique, eternally self-existent, spiritual being, completely distinct from all other entities, which were created from nothing. The orthodox response to Aryanism was that the church had always believed that Jesus was truly God, and there cannot be more than one unique divine essence."[14] Both of these doctrines had been influenced by the infusion of Greek philosophy into the Christian teachings following the demise of the apostles.

Hugh Nibley, in *Apostles and Bishops in Early Christianity*, writes: "the Arian controversy was merely an aspect of the great struggle for episcopal authority. It is not a contest between theologians, but between bishops, and the issue is not doctrine but power. . . . Was the nature of the Trinity the real issue at Nicaea? Not for a moment!"[15] The bishops, who participated in this first ecumenical council of the newly sanctioned church, preceded the conference by letters to Constantine, trying to win him over to their point of view and condemning the errors of their fellow bishops. "At the opening of the Nicene Council, while all were waiting for latecomers, the emperor presided at the burning of a mountain of letters that had been submitted to him by the clergy from all over the world during the days when the council was being prepared. This huge pile of documents consisted almost entirely of charges by various churchmen against each other."[16]

In his article about Christian councils, LDS author Barry R. Bickmore states that at the conference were "three primary groups: (1) the Nicenes, including Athanasius, who believed that the Father and the Son were separate persons coexisting in the same being, (2) the Arians [who asserted that Christ as the son was of a different essence than God the Father], and (3) . . . 'the great conservative middle party,' who taught that there were three divine persons, 'separate in rank and glory but united in harmony of will.'"[17] The result of the conference was the Nicene Creed, which is presented in chapter 4 of this book.

THE HELLENIZATION OF ORTHODOX CHRISTIANITY

Although the Early Church Fathers vigorously fought the heretical influence of the Gnostics, their theology was nevertheless influenced by Greek philosophy. First the Greeks, under Alexander the Great, and then the Romans had conquered Judea and spread their influence and culture to include their languages. "Religious terms and concepts from Hebrew and Aramaic were rendered into Greek, and then Latin."[18] The Apostle Paul and Luke, his missionary companion, used their knowledge of Hebrew and Greek to proselytize the Gentiles, and many of the epistles of Paul would have been written originally in Greek. Noel B.

Reynolds paraphrased Paul's warning to the Saints: "See to it that no one takes you captive through hollow and deceptive philosophy, which depends on human tradition and the basic principles of this world rather than on Christ."[19] By the third century, with the apostasy already in full swing, the Christians found themselves without central leadership to refute the false doctrines that were prevalent in many divergent congregations of the church. The Gnostics and the orthodox congregations, as well as the Arians and many other sects, all claimed to have the truth. These converts brought with them their cultural backgrounds and philosophical beliefs, and in the absence of guidance from the apostles, their concepts and understanding of the gospel began to blend with the popular ideas of their cultures.

Clement of Alexandria (c. 150–215) and his student Origen (c. 185–254) believed that God had inspired the Greeks with wisdom. Clement wrote, "Perchance, too, philosophy was given to the Greeks directly and primarily, till the Lord should call the Greeks."[20] Graham and Seibach, writing *The Introduction of Philosophy into Early Christianity*, stated, "According to Clement, God had inspired the pagans with wisdom, which was to be found randomly in all the philosophical schools. He sent philosophy to the Greeks as a schoolmaster to bring them to Christ, as he had provided the Hebrews with the law of Moses."[21]

Noel B. Reynolds states,

> Even Protestant historians, who used to criticize the hellenization of the early churches, now recognize that the Christian movement would have dwindled into an insignificant folk religion without the infusion of Greek thought. Soon, the third century Christian thinkers came to share Clements's appreciation for the work of Plato and his successors. They went so far as to claim, echoing Origen, that God had sent the Greeks to prepare the systems of thought that would bring Christianity to its divinely intended completion. . . . Though the incorporation of Greek philosophy was not the cause of the apostasy, the apostate Christian churches reached out to embrace philosophy as a means of bringing common standards and rationality to Christian belief. It is widely recognized today by Christian historians that the apostate Christian churches saved the Christian tradition by so doing. But the Christian tradition that resulted was far different than the one established by Jesus and his apostles in the first century."[22]

COVENANTS REPLACED BY SACRAMENTS

Noel B. Reynolds shows that in the second century the early Christian churches had replaced the covenants between man and God, such as baptism, priesthood ordinations, and marriage, with sacraments performed by a priest. From the time of Abraham, the Hebrews had always been a covenant people—or at least were expected by the God of Israel to be, though they frequently rebelled and forsook their covenants. Nevertheless, the covenants of baptism, circumcision, and sacrifice were a way of life for the righteous Israelites. The covenants included sacred promises to follow God, forsake sins, and offer sacrifices as a symbol of the atonement of the Messiah, who would someday be their salvation. The New Testament shows that the commitment of the Jews to their ancestral covenants, such as circumcision, prevented many of them from accepting Christ. Jesus and his apostles introduced the covenant ordinances of baptism and the last supper into the primitive church, but "no clear description of the Christian covenant survives in any New Testament text or in the teachings of the early Christian writers."[23] In the early church after the apostles, however, these ordinances were reinvented, not as sacred promises between man and God, but as blessings offered from God by the intervention of priests or bishops. These blessings did not require any commitment on the part of the recipient and were considered a gift from God through the mediation of the clergy.[24]

Since, in the post-apostolic church, baptism was no longer a covenant with sacred promises to forsake sin and obey God in exchange for the promise of forgiveness but a sacrament requiring no commitment from the recipient, it became commonplace for priests to bestow God's blessings on all people, including infants and sinners who were about to die without baptism. The same is true of the covenant of partaking of the emblems of the body and blood of Christ. Jesus said, "This is my blood of the new covenant" (Mark 14:24). "And he took bread, and gave thanks, and brake it, and gave unto them, saying, This is my body which is given for you: this do in remembrance of me" (Luke 22:19). So the ordinance commonly known today as communion or the sacrament was indeed changed, from a covenant between the partaker and the Lord to remember him always, into a sacrament administered by the priest who miraculously changed the bread and wine representing the body and blood of Christ into the actual flesh and blood of Christ, leaving the recipient beholden to the priest for the performance of this blessing.

THE SEARCH FOR APOSTOLIC SUCCESSION

Although Constantine tried to resolve conflicts between various religious doctrines espoused by the 318 bishops of the multitude of cities of the Roman Empire, the conflicts nevertheless continued as the ambitious bishops contended for authority over each other. Every bishop had his office designated by the name of a city. The office of bishop was clearly a local office. The earliest bishops made no claim to apostolic authority, but with the passing of the apostles, the bishops were lost without central leadership to resolve doctrinal disputes, so they looked to the bishops of the most ancient branches of the church, where the apostles were known to have resided for some time.

By the time of Constantine, bishops in the larger cities claimed superiority over those in outlying areas. Bishops of ancient cities where the apostles had established congregations claimed superiority over bishops of cities with no such distinctions. Hugh Nibley says, "The principle that a bishop was exactly as important as his city is certainly not a holy one and certainly was not known to the ancient church, but by the fourth century it became the guiding principle of general church organization."[25]

Duchesne writes, "At the Council of Nicaea, the grouping of bishops by provinces and their subordination to the bishop of the civil metropolis are already an accomplished fact. . . . The provinces to which the council refers are those which Diocletian had formed."[26]

Nibley comments on Duchesne's observation:

> So they were formed by Diocletian, not the apostles. There is nothing apostolic about this—but is there anything wrong with it? There is, for the inevitable hierarchy among the bishops not only wiped out the basic principle of episcopal equality, but introduced an "order of the priesthood" in which rank was assigned purely by the census taker, and this rank inevitably and quickly was taken as a degree of holiness. The bigger the city, the holier its head. God does not work that way.[27]

Still, this was the system used. And since the Church in Jerusalem was gone, due to the Roman invasion in AD 70, they turned to the Church of Rome. Irenaeus described a solution to resolving any disagreement

> by indicating that tradition, derived from the apostles, of the very great, the very ancient, and universally known church founded and organized at Rome by the two most glorious apostles, Peter and Paul . . . and by indicating the faith . . . which came down to our time by means of the succession of bishops. For it is necessary that every church should agree with this church, on account of its preeminent authority."[28]

The most ancient church was in Jerusalem, but that city had been destroyed by the Romans in AD 70. James, the brother of Jesus, was the bishop of Jerusalem before being killed by order of the high priest between the reigns of different Roman governors.

Eusebius records, "Peter and James and John, after the ascension of the Savior, as those set at the head by the Savior, did not set themselves up, establishing their relative degrees of authority, but chose James the Just to be bishop of Jerusalem."[29] Scholars have concluded that James, Bishop of Jerusalem, was a bishop of bishops (a presiding bishop), who presided at the Jerusalem Conference of AD 42 regarding the question of circumcision of the gentile converts, while Peter and Paul and the other apostles were present. This indicates that James the Just was the Presiding Bishop of the church, but not an apostle. He remained in his office in Jerusalem until his execution in AD 66 and was not a traveling General Authority, as were the apostles. The office of bishop was an office of the Aaronic Priesthood, the same priesthood held by John the Baptist and the other priests of the Jerusalem temple at the time of Jesus. The bishop presides over priests, teachers, and deacons in the Aaronic Priesthood in a local congregation. The office of apostle was an office of the Mechizedek Priesthood, and an apostle's function was to be a special witness of the resurrection of Jesus Christ to the whole Church. It is clear that the bishops, who were local authorities, were not the successors of the apostles but served concurrently with them. According to the *Didache*, "Bishops shall minister to the traveling general brethren as their superiors."[30]

Nibley writes,

> The discovery of the *Didache*, in 1875 led Harnack to announce a realization which 'was in opposition to everything that had ever been claimed before'—namely, that the primitive church was endowed not with one priesthood but with two. Harnack pointed out what has since been universally accepted—the presence in the

earliest church of traveling general authorities, an institution of great significance for the study of the existence of an original centralized church organization. These traveling agents, he noted were not elected but were appointed to their office by 'a mandate from God'; they were apostles, prophets, and teachers, and they had, Harnack concluded, no administrative or judicial function. The bishops and deacons, on the other hand, had such functions, but they were exercised only in the local branches.[31]

Nibley quotes Tertullian, who

> makes a sharp distinction between two clearly marked levels of religious operation: both are good and necessary, but the higher one has departed from the church. The higher type is apostolic and prophetic and its genius is power—*potestas*. Against this the present church, according to Tertullian, can only set up a succession of bishops with discipline, *officium*, in the place of *potestas*.
>
> The old church had *imperium*—the authority to initiate organization, doctrine, etc.—while the new one had instead *ministerium*—a prescribed routine.[32]

Eusebius and Irenaeus both set out to trace their line of authority to the apostles. Irenaeus wanted only to establish proof of certain doctrines to refute false teachings of the heretics. Eusebius announced, "I have not found a single writer on ecclesiastical affairs who has concerned himself with this question [of episcopal succession]."[33]

"Eusebius reviews the bishops lists of Jerusalem, Rome, Antioch, and Alexandria. . . . Addressing himself to this task, Eusebius quickly discovers that the documents are totally inadequate even in those great churches to prove direct derivation of office from the apostles: the beginnings of these churches, he finds, are a complete mystery."[34]

Though Jerusalem was the original "mother church," according to Albert Dufourcq, "As early as the year 42, Antioch had dethroned Jerusalem. Antioch appeared as the metropolis of infant Christianity; it was from there that the apostles gradually spread the gospel throughout the world."[35]

Rome, being the greatest city in the world at that time, gave justification to the bishop of Rome to consider himself more important than all other bishops. That caused no small conflict when Constantine moved the capital of the Roman Empire to Byzantium, which was renamed after his death as Constantinople, now Istanbul, Turkey. "The famous third canon of the Council of Constantinople in 381 declared that the bishop of Constantinople should stand in honor to the bishop of Rome '*because the city of which he is bishop is the New Rome*.'"[36] This conflict continued until 1054, when the bishops of Rome and Constantinople excommunicated each other, cementing the split between the Roman Catholic Church and the Greek Orthodox Church.

The bishops of Rome, attempting to justify their claim to superiority over all congregations of the universal, or Catholic, church, began to claim apostolic succession from Peter, who they said was the bishop of Rome. Hugh Nibley writes, "What the Roman Catholics have to prove is not that the Savior bestowed office on Peter, but that Peter bestowed office on them; to date they have thought to settle the whole question by endless repetition of "thou art Peter."[37] According to Nibley, "There is no proof that Peter was ever a bishop of Rome."[38] Peter was an apostle, a traveling General Authority, who ordained other bishops of Rome. "In the *Apostolic Constitutions*, Peter is represented as saying,

> Of the church of the Romans, first Linus, the son of Caludius was ordained by Paul, and then after the death of Linus, Clement was ordained by me, Peter, being the second one.

"Here we have apostles ordaining bishops in Rome as they did elsewhere, but not acting as bishops themselves at all."[39]

CONCLUSIONS

The church established by Constantine was not the same Church established by the apostles. Apostasy, or rebellion from within the membership of the Church, and the death of the apostles had already resulted in the loss of priesthood authority, and church leaders began to be appointed by the Roman Emperor or by acclamation by the people in civil elections, not by divine appointment. With the loss of the apostles, the authority to ordain others to the priesthood was lost, resulting in the loss of divine authority and revelation, as evidenced by the atrocities committed in the name of God during the long, dark centuries of the middle ages and by the changes in the ordinances and doctrines of the ancient Church established by the apostles. Confusion about the nature of Heavenly Father and Jesus was rampant, and this controversy was decided by councils of ambitious bishops who contended with each other for power and jurisdiction over the whole church. The philosophies of Plato and other Greek thinkers were blended with the teachings of the apostles, and the ordinances and forms of worship were changed from the simple pattern established in the ancient Church. The bishops of Rome in the third and fourth centuries began to usurp authority over the whole church and tried to justify their position by claiming direct succession from the Apostle Peter, who they set up to have been the bishop of Rome when in fact he was an apostle who ordained other bishops of Rome. The falling away prophesied by Jesus and the apostles was in full swing.

NOTES

1. Hugh Nibley, *Apostles and Bishops in Early Christianity* (Salt Lake City and Provo, UT: Deseret Book and FARMS, 2005), 75.
2. Ibid., 2.
3. Ibid., 79.
4. James E. Talmage, *The Great Apostasy* (Salt Lake City: Deseret Book, 1909), 76.
5. Noel B. Reynolds, "What Went Wrong for the Early Christians?," in *Early Christians in Disarray*, ed. Noel B. Reynolds (Provo, UT: Brigham Young University Press, 2005), 24.
6. David L. Paulsen, "The Doctrine of Divine Embodiment," in *Early Christians in Disarray*, 244.
7. Origen, *De Principiis*, in *The Ante-Nicene Fathers*, ed. Alexander Roberts and James Donaldson (1885; reprint, Grand Rapids, MI: Eerdmans, 1951), 4:239–41, quoted in David L. Paulsen, "The Doctrine of Divine Embodiment," 256–57.
8. Barry R. Bickmore, "A Guide to Christian Documents and Writers," in *Early Christians in Disarray*, 327–28.
9. Walker, Norris, Lotz, and Handy, *A History of the Christian Church*, fourth edition, (New York: Charles Scribner's Sons, 1985), 131–34.
10. Ibid., 81.
11. Tertullian, *Against Praxeas,* 2 [AD 216], translation from The Catholic Encyclopedia, Chapter 2, The Catholic Doctrine of the Trinity and Unity, Sometimes Called the Divine Economy, or Dispensation of the Personal Relations of the Godhead.
12. Tertullian, *Against Praxeas,* 9 [AD 216], translation from The Catholic Encyclopedia, Chapter 9, the Trinity
13. David L. Paulsen, "The Doctrine of Divine Embodiment," in *Early Christians in Disarray*, 270.
14. Barry R. Bickmore and Adam W. Bentley, "Christian Councils," in *Early Christians in Disarray*, 346.

15. Nibley, *Apostles and Bishops in Early Christianity*, 108.
16. Ibid., 109.
17. Bickmore and Bentley, "Christian Councils," 346–47.
18. Daniel W. Graham and James L. Seibach, "The Introduction of Philosophy into Early Christianity," in *Early Christians in Disarray*, 233.
19. Noel B. Reynolds, "What Went Wrong for the Early Christians?," 10.
20. Clement, *Miscellanies* 1.5 (alluding to Galatians 3:24), in *The Ante-Nicene Fathers*, ed. Alexander Roberts and James Donaldson 1885 reprint (Peabody MA: Hendrickson, 1994), 2:305, quoted by Reynolds, "What Went Wrong for the Early Christians?," 11.
21. Graham and Seibach, "The Introduction of Philosophy into Early Christianity," 234–35.
22. Reynolds, "What Went Wrong for the Early Christians?," 12–14.
23. Noel B. Reynolds, "The Decline of Covenant in Early Christian Thought," in *Early Christians in Disarray*, 322–23.
24. Reynolds, "What Went Wrong for the Early Christians?" 6.
25. Nibley, *Apostles and Bishops in Early Christianity*, 85.
26. Duchesne, Origines du Culte Chretien, 24: Duchesne, Historie Ancienne de l'Eglise, 2:661–62, quoted by Nibley, *Apostles and Bishops in Early Christianity*, 87.
27. Nibley, *Apostles and Bishops in Early Christianity*, 87.
28. Irenaeus, AH 3.3.2, quoted by Elaine Pagels, *The Gnostic Gospels* (New York: Random House, 1979), 24.
29. Eusebius Historica Ecclesiastica 2.1.3, in PG 20:136, quoted by Nibley, *Apostles and Bishops in Early Christianity*, 34.
30. *Didache*, 11.3–12.2, quoted by Nibley, *Apostles and Bishops in Early Christianity*, 66.
31. Nibley, *Apostles and Bishops in Early Christianity*, 19–20.
32. Tertullian, *De Pudicitia* 21, in PL 2:1077–80, quoted by Nibley, *Apostles and Bishops in Early Christianity*, 22.
33. Eusebius Historica Ecclesiastica 1.1.5, in PG 20:52, quoted by Nibley, *Apostles and Bishops in Early Christianity*, 32.
34. Nibley, *Apostles and Bishops in Early Christianity*, 32–33.
35. Ibid., 93.
36. Ibid., 90, italics in original.
37. Ibid., 147.
38. Ibid., 84.
39. *Constitutiones Apostolicae* 7.46.6, in PG 1:1052–53, quoted by Nibley, *Apostles and Bishops in Early Christianity*, 159.

CHAPTER 12

THE CHURCH IN THE MIDDLE AGES

And they shall wander from sea to sea, and from the north even to the east, they shall run to and fro to seek the word of the Lord, and shall not find it.

Amos 8:12

AFTER THE DEATH OF CONSTANTINE, HIS SONS FOLLOWED HIM AS emperors of a united Roman Empire, which remained united until AD 394. The two principal centers for the church were Rome and Constantinople. Since bishops were the civil as well as the religious leaders of their cities, every city had to have a bishop. The church spread rapidly throughout the Roman Empire after Constantine adopted Christianity as the official state religion. Church councils continued to be called by the Roman emperors, following the pattern established by Constantine I. As noted in the last chapter, the emperor Theodosius the Great called the First Council of Constantinople in 381, which "declared that the bishop of Constantinople should stand in honor to the bishop of Rome '*because the city of which he is bishop is the New Rome.*'"[1] However, contention between the bishops of these two cities of the empire continued until the final split between the Roman and Greek Catholic churches in AD 1054.

THE FALL OF THE ROMAN EMPIRE

In AD 376 the Visigoths (Western Goths) and the Ostrogoths

(Eastern Goths) invaded the Roman borders and destroyed the Roman army at the Battle of Adrianople. Theodosius pushed the Goths back to the east, but they moved to the northern borders and invaded Rome from the north. In AD 410 Rome was sacked by the Visigoths. The Vandals plundered Rome again in AD 455. In AD 476 Rome was conquered by German invaders, which marked the end of the Western Roman Empire. The Eastern Empire continued to battle the barbarians and the Muslim invaders until their final defeat by the Muslims in 1453, when the city of Constantinople was renamed Istanbul and the remaining Christians were either driven out or converted to Islam.

Because many of the barbarian tribes were professing Christians, although they followed the teachings of Arius, they were somewhat sympathetic and spared many of the Christian inhabitants of Rome from death and destruction of property. The barbarian invasions broke up the Western Empire into various states and brought about the feudal system, where kings gave land to their aristocracy, designated as lords, who ruled as judges and landlords over the peasants, who farmed the land for their subsistence. The invading Arian Christians settled with the orthodox Catholic inhabitants, causing local religious conflicts.

THE DARK AGES AND FEUDALISM

The fall of the Western Roman Empire brought on the beginning of the era known as the Dark Ages, although the Eastern, or Byzantine, Empire continued to advance art and culture until conquered by the Muslims in 1453. Without a strong central government, the former Western Empire was broken into many smaller kingdoms, ruled by kings and king nobles known as lords, and the clergy began to be appointed by nobility. Vassals were free people, but serfs, who comprised 98 percent of the populace, were the peasants enslaved to work the land and provide food for the nobles in exchange for protection from invading barbarians. The lords of the land (landlords) controlled the populace and administered justice on parcels of land known as manors. Almost everyone lived on a manor. There was no need for trade because everything needed was produced on the manor. This system of government is known as feudalism. The kings of this era had less power because local areas were governed by feudal lords, who protected their nobles and vassals in castles and raised armies of knights and soldiers to war against invasions of their local territories by barbaric tribes. Just as in the Roman Empire of Constantine and his successors, there was no separation of church and state in the feudal systems of the middle ages. Bishops and abbots, who would read and write for the king, served at the pleasure of lords and kings, who also appointed local priests to serve under their direction.

Since 98 percent of the population were serfs who worked the land, education was limited to the 2 percent of the populace who were nobles and vassals, and most education was limited to the monasteries established by the abbots. With a loss of a central government, the Roman Catholic (universal) church became the most influential force to unify medieval Europe because it was the only central authority with a hierarchical structure of leadership under the bishop of Rome. Almost everyone, except for a small number of Jews, were Christians, from kings to lords, nobles, vassals, and serfs. The church collected taxes based on tithing laws and became the largest landowner in Europe. In addition to taxes, church leaders received large donations from those who wanted to influence them in their favor or who were promised a place in heaven for their gifts. In return, the church used its wealth and power to influence kings to follow its desires. The bishop of Rome became known as the Pope (papa, or father). The Pope had the power to excommunicate even kings and deny them membership in any congregation of the church—and any hope of eternal salvation. So by claiming to be direct representatives of God, Popes began to exercise power over kings. James E. Talmage states in *The Great Apostasy*, "Not content with assumed supremacy in all church affairs, the popes 'carried their insolent pretensions so far as to give themselves out for lords of the universe, arbiters of the fate of kingdoms and empires, and supreme rulers over kings and princes of the earth.' They claimed the right to authorize and direct the internal affairs of nations, and to make lawful the rebellion of subjects against their rulers if the latter failed to keep favor with the papal power."[2]

The local church was called a parish, and every town had one, which was the center of social and religious life, from birth and christening to death and burial. Religion was very important to family life in the middle ages, and the most devout people dedicated some of their children to serve God as monks or nuns, who lived in monasteries and nunneries and who denied themselves worldly pleasure to live lives of prayer and study. The greatest contribution of the monasteries was the preservation of knowledge during an era in which education of the masses was almost nonexistent. The monks copied and preserved ancient manuscripts of the scriptures as well as manuscripts of classical Greek writings.

CLOVIS, KING OF THE FRANKS, CONVERTS HIS WHOLE NATION

In AD 481, Clovis, the most famous of the Merovingian kings, became king of the Franks. By AD 486, Clovis had conquered most of what is now France and half of what is now Germany, becoming one of the most powerful kings in western Europe. His wife, Clotilde, was a Roman Christian, while most of Gaul, now France, were Arian Christians, who denied the divinity of Jesus and insisted on his humanity. At that time, the bishop of Rome had no more power than the bishop of Constantinople, and the Roman Church was surrounded by the Arian Christians of the Franks and other tribes. Clovis's conversion to Christianity had a history-changing influence on the future of the Roman Church for a thousand years, because, as a result of his conversion, his entire nation of the Franks was converted by his decree. Traditional history records that Clovis made an accord with the Roman Church through St. Remey. This was a major political triumph for the church that extended its influence throughout the region of western Europe. Rome now claimed equal, if not superior, status to Constantinople in leadership of the church. In return, Clovis was granted the title "Novus Constantinus," or "New Constantine," and became the first Catholic king of the "Holy Roman Empire." He was not crowned king by the Pope because he was already king of the Franks, but the marriage of royalty with religious authority strengthened both Clovis and the church.[3]

THE EXPANDING POWER OF THE POPE OF THE ROMAN CHURCH

Robert A. Guisepi writes in "Europe's Search for Stability: The Church of the Middle Ages":

> As Europe gradually emerged from the destruction of the Roman Empire, the church became one of the mainstays of civilization. During the pontificate of Gregory I the Great (590–604), the medieval papacy began to assert its authority. Gregory's achievement

> was to go beyond the claim of papal primacy in the church by beginning to establish the temporal power of the papacy. . . .
>
> Concluding that the world was coming to an end, Gregory withdrew from it to become a Benedictine monk. In 579 the pope convinced him to undertake a fruitless mission seeking Byzantine aid against the Lombards, who had invaded Italy a few years before. After Gregory was elected pope in 590, he assumed the task of protecting Rome and its surrounding territory from the Lombard threat. Thus Gregory was the first pope to act as temporal ruler of a part of what later became the Papal States.
>
> Gregory the Great also laid the foundation for the elaborate papal machinery of church government. He took the first step toward papal control of the church outside of Italy by sending a mission of Benedictine monks to convert the pagan Anglo-Saxons. The pattern of church government Gregory established in England—bishops supervised by archbishops, and archbishops by the pope—became standard in the church."[4]

Charlemagne (Charles the Great) became the leader of the Franks in 768. In 800, on Christmas day, he was crowned by Pope Leo III as the Emperor of the Holy Roman Empire. Even though he was a strong Christian, he didn't like the Pope crowning him because he feared the Pope would have more power. In 804, Charlemagne conquered the Saxons of Briton and forced them to become Christians.

Beginning in the early 600s, the Eastern church in the Byzantine Empire was rapidly being conquered by the followers of Muhammad. By 1071, Jerusalem, Antioch, and Alexandria had all fallen to the Muslims. The Christian inhabitants of these ancient cities fled, were killed, or were converted by the persuasive influence of the Muslims. Some Christian communities continued to exist in Egypt, Palestine, North Africa, Arabia, and Persia. Christians in Constantinople remained under siege by the Muslims until the city was finally conquered in 1453. As the Eastern church was weakened, the Western church of Rome became more powerful and influential because Roman Catholic missionaries continued to convert countries to the north.

THE CRUSADES

In 1071, Turkish Muslims captured Jerusalem and stopped the Christians from visiting the holy places in Palestine. The Byzantine emperor in Constantinople and the Pope in Rome formed an alliance to recapture the Holy Lands from the Turks. As an incentive to recruit soldiers for the cause, Pope Urban II promised forgiveness of sins of all who took up the sword in the Crusades to recover the Holy Lands. Besides the Turks, along the way, the Christians slaughtered thousands of Hungarians, Germans, Greeks, and Jews. The Christians defeated the Turks and conquered Jerusalem in 1099. Eight Crusades took place from 1096 to 1291. When the Muslims took Jerusalem in 1187, the third Crusade, led by Richard Lion Heart, massacred three thousand innocent Muslim villagers. When they got to the Holy Land, the Crusaders were defeated by the Muslim general, Saladin. By 1291, the Muslims had taken the last remaining Christian city at Acre.

THE KNIGHTS TEMPLAR

In 1118, the Order of the Knights Templar, a monastic order of warrior monks, was established, purportedly to protect tourists from bandits on their journey to the Holy Lands. The Templars took the three vows of obedience, poverty, and chastity and swore an oath to safeguard and protect pilgrims against attacks of brigands and infidels. Those who joined this noble order were required to consecrate all of their earthly property to the order, including lands and gold, and live a life of poverty. The Order of the Knights Templar became a prestigious group because of their chivalry in combat in the succeeding Crusades, and many prominent families had sons who joined this order, contributing large tracts of land and all manner of wealth. In 1127, a council of the church was called at Troyes, where the Templars were officially recognized by the church as a religious-military order called the "militia of Christ." In 1139, Pope Innocent II issued a papal bull decreeing that "the Templars would owe allegiance to no secular order or ecclesiastical power other than the Pope himself. In other words, they were rendered totally independent of all kings, princes, and prelates, and of all interference from both political and religious authorities. They had become, in effect, a law unto themselves, an autonomous, international empire."[5]

Although the individual Templars made vows of poverty, the consecration of their lands and property to the Templars made the Order extremely wealthy. Soon the Templars became the most powerful economic force in Europe and became bankers, lending money to kings of nations, who were in great debt to them. In 1306, Philippe IV of France conspired to rid his empire of the Templars' influence and erase his debts to them, but to do this he had to dissolve their affiliation with the Pope.

> Between 1303 and 1305 the French king and his ministers engineered the kidnapping and death of one Pope (Boniface VIII) and then quite possibly the murder by poison of another (Benedict XI). Then, in 1305, Philippe managed to secure the election of his own candidate, the archbishop of Bordeaux, to the vacant papal throne. The new pontiff took the name Clement V. Indebted as he was to Philippe's influence, he could hardly refuse the king's demands. And these demands included the eventual suppression of the Knights Templar. . . . At dawn on Friday, October 13, 1307, all Templars in France were to be seized and placed under royal sequestration, their goods confiscated.[6]

This marked the end of the Order of the Knights Templar, who were persecuted and tortured into admission of all manner of sins and debauchery. Many were executed, and others were imprisoned. The Templars' lands and wealth were confiscated, and the Order ceased to exist officially, although many believe that it continued underground and eventually evolved into the Freemasons.

THE CATHAR CRUSADES

The church in the thirteenth century waged an official crusade of death and destruction against an entire group of people in France known as the Cathars, or Albegensians, to stamp out the perceived heresies of their religious beliefs.

The Cathars were a religious group that formed in northern Europe in the eleventh century. Their beliefs were likely influenced by Gnostic traditions from the Eastern Empire by commerce with Constantinople and perhaps by participants in the Crusades. "The term 'Cathars' (Catharos) is of Greek origin and means 'Pure Ones.'" The Roman Church considered them heretics, but they considered themselves true Christians.[7]

The authors of *Holy Blood, Holy Grail* describe the beliefs and extermination of the Cathars in a Crusade directed by the Pope:

> In general, the Cathars subscribed to a doctrine of reincarnation and to a recognition of the feminine principle in religion. Indeed, the preachers and teachers of Cathar congregations were of

both sexes. At the same time, the Cathars rejected the Orthodox Catholic Church, and denied the validity of all clerical hierarchies, and official and ordained intercessors between man and God. At the core of this position lay an important Cathar tenant—the repudiation of 'faith,' at least as the Church insisted upon it. In the place of 'faith,' accepted at second hand, the Cathars insisted upon a direct personal knowledge, a religious or mystical experience apprehended at first hand. This experience has been called *gnosis,* from the Greek word for 'knowledge,' and for the Cathars it took precedence over all creeds and dogma. Given such an emphasis on direct personal contact with God, priests, bishops, and other clerical authorities became superfluous.[8]

THE DESTRUCTION OF THE CATHARS

In 1209 an army of some thirty thousand knights and foot soldiers from northern Europe descended like a whirlwind on the Languedoc—the mountainous northeastern foothills of the Pyrenees in what is now southern France. In the ensuing war the whole territory was ravaged, crops were destroyed, towns and cities were razed, a whole population was put to the sword. This extermination occurred on so vast, so terrible a scale that it may well constitute the first case of 'genocide' in modern European history. In the town of Béziers alone, for example, at least fifteen thousand men, women, and children were slaughtered wholesale—many of them in the sanctuary of the church itself. When an officer inquired of the Pope's representative how he might distinguish heretics from true believers, the reply was, 'Kill them all. God will recognize His own.' This quotation, though widely reported, may be apocryphal. Nevertheless, it typifies the fanatical zeal and bloodlust with which the atrocities were perpetrated. The same papal representative, writing to Innocent III of Rome, announced proudly that "neither age nor sex nor status was spared."[9]

THE BISHOPS OF ROME

The struggle for supremacy between the bishops of Rome and the bishops of Constantinople continued to rage for five hundred years until AD 855, when the bishop of Constantinople disavowed any further allegiance to the bishop of Rome, resulting in the division of the universal, or Catholic, church into the Roman Catholics and the Greek

Catholics, neither being universal after that separation, which continues to this day.[10] Until the eleventh century, the bishop of Rome was chosen by local election of the people and the clergy, but from that time forward, this authority was vested in the College of Cardinals.

THE SALE OF INDULGENCES

James E. Talmage, writing in *The Great Apostasy*, states:

> In the eleventh century, and later, we find the Church imposing punishment of fine, imprisonment, bodily torture, and even death, as penalties for infraction of church regulations, and more infamous still, providing for mitigation or annulment of such sentences on payment of money. This led to the practice of selling indulgences, or pardons, which was afterwards carried to the awful extreme of issuing such before the commission of the specific offense, thus literally offering for sale licenses to sin, with assurance of temporal and promise of spiritual immunity.[11]

John Tetzel, agent of the Pope in the sixteenth century, "boasted that he had saved more souls from hell by his indulgences than St. Peter had converted to Christianity by his preaching."[12]

Talmage continues,

> The awful sin of blasphemy consists in taking to one's self the divine prerogatives and powers. Here we find the pope of Rome, head of the only church recognized at the time, assuming to remit the punishments due in the hereafter for sins committed in mortality. A pope assuming to sit in judgment as God himself! Is this not fulfillment of the dread conditions of apostasy foreseen and foretold as antecedent to the second advent of Christ? Read for yourselves, "Let no man deceive you by any means; for that day shall not come, except there come a falling away first, and that man of sin be revealed, the son of perdition; who opposeth and exhalteth himself above all that is called God, or that is worshiped; so that he as God sitteth in the temple of God, shewing himself that he is God." [2 Thesseloinans 2:3–4][13]

The history of the succession of popes from the time of the fall of Rome to the eleventh century, when popes began to be selected by the College of Cardinals, leaves a horrific image in the mind of any student of this tragic period of the medieval church. Popes committed all manner of atrocities to claim the power and authority of the papal seat. Torture was inflicted upon those who opposed their rule. Rebellion against popes was frequent, and the rebels installed their own successor to the papal throne. Talmage continues his description of the dark history of papal succession:

> Sergius III, by the aid of a military force, seized the pontificate, AD 905. This man, according to the testimony of the times, lived in criminal intercourse with the prostitute, Theodora, who, with her daughters Marozia and Theodora, also prostitutes, exercised an extraordinary control over him. The love of Theodora was also shared by John X: she gave him first the archbishopric of Ravenna, and then translated him to Rome, AD 915, as pope. John was not unsuited to the times; he organized a confederacy which perhaps prevented Rome from being captured by the Saracens, and the world was astonished and edified by the appearance of this war-like pontiff at the head of his troops. By the love of Theodora, as was said, he had maintained himself in the papacy for fourteen years; by the intrigue and hatred of her daughter Marozia he was overthrown. She surprised him in the Lateran Palace; killed his brother Peter before his face; threw him into prison, where he soon died, smothered, as was asserted, by a pillow. After a short interval, Marozia made her own son pope as John XI, AD 931. . . . A synod was summoned for his trial in the Church of St. Peter, before which it appeared that he had accepted bribes for the consecration of bishops; that he had ordained one who was only ten years old, and had performed that ceremony over another in a stable; he was charged with incest with one of his fathers' concubines, and with so many adulteries that the Lateran Palace had become a brothel; he put out the eyes of one ecclesiastic, and castrated another, both dying in consequence of their injuries; he was given to drunkenness, gambling, and the invocation of Jupiter and Venus. [14]

CONCLUSIONS

Although the apostasy and loss of priesthood authority from Christ was complete by the third century, before the establishment of the universal, or Catholic, church by Constantine, the evidence and the results of this apostasy and loss of priesthood authority continued to mushroom throughout the middle ages, culminating in rebellion against the church by the reformers who started the Protestant revolution in the fifteenth century. The fall of the Roman Empire in AD 476 empowered the Roman Church as the only central authority in Western Europe, and the conversion of the entire nation of the Franks by Clovis I gave the Roman bishop more power than the bishop of Constantinople. Bishops of the Roman Church in the eleventh to the thirteenth centuries committed all manner of corruption, torture, murder, and fornication to obtain and maintain the papal throne, while selling indulgences, or forgiveness for future sins, in order to raise funds for the expansion of their authority. The popes sponsored the Crusades against the Muslims in the Holy Lands, which resulted in the slaughter of many innocents, and continued this campaign of genocide against the Cathars of France for their perceived heretical beliefs. The persecution of perceived heretics by the church was as heinous, if not more so, than the persecution of early Christians by the Roman Emperors. The papal office, which promised autonomy to the Order of the Knights Templar, turned against them to please Philippe IV, King of France, resulting in great persecutions and in the near extinction of this supposedly sacred monastic order. Although the Roman Church claims an unbroken chain of priesthood authority from the Apostle Peter, it is obvious to the most casual observer that this chain of authority was broken over and over again by installation of bishops and popes by civil and not divine authority, and by vile wickedness by those who claimed to act for God as the supreme leaders of his church.

NOTES

1. Hugh Nibley, *Apostles and Bishops in Early Christianity* (Salt Lake City and Provo, UT: Deseret Book and FARMS, 2005), 90, italics in original.
2. James E. Talmage, *The Great Apostasy*, (Deseret Book Company, Salt Lake City, UT 1909), 133–34.
3. Michael Baigent, Richard Leigh, and Henry Lincoln, *Holy Blood, Holy Grail* (New York: Bantam Dell, 1982), 244.
4. Robert A. Guisepi, ed., "Europe's Search for Stability: The Church in the Early Middle Ages," International World History Project, http://history-world.org/churchmiddleages.htm.
5. Baigent, Leigh, and Lincoln, *Holy Blood, Holy Grail*, 68.
6. Ibid., 75.
7. Walker, Norris, Lotz, and Handy, *A History of the Christian Church*, 4th ed. (New York: Charles Scribner's Sons, 1985), 301.
8. Baigent, Leigh, and Lincoln, *Holy Blood, Holy Grail*, 52.
9. Ibid., 49.
10. James E. Talmage, *The Great Apostasy* (Salt Lake City, Utah: Deseret Book Company, 1909), 133.
11. Ibid., 134–35.
12. Ibid., 137.
13. Ibid., 138–39.
14. Ibid., 145–46.

CHAPTER 13

THE PROTESTANT REFORMATION

I have sought nothing beyond reforming the Church in conformity with the Holy Scriptures. The spiritual powers have been not only corrupted by sin, but absolutely destroyed; so that there is now nothing in them but a depraved reason and a will that is the enemy and opponent of God. I simply say that Christianity has ceased to exist among those who should have preserved it.

Martin Luther

THE DOMINATION OF THE ROMAN CHURCH CONTINUED INTO THE fourteenth century, when all nations of western Europe professed the faith of the Latin or Roman Catholic Church. Papal agents collected taxes from subjects in all nations over which the church exerted authority. Rulers of nations were beginning to resent the authority that the church exercised over them and the taxes that left their borders and were sent to Rome. Society was transitioning from one dominated by the Church to one in which the Church was to become subject to the will of the rulers of the nations. The higher levels of the clergy sought to live in luxury and continued to seek to expand their wealth and power, while the lower levels of the clergy lived in poverty and oppression. The dual role of ecclesiastical and civil authority exercised by the clergy in many localities afforded them excessive power and opportunities for expansion of their wealth. The prestige of the clergy suffered, and in many places its members were regarded with scorn.

The Catholic Encyclopedia gives this description of the conditions during this period:

> The authority of the Holy See had also been seriously impaired, partly through the fault of some of its occupants and partly through that of the secular princes. . . . Humanism and the ideals of the Renaissance were zealously cultivated in Rome, and unfortunately the heathen tendencies of this movement, so opposed to the Christian moral law, affected too profoundly the life of many higher ecclesiastics, so that worldly ideas, luxury, and immorality rapidly gained ground at the centre of ecclesiastical life. When ecclesiastical authority grew weak at the fountain-head, it necessarily decayed elsewhere. There were also serious administrative abuses in the Papal Curia. The ever-increasing centralization of ecclesiastical administration had brought it about that far too many ecclesiastical benefices in all parts of Christendom were conferred at Rome, while in the granting of them the personal interests of the petitioner, rather than the spiritual needs of the faithful, were too often considered.[1]

JOHN WYCLIFFE

It was in this environment that John Wycliffe (1325–1384), an English theologian, began to challenge the ideas of infallible papal authority and urged a return to the Bible rather than church tradition to understand the doctrines of salvation. His fundamental belief was that the church should be poor, as in the days of the apostles. John Wycliffe "provided the inspiration and impetus for the translation of the Vulgate Bible into English. It appears that he did not contribute directly to the work of translation, which was carried out and completed after his death, by a group of disciples."[2]

The result was the first handwritten manuscripts of the Bible in English in the 1380s before the invention of the printing press in 1440. Wycliffe was well-known throughout Europe for his opposition to the teaching of the organized church, which he believed to be contrary to the Bible. Wycliffe produced dozens of English language manuscript copies of the scriptures, translated from the Latin Vulgate, which was the only source text available to him.

John Foxe (1516–1587), in *Foxe's Christian Martyrs*, writes:[3]

> The following points, taken from Wycliffe's sermons, summarize his teachings:

> The holy Eucharist, after consecration, is not the actual body of Christ.
>
> The Church of Rome is no more important than any other church, and Peter had no more power given to him by Christ than any other Apostle.
>
> The pope has no more power than any other priest.
>
> The gospel is enough for any man, without the rules of men, which add nothing to the gospel.
>
> Neither the pope nor any other church official has the power or right to punish transgressors.

The Church was so infuriated by his teachings and his translation of the Bible into English, that forty-four years after Wycliffe had died, his bones were dug up, crushed, and scattered in the river!

THE PRINTING PRESS

Johann Gutenberg invented the printing press in Germany in 1440, which was used to spread the views of Protestant reformers like Wycliffe, Hus, and Luther across national boundaries and make the scriptures, once read by only the clergy, available to the common people. This invention, with its publication of the scriptures, aroused popular discontent at the moral corruption in the church and provided support for a reformation as never before.

JAN HUS

Jan Hus (1372–1415), a Czech religious thinker, philosopher, reformer, and master at Charles University in Prague, was influenced by the doctrines of Wycliffe after the Bohemian princess Ann married King Richard II of England, and Czech students attracted to Oxford, where Wycliffe taught, brought back his religious views to the University of Prague.[4]

Condemned as a heretic by the church, Hus was excommunicated in 1411 and burned at the stake in 1415. Like Wycliffe, Hus had a strong influence on Martin Luther, who lived a century later. Among Hus's last words allegedly are, "in 100 years, God will raise up a man whose calls for reform cannot be suppressed."[5] Martin Luther nailed his Ninety-Five Theses of Contention to a church door in Wittenberg 102 years later.

MARTIN LUTHER

Over one hundred years after the deaths of Wycliffe and Hus, on 31 October 1517, in Saxony (in what is now Germany), Martin Luther nailed his Ninety-Five Theses *On the Power of Indulgences* to the door of the Wittenberg Castle Church. His theses criticized the church and the Pope for the sale of indulgences, whereby one could pay for forgiveness of the sins of one's ancestors to free them from purgatory or even pay in advance for personal sins to be committed in the future. This doctrine, fabricated by the Pope to raise money for the construction of cathedrals, was seen by Luther to be an abomination and not supported by the scriptures.

Luther was greatly influenced by the writings of John Wycliffe and Jan Hus. His challenge to the church's authority on this doctrine was quickly disseminated by the advent of the printing press, and he influenced other reformers, such as Ulrich Zwingli and John Calvin, who soon followed his lead in protesting church doctrines and practices including purgatory, devotion to Mary, the intercession of the saints, most of the sacraments, and the authority of the Pope.

Luther espoused the notion of salvation by faith alone, that each man can be his own priest, and that the only true authority is the Bible, once again limiting the authority of the Pope. Luther escaped condemnation to be burned at the stake like Hus and other reformers due to the protection of Emperor Charles V and Elector Frederick of Saxony. He translated the Bible from Latin into German and became the founder of the Lutheran church, which galvanized the Protestant movement.

ULRICH ZWINGLI AND JOHN CALVIN

In Switzerland, Ulrich Zwingli led the reform movement, and he was accused of heresy. In 1531 the Catholics and the Protestants engaged in a battle in which Zwingli was killed and his body mutilated. John Calvin took up the reform effort of the Swiss, although he was opposed to many of Zwingli's doctrines. "He [Calvin] advocated and vehemently defended the doctrine of absolute predestination, thus denying the free agency of man."[6]

THE CHURCH OF ENGLAND

In 1522, King Henry VIII of England, a devout member of the

Catholic faith, wrote a book refuting Luther's doctrines. Pope Leo X was so pleased with the king that he conferred upon him the title "Defender of the Faith," a title still claimed by the Kings and Queens of England to this day. However, the pleasure of the Pope would not be long lasting, since King Henry requested papal authority to divorce his queen, Catherine, in order to marry Ann Boleyn. When the Pope hesitated in granting the divorce, Henry became impatient and secretly married Ann Boleyn. The Pope then excommunicated King Henry, who responded by enticing the English Parliament to enact a law that established the Church of England with the King as its supreme head and severed all allegiance to papal authority and the Church of Rome.[7]

THE COUNCIL OF TRENT

In response to the crisis caused by the Protestant Reformation, the church called the Council of Trent, which lasted eighteen years, from AD 1545 to 1563. A number of reforms were instituted, but the church continued to defend itself against the reformers, including

> restrictions placed on reading and interpretation of scriptures. The same Council of Trent, which disclaimed authority or blame for the acts of church officials regarding the scandalous traffic in indulgences, prescribed most rigid regulations forbidding the reading of the scriptures by the people. Mosheim describes the outcome of this council as follows:
>
> A severe and intolerable law was enacted, with respect to interpreters and expositors of the scriptures, by which they were forbidden to explain the sense of these divine books, in matters of faith and practice, in such a manner as to make them speak a different language from that of the church and the ancient doctors. The same law declared that the church alone (i.e., its ruler, the Roman pontiff) had the right of determining the true meaning and signification of scripture. To fill up the measure of these tyrannical and iniquitous proceedings, the Church of Rome persisted obstinately in affirming, though not always with the same imprudence and plainness of speech, that *the holy scriptures were not composed for the use of the multitude, but only for that of their spiritual teachers*; and of consequence ordered these divine records to be taken from the people in all places where it was allowed to execute its imperious demands.[8]

THE SPANISH INQUISITION

King Ferdinand and Queen Isabella, who ruled in Spain near the end of the fifteenth century, were likewise "Defenders of the Faith," and they established the "Holy Office" for the punishment of heresy. Talmage quotes *Myers General History*, which says,

> The Holy Office, as the tribunal was styled, thus became the instrument of the most incredible cruelty. Thousands were burned at the stake, and tens of thousands more condemned to endure penalties scarcely less terrible. Queen Isabella, in giving her consent to the establishment of the tribunal in her dominions, was doubtless actuated by the purest religious zeal, and sincerely believed that in suppressing heresy she was discharging a simple duty, and rendering God good service. 'In love of Christ and his Maid-Mother,' she says, 'I have caused great misery. I have depopulated towns and districts, provinces and kingdoms.'[9]

RELIGIOUS INTOLERANCE OF THE PROTESTANTS

Talmage quotes from *Myers General History* about the religious intolerance of the protestant reformation,

> At this point, in connection with the persecutions of the Inquisition, we should not fail to recall that in the sixteenth century a refusal to conform to the established worship was regarded by all, by Protestants as well as Catholics, as a species of treason against society and was dealt with accordingly. Thus we find Calvin at Geneva consenting to the burning of Servetus (1553) because he published views that the Calvinists thought heretical; and in England we see Anglican Protestants waging the most cruel, bitter, and persistent persecutions, not only against the Catholics but also against the Protestants that refused to conform to the Established Church.[10]

EARLY PURITAN MOVEMENT

One of the earliest Protestants in England was William Tyndale, who was the first to translate major sections of the Bible into English from the Greek and Hebrew texts and the first to publish his translations (in 1524) since the invention of the printing press (in 1440).

The Protestant Reformation in England can be traced to the divorce of Henry VIII (1509–1547) and to his three children and successors,

Edward VI (1547–1553), Mary (1553–1558) and Elizabeth (1558–1603), who alternately supported Catholicism and the Protestant reformers.[11] Henry's divorce from his queen, Catherine, resulted in his excommunication from the Catholic Church by the Pope and his decision in 1553 to sever ties with Rome and organize the Church of England with himself as its head. Upon his death in 1547, his son, Edward, became king at the age of nine, and England was ruled by a privy council that rescinded laws allowing religious persecutions and sustained the schism enacted by Henry.[12] Mary took the throne in 1553 upon the untimely death of Edward from tuberculosis at age fifteen, and she began to reconcile with Catholicism. Under Mary's leadership, Parliament reenacted ancient heresy laws. Mary felt that her childless state was due to a failure to satisfy the judgment of God, so she increased persecutions for heresy until her death in 1558. During her reign, nearly three hundred persons were burned to death for heresy, which intensified anti-Roman sentiment among the people.[13] Elizabeth, born to Henry and his second wife, Ann Boleyn, after Henry's excommunication, was considered illegitimate by the Pope, and she was thus disposed to Protestant views. Elizabeth's reforms to distance England from the Pope's authority were too slow for the House of Commons, which passed the Act of Supremacy, once again establishing an English liturgy, restoring the ornaments and vestments of the clergy enacted under Edward's rule, and abolishing persecutions for heresy.[14]

It was in this setting of religious confusion and ghastly persecutions that Protestants in England, who followed the ideas of Luther, Calvin, Zwingly, and Knox, began their quest to purify the church and their own lives by rejecting the political struggles and man-made doctrines of both of these churches. They saw the Bible as their guide to provident living and rejected the ornaments and vestments of the clergy. Initially, they only desired to purify the Anglican Church of England, which held onto many of the ceremonial trappings of the Catholic Church, but Queen Elizabeth, the head of the Anglican Church, refused to grant changes in the structure and liturgy and enforced laws against separation from the established religion. Puritans who became separatists fled to Holland. To escape religious persecution in England, a group of Puritan separatists sailed on the Mayflower in 1620 from Plymouth, England, and established the Plymouth Massachusetts Colony with their governor, William Bradford.

CONCLUSIONS

The Renaissance, or awakening from the Dark Ages, and the invention of the printing press enabled reformist ideas that had been brewing for centuries to arouse the desire of the common people to learn more about the gospel and to free themselves from the domination of unrighteous clerics who sought to enrich themselves at the expense of the salvation of those they were supposedly called to save. But not one of the reformers claimed to have received revelation or a divine calling. Instead they based their reforms on the discrepancies between the scriptures and the practices of the papal office and their delegates, and upon their own uninspired interpretation of these scriptures, leading to further controversy. The reformers disagreed on many points of doctrine and fell into the same wicked practices as the church they rejected by inflicting persecutions on those who disagreed with them. The rebellions incited by the Protestant Reformers resulted in many religious schisms but eventually led to religious freedom in the new world and some limited reformation of the Catholic Church, which they sought to reform but from which they were expelled. Surely, this was the time prophesied by Amos, who said, "Behold, the days come, saith the Lord God, that I will send a famine in the land, not a famine of bread, nor a thirst for water, but of hearing the words of the Lord: And they shall wander from sea to sea, and from the north even to the east, they shall run to and fro to seek the word of the Lord, and shall not find it" (Amos 8:11–12).

The simple gospel of Jesus Christ and his apostles, in its clarity with the interpretations of those who held the legitimate priesthood and spirit of prophecy, was not to be found on the earth. The doctrines of Jesus had been so perverted and embellished by the philosophies of men that they became obscure even to those who sought to correct and reform them. However, the Protestant Reformation, the discovery of the new world, and the inspired constitution of the United States of America established an environment of religious freedom in which the Lord could finally restore his Apostolic Church to the earth, as promised.

NOTES

1. Catholic Encyclopedia, New Advent, *Reformation*, C.
2. Walker, Norris, Lotz, and Handy, *A History of the Christian Church*, 4th

ed. (New York: Charles Scribner's Sons, 1985), 380.

3. John Foxe, *Foxe's Christian Martyrs* (Uhrichsville, OH: Barbour Publishing, 2010), 43.
4. Walker, Norris, Lotz, and Handy, *A History of the Christian Church*, 381.
5. See *English Bible History*, s.vv. "Jon Hus."
6. James E. Talmage, *The Great Apostasy* (Salt Lake City: Deseret Book, 1909), 153–54.
7. Ibid., 156.
8. Mosheim, *Eccl. Hist.*, Cent. XVI, Part I, ch. 1:25, quoted by Talmage, *The Great Apostasy,* 139. Italics introduced by Talmage.
9. Myers, "Gen. History," 500, quoted by Talmage, *The Great Apostasy,* 154–55.
10. Myers, "Gen. Hist.," 527, quoted by Talmage, *The Great Apostasy*, 155.
11. Walker, Norris, Lotz, and Handy, *A History of the Christian Church*, 4th ed. (New York: Charles Scribner's Sons, 1985), 481.
12. Ibid., 488–89.
13. Ibid., 493.
14. Ibid., 494. See *A History of the Christian Church,* 481–94.

SECTION 3

THE RESTITUTION OF ALL THINGS

CHAPTER 14

HEAVENLY VISITATIONS

And I saw another angel fly in the midst of heaven, having the everlasting gospel to preach unto them that dwell on the earth, and to every nation, and kindred, and tongue, and people.

Revelation 14:6

As Peter and John were about to enter the temple at Jerusalem, they saw a man who was lame from his birth begging for alms.

> Then Peter said, Silver and gold have I none; but such as I have give I thee: In the name of Jesus Christ of Nazareth rise up and walk.
>
> And he took him by the right hand, and lifted him up: and immediately his feet and ankle bones received strength.
>
> And he leaping up stood, and walked, and entered with them into the temple, walking, and leaping, and praising God.
>
> And all the people saw him walking and praising God:
>
> And they knew that it was he which sat for alms at the Beautiful gate of the temple: and they were filled with wonder and amazement at that which had happened unto him.
>
> And as the lame man which was healed held Peter and John, all the people ran together unto them in the porch that is called Solomon's, greatly wondering. (Acts 3:6–11)

The courtyard of the temple was filled with throngs of people who had daily seen this lame man begging for alms, and now he was walking and leaping and praising God. Peter attributed this miracle to Jesus Christ, who had been condemned by the rulers of the temple, and then said to the multitude,

> Repent ye therefore, and be converted, that your sins may be blotted out, when the times of refreshing shall come from the presence of the Lord;
>
> And he shall send Jesus Christ, which before was preached unto you:
>
> Whom the heaven must receive until *the times of restitution of all things,* which God hath spoken by the mouth of all his holy prophets since the world began. (Acts 3:19–21; emphasis added)

Here Peter prophesied of the "restitution of all things." Why would there need to be a "restitution of all things" if these things were not to be lost? When and how would this restitution be made? When would the times of refreshing occur, which should come from the presence of the Lord?

John, in the book of Revelation, records a vision that this restitution would come by an angel.

> And I saw another angel fly in the midst of heaven, having the everlasting gospel to preach unto them that dwell on the earth, and to every nation, and kindred, and tongue, and people, Saying with a loud voice, Fear God, and give glory to him; for the hour of his judgment is come: and worship him that made heaven, and earth, and the sea, and the fountains of waters. (Revelation 14:6–7)

The beginning of the restitution of all things occurred in the spring of 1820, when a young farm boy living with his poor family in Palmyra, New York, went into a grove of trees near his father's farm and uttered his first vocal prayer to God to learn which church was the true church and which he should join. This area of the state of New York had been the scene of a number of recent religious revivals, and Joseph's family had been torn between contending sects, each claiming to have the true religion, but each interpreting the same passages of scripture differently. The Smith family read the Bible regularly, so young Joseph, at the age of fourteen, was acquainted with the scriptures though certainly not a learned gospel scholar. As he puzzled over the conflicting claims of the competing ministers of his community, Joseph read this passage from the Book of James: "If any of you lack wisdom, let him ask of God, that giveth to all men liberally, and upbraideth not; and it shall be given him. But let him ask in faith, nothing wavering. For he that wavereth is like a wave of the sea driven with the wind and tossed" (James 1:5–6).

JOSEPH SMITH'S FIRST VISION

Joseph determined to ask with faith which church to join. In his own words,

> At length I came to the conclusion that I must either remain in darkness and confusion, or else I must do as James directs, that is, ask of God. I at length came to the determination to "ask of God," concluding that if he gave wisdom to them that lacked wisdom, and would give liberally, and not upbraid, I might venture.
>
> So, in accordance with this, my determination to ask of God, I retired to the woods to make the attempt. It was on the morning of a beautiful, clear day, early in the spring of eighteen hundred and twenty. It was the first time in my life that I had made such an attempt, for amidst all my anxieties I had never as yet made the attempt to pray vocally.
>
> After I had retired to the place where I had previously designed to go, having looked around me, and finding myself alone, I kneeled down and began to offer up the desires of my heart to God. I had scarcely done so, when immediately I was seized upon by some power which entirely overcame me, and had such an astonishing influence over me as to bind my tongue so that I could not speak. Thick darkness gathered around me, and it seemed to me for a time as if I were doomed to sudden destruction.
>
> But, exerting all my powers to call upon God to deliver me out of the power of this enemy which had seized upon me, and at the very moment when I was ready to sink into despair and abandon myself to destruction—not to an imaginary ruin, but to the power of some actual being from the unseen world, who had such marvelous power as I had never before felt in any being—just at this moment of great alarm, I saw a pillar of light exactly over my head, above the brightness of the sun, which descended gradually until it fell upon me.
>
> It no sooner appeared than I found myself delivered from the enemy which held me bound. When the light rested upon me I saw two Personages, whose brightness and glory defy all description, standing above me in the air. One of them spake unto me, calling me by name and said, pointing to the other—*This is My Beloved Son. Hear Him!*

> My object in going to inquire of the Lord was to know which of all the sects was right, that I might know which to join. No sooner, therefore, did I get possession of myself, so as to be able to speak, than I asked the Personages who stood above me in the light, which of all the sects was right (for at this time it had never entered into my heart that all were wrong)—and which I should join.
>
> I was answered that I must join none of them, for they were all wrong; and the Personage who addressed me said that all their creeds were an abomination in his sight; that those professors were all corrupt; that: "they draw near to me with their lips, but their hearts are far from me, they teach for doctrines the commandments of men, having a form of godliness, but they deny the power thereof." (Joseph Smith—History 1:13–19)

Joseph suffered repeated persecutions from religious leaders and locals for asserting that he had seen the Father and the Son in a vision. He stated,

> It caused me serious reflection then, and often has since, how very strange it was that an obscure boy, of a little over fourteen years of age, and one, too, who was doomed to the necessity of obtaining a scanty maintenance by his daily labor, should be thought a character of sufficient importance to attract the attention of the great ones of the most popular sects of the day, and in a manner to create in them a spirit of the most bitter persecution and reviling. But strange or not, so it was, and it was often the cause of great sorrow to myself.
>
> However, it was nevertheless a fact that I had beheld a vision. I have thought since, that I felt much like Paul, when he made his defense before King Agrippa, and related the account of the vision he had when he saw a light, and heard a voice; but still there were but few who believed him; some said he was dishonest, others said he was mad; and he was ridiculed and reviled. But all this did not destroy the reality of his vision. He had seen a vision, he knew he had, and all the persecution under heaven could not make it otherwise; and though they should persecute him unto death, yet he knew, and would know to his latest breath, that he had both seen a light and heard a voice speaking unto him, and all the world could not make him think or believe otherwise.
>
> So it was with me. I had actually seen a light, and in the midst of that light I saw two Personages, and they did in reality speak to me; and though I was hated and persecuted for saying that I had seen a

> vision, yet it was true; and while they were persecuting me, reviling me, and speaking all manner of evil against me falsely for so saying, I was led to say in my heart: Why persecute me for telling the truth? I have actually seen a vision; and who am I that I can withstand God, or why does the world think to make me deny what I have actually seen? For I had seen a vision; I knew it, and I knew that God knew it, and I could not deny it, neither dared I do it; at least I knew that by so doing I would offend God, and come under condemnation. (Joseph Smith—History 1:23–25)

Joseph continued to suffer ridicule from his community for claiming to have seen a vision, and he continued to labor with his hands to help support his family until three years later, when, in response to another sincere prayer, an angel named Moroni appeared at his bedside.

THE ANGEL MORONI

Quoting from Joseph Smith's history:

> While I was thus in the act of calling upon God, I discovered a light appearing in my room, which continued to increase until the room was lighter than at noonday, when immediately a personage appeared at my bedside, standing in the air, for his feet did not touch the floor.
>
> He had on a loose robe of most exquisite whiteness. It was a whiteness beyond anything earthly I had ever seen; nor do I believe that any earthly thing could be made to appear so exceedingly white and brilliant. His hands were naked, and his arms also, a little above the wrist; so, also, were his feet naked, as were his legs, a little above the ankles. His head and neck were also bare. I could discover that he had no other clothing on but this robe, as it was open, so that I could see into his bosom.
>
> Not only was his robe exceedingly white, but his whole person was glorious beyond description, and his countenance truly like lightning. The room was exceedingly light, but not so very bright as immediately around his person. When I first looked upon him, I was afraid; but the fear soon left me.
>
> He called me by name, and said unto me that he was a messenger sent from the presence of God to me, and that his name was Moroni; that God had a work for me to do; and that my name should be had for good and evil among all nations, kindreds, and tongues, or that it should be both good and evil spoken of among all people.

> He said there was a book deposited, written upon gold plates, giving an account of the former inhabitants of this continent, and the source from whence they sprang. He also said that the fulness of the everlasting gospel was contained in it, as delivered by the Savior to the ancient inhabitants;
>
> Also, that there were two stones in silver bows—and these stones, fastened to a breastplate, constituted what is called the Urim and Thummim—deposited with the plates; and the possession and use of these stones were what constituted "seers" in ancient or former times; and that God had prepared them for the purpose of translating the book. (Joseph Smith—History 1:30–35)

The angel Moroni explained to Joseph that he was a resurrected being who had been the last prophet to write in the sacred record on the gold plates. He further explained that this record included a history of the ancient inhabitants of this, the American continent; their migration from Jerusalem in 600 BC; and the prophecies received by their prophets down to and including the visit of Jesus Christ to these ancient Americans after his resurrection in Jerusalem. Moroni's father was a prophet-historian named Mormon who had abridged the sacred record on the plates of gold.

ANCIENT BURIED RECORD: THE GOLD PLATES OF THE BOOK OF MORMON

On the morning following this angelic visitation, Joseph was led by the angel Moroni to a hillside near the city of Palmyra, New York, where he was shown a rounded stone that covered a buried stone box, which contained the gold plates the angel had described the night before.

Although Joseph was allowed to lift the stone lid and look into the buried box, the angel forbade him to remove the plates at that time.

He finally was allowed to remove the plates five years later:

> On the twenty-second day of September, one thousand eight hundred and twenty-seven, having gone as usual at the end of another year to the place where they were deposited, the same heavenly messenger delivered them up to me with this charge: that I should be responsible for them; that if I should let them go carelessly, or through any neglect of mine, I should be cut off; but that if I would use all my endeavors to preserve them, until he, the messenger, should call for them, they should be protected.

> I soon found out the reason why I had received such strict charges to keep them safe, and why it was that the messenger had said that when I had done what was required at my hand, he would call for them. For no sooner was it known that I had them, than the most strenuous exertions were used to get them from me. Every stratagem that could be invented was resorted to for that purpose. The persecution became more bitter and severe than before, and multitudes were on the alert continually to get them from me if possible. But by the wisdom of God, they remained safe in my hands, until I had accomplished by them what was required at my hand. When, according to arrangements, the messenger called for them, I delivered them up to him; and he has them in his charge until this day, being the second day of May, one thousand eight hundred and thirty-eight. (Joseph Smith—History 1:51–54, 59–60)

THE TRANSLATION OF THE BOOK OF MORMON

The following account is taken from "Book of Mormon Translations," in the *Encyclopedia of Mormonism*, ed. Daniel H. Ludlow:

> The Book of Mormon was translated from ancient gold plates by the Prophet Joseph Smith, who testified that he translated it through the power of God, though he knew no ancient languages at the time of the translation. Joseph Smith, at the age of twenty-two, first obtained the plates at the Hill Cumorah near Palmyra, New York, on September 22, 1827, and began translation shortly thereafter. His wife, Emma, "recalled that Joseph dictated the translation to her [or a scribe, primarily Oliver Cowdery] word for word, spelled out the proper names, and would correct her scribal errors even though he could not see what she had written. . . . After a meal or a night's rest, Joseph would begin, without prompting, where he had previously left off."[1]

Most reports state that throughout the project, Joseph used the "Nephite interpreters' or, for convenience, he would use a SEER STONE [objects included in the stone box with the gold plates]. Both instruments were sometimes called by others the URIM AND THUMMIM [see Exodus 28:30]." In 1830, Oliver Cowdrey is reported to have testified in court that these tools enabled Joseph "to read in English, the reformed Egyptian characters, which were engraved upon the plates."[2]

Despite persecution and the constant threat that the gold plates would be stolen, virtually all of the English text of the Book of Mormon was translated within sixty working days in April, May, and June of 1829.[3] Reports state that at times Joseph used a seer stone, or Urim and Thummim, which had been buried in the stone box with the plates, to discern the Reformed Egyptian characters, but the progress of the translation depended primarily on his own spiritual efforts and righteousness.

The Book of Mormon: Another Testament of Jesus Christ, published by The Church of Jesus Christ of Latter-day Saints, is a religious history of the ancient inhabitants of the American continent and the revelations received by their prophets. This history begins in Jerusalem in 600 BC with a prophet named Lehi, who received a revelation in a vision commanding him to preach repentance to the people, telling them of their wickedness and that if they did not repent they would be destroyed. This occurred a few years before the Babylonian captivity of the Israelite nation from 597 to 586 BC.

Lehi's preaching was not well received by the people of Jerusalem, and his life was threatened. The Book of Mormon tells that the Lord then commanded Lehi to take his family and flee Jerusalem, promising that he would lead them to a new promised land. Lehi took his family on a journey into the wilderness, along the banks of the Red Sea, to an oasis in the desert, where his son Nephi was instructed by the Lord how to build a ship. The story chronicles the journey of Lehi's family across the ocean and describes a new land that closely resembles Central America in its geographical descriptions in the Book of Mormon.

Lehi brought to America a record of the Old Testament up to 600 BC written on plates of brass. Lehi recorded the history of his family and his revelations from the Lord on gold plates, which he passed on to his son Nephi, who also recorded history and revelations. Each prophet-leader preserved these plates and added to them before passing them on to a son or a spiritual follower.

The plates also contain a record of the wars and contentions between the followers of Nephi, Lehi's righteous son, and the descendants of Laman and Lemuel, Nephi's older brothers who rebelled against him and his teachings. The gold plates tell of Jesus Christ's visit to the American continent after his resurrection in Jerusalem, and they tell of his ministry among his other sheep there. They tell of two hundred years of peace after his visit, after which the Nephites and the Lamanites engaged in wars that lasted until the Nephites were destroyed by the Lamanites in about AD 400. Mormon, one of the last Nephite prophets, abridged the record, and his son, Moroni, the last prophet to write in the record, buried the plates in the hillside in Palmyra, New York.

As a resurrected being, this same Moroni appeared to young Joseph Smith and led him to the hill where the plates were buried. Following the translation, the angel Moroni appeared to three witnesses, who heard him declare that this record was the work of God. They were allowed to handle the gold plates and examine the ancient Egyptian characters on them. The Lord allowed Joseph Smith to show the plates to eight other witnesses, after which they were returned to the angel Moroni as commanded by the Lord.

According to LDS author Dr. Joseph L. Allen, the Book of Mormon describes three different migrations to the Americas, and many modern archaeologists believe that these migrations correspond remarkably with three ancient American civilizations documented by archaeologists:[4]

Archaeology Name	Book of Mormon Name	Time Period (Archaeology & Book of Mormon)
Olmecs/Tultecas	Jaredites	2500–600 BC
Mayas	Lamanites/Nephites	600 BC–AD 1519
Zapotecs	Mulekites	580 BC–200 BC

The Book of Mormon, published by Joseph Smith in 1830, long before chronicles of archaeological discoveries in America were available for publication, tells of great highways and aqueducts, of fortified cities, and of the building of ancient temples. It also tells of cities buried under lakes and oceans by earthquakes and volcanoes at the time of the crucifixion of Jesus Christ in Jerusalem.

THE AARONIC PRIESTHOOD RESTORED BY JOHN THE BAPTIST

While translating the record from the gold plates, Joseph Smith and his scribe, Oliver Cowdery encountered the subject of baptism for the remission of sins, which caused them to inquire of the Lord. When they did so, another heavenly visitor appeared:

We still continued the work of translation, when, in the ensuing month (May 1829), we on a certain day went into the woods to pray and inquire of the Lord respecting baptism for the remission of sins, that we found mentioned in the translation of the plates. While we were thus employed, praying and calling upon the Lord, a messenger from heaven descended in a cloud of light, and having laid his hands upon us, he ordained us, saying:

Upon you my fellow servants, in the name of Messiah, I confer the Priesthood of Aaron, which holds the keys of the ministering of angels, and of the gospel of repentance, and of baptism by immersion for the remission of sins; and this shall never be taken again from the earth until the sons of Levi do offer again an offering unto the Lord in righteousness.

He said this Aaronic Priesthood had not the power of laying on hands for the gift of the Holy Ghost, but that this should be conferred on us hereafter; and he commanded us to go and be baptized, and gave us directions that I should baptize Oliver Cowdery, and that afterwards he should baptize me.

Accordingly we went and were baptized. I baptized him first, and afterwards he baptized me—after which I laid my hands upon his head and ordained him to the Aaronic Priesthood, and afterwards he laid his hands on me and ordained me to the same Priesthood—for so we were commanded.

The messenger who visited us on this occasion and conferred this Priesthood upon us, said that his name was John, the same that is called John the Baptist in the New Testament, and that he acted under the direction of Peter, James and John, who held the keys of the Priesthood of Melchizedek, which Priesthood, he said, would in due time be conferred on us, and that I should be called the first Elder of the Church, and he (Oliver Cowdery) the second. It was on the fifteenth day of May, 1829, that we were ordained under the hand of this messenger, and baptized.

Immediately on our coming up out of the water after we had been baptized, we experienced great and glorious blessings from our Heavenly Father. No sooner had I baptized Oliver Cowdery, than the Holy Ghost fell upon him, and he stood up and prophesied many things which should shortly come to pass. And again, so soon as I had been baptized by him, I also had the spirit of prophecy, when, standing up, I prophesied concerning the rise of this Church, and many other things connected with the Church, and this generation of the children of men. We were filled with the Holy Ghost, and rejoiced in the God of our salvation.

> Our minds being now enlightened, we began to have the scriptures laid open to our understandings, and the true meaning and intention of their more mysterious passages revealed unto us in a manner which we never could attain to previously, nor ever before had thought of. In the meantime we were forced to keep secret the circumstances of having received the Priesthood and our having been baptized, owing to a spirit of persecution which had already manifested itself in the neighborhood. (Joseph Smith—History 1:68–74)

Oliver Cowdery, Joseph's scribe, described this miraculous visitation in these words:

> These were days never to be forgotten—to sit under the sound of a voice dictated by the inspiration of heaven, awakened the utmost gratitude of this bosom! Day after day I continued, uninterrupted, to write from his mouth, as he translated with the Urim and Thummim, or, as the Nephites would have said, "Interpreters," the history or record called "The Book of Mormon."
>
> To notice, in even few words, the interesting account given by Mormon and his faithful son, Moroni, of a people once beloved and favored of heaven, would supersede my present design; I shall therefore defer this to a future period, and, as I said in the introduction, pass more directly to some few incidents immediately connected with the rise of this Church, which may be entertaining to some thousands who have stepped forward, amid the frowns of bigots and the calumny of hypocrites, and embraced the gospel of Christ.
>
> No men, in their sober senses, could translate and write the directions given to the Nephites from the mouth of the Savior, of the precise manner in which men should build up His Church, and especially when corruption had spread an uncertainty over all forms and systems practiced among men, without desiring a privilege of showing the willingness of the heart by being buried in the liquid grave, to answer a "good conscience by the resurrection of Jesus Christ."
>
> After writing the account given of the Savior's ministry to the remnant of the seed of Jacob, upon this continent, it was easy to be seen, as the prophet said it would be, that darkness covered the earth and gross darkness the minds of the people. On reflecting further it was as easy to be seen that amid the great strife and noise concerning religion, none had authority from God to administer the ordinances of the gospel. For the question might be asked, have men authority to administer in the name of Christ, who deny revelations, when His testimony is no less than the spirit of prophecy, and His religion

based, built, and sustained by immediate revelations, in all ages of the world when He has had a people on earth? If these facts were buried, and carefully concealed by men whose craft would have been in danger if once permitted to shine in the faces of men, they were no longer to us; and we only waited for the commandment to be given "Arise and be baptized."

This was not long desired before it was realized. The Lord, who is rich in mercy, and ever willing to answer the consistent prayer of the humble, after we had called upon Him in a fervent manner, aside from the abodes of men, condescended to manifest to us His will. On a sudden, as from the midst of eternity, the voice of the Redeemer spake peace to us, while the veil was parted and the angel of God came down clothed with glory, and delivered the anxiously looked for message, and the keys of the gospel of repentance. What joy! what wonder! what amazement! While the world was racked and distracted—while millions were groping as the blind for the wall, and while all men were resting upon uncertainty, as a general mass, our eyes beheld, our ears heard, as in the "blaze of day"; yes, more—above the glitter of the May sunbeam, which then shed its brilliancy over the face of nature! Then his voice, though mild, pierced to the center, and his words, "I am thy fellow-servant," dispelled every fear. We listened, we gazed, we admired! 'Twas the voice of an angel from glory, 'twas a message from the Most High! And as we heard we rejoiced, while His love enkindled upon our souls, and we were wrapped in the vision of the Almighty! Where was room for doubt? Nowhere; uncertainty had fled, doubt had sunk no more to rise, while fiction and deception had fled forever!

But, dear brother, think, further think for a moment, what joy filled our hearts, and with what surprise we must have bowed, (for who would not have bowed the knee for such a blessing?) when we received under his hand the Holy Priesthood as he said, "Upon you my fellow-servants, in the name of Messiah, I confer this Priesthood and this authority, which shall remain upon earth, that the Sons of Levi may yet offer an offering unto the Lord in righteousness!"

I shall not attempt to paint to you the feelings of this heart, nor the majestic beauty and glory which surrounded us on this occasion; but you will believe me when I say, that earth, nor men, with the eloquence of time, cannot begin to clothe language in as interesting and sublime a manner as this holy personage. No; nor has this earth power to give the joy, to bestow the peace, or comprehend the wisdom which was contained in each sentence as they were delivered

> by the power of the Holy Spirit! Man may deceive his fellow-men, deception may follow deception, and the children of the wicked one may have power to seduce the foolish and untaught, till naught but fiction feeds the many, and the fruit of falsehood carries in its current the giddy to the grave; but one touch with the finger of his love, yes, one ray of glory from the upper world, or one word from the mouth of the Savior, from the bosom of eternity, strikes it all into insignificance, and blots it forever from the mind. The assurance that we were in the presence of an angel, the certainty that we heard the voice of Jesus, and the truth unsullied as it flowed from a pure personage, dictated by the will of God, is to me past description, and I shall ever look upon this expression of the Savior's goodness with wonder and thanksgiving while I am permitted to tarry; and in those mansions where perfection dwells and sin never comes, I hope to adore in that day which shall never cease." (*Messenger and Advocate,* vol. 1 [October 1834], 14–16)

The divine authority of the priesthood to act for Jesus Christ, which had been lost with the passing of the apostles and the selection of bishops by Roman Emperors, had finally been restored to the earth. The restoration was accomplished by the last legitimate holder of this Aaronic Priesthood, who was John the Baptist, who had been beheaded by Herod during the Savior's mortal ministry but who was now a resurrected being. This authority had been assumed by men for centuries, but it was now conferred by a heavenly messenger sent from the Savior himself to his chosen prophet.

THE MELCHIZEDEK PRIESTHOOD RESTORED BY PETER, JAMES, AND JOHN

As promised by John the Baptist in his ordination of Joseph and Oliver to the Aaronic Priesthood, Peter, James, and John, the resurrected apostles and presidency of the early Church organized by Jesus himself, appeared to Joseph Smith and Oliver Cowdery in the spring of 1829 and ordained them to the higher, or Melchizedek, priesthood. They also set them apart as apostles of Christ's Church, which was soon to be restored to the earth after centuries of apostasy.

THE RESTORED CHURCH

With the authority of the Aaronic and Melchizedek Priesthoods and his ordination as an apostle by Peter, James, and John, the last legitimate presidency of the Church organized by Jesus Christ, Joseph Smith was commanded by the Lord to organize his Church on the earth again. This was accomplished on April 6, 1830, in Fayette, New York, and the Lord revealed that the name of the Church should be The Church of Jesus Christ of Latter-day Saints. Joseph Smith was the First Elder of the Church, with Oliver Cowdery as the Second Elder. Later, the Lord commanded Joseph to call and ordain twelve other apostles.

The Church of Jesus Christ of Latter-day Saints is organized according to the ancient pattern of the Primitive Church, with a quorum of twelve apostles; a president, or prophet, with two counselors (following the pattern of Peter, James, and John, which was established by Jesus when he was on the earth); quorums of Seventy (traveling evangelists proclaiming the gospel); and bishops over local congregations. Within each congregation, the Aaronic Priesthood, consisting of deacons, teachers, priests, and bishops, prepare, bless, and pass the sacrament, or emblems of the Last Supper, to the congregation. The priests also have the power to baptize but not to confer the gift of the Holy Ghost. The leadership of the Church is based in the Melchizedek Priesthood, of which Jesus Christ is the great high priest. This priesthood includes the offices of elder, Seventy, and high priest. Members of the Mechizedek Priesthood confer the gift of the Holy Ghost, or the baptism of the Spirit, since Jesus told Nicodemus, "Except a man be born of water and of the Spirit, he cannot enter into the kingdom of God" (John 3:5).

THE BUILDING OF TEMPLES

Another practice of the restored Church that brings it into harmony with the primitive Church is the restored ordinance of baptisms for the dead. The baptismal fonts in the temples of the LDS Church today are patterned after the font in Solomon's temple, with the font resting on the backs of twelve oxen as described in 1 Kings 7:23–25 and 2 Chronicles 4. Worthy members of the Church enter into the font and are baptized in behalf of their ancestors, who may not have had the chance to hear the gospel in its fulness and be baptized by someone holding the proper priesthood authority.

The Lord commanded Joseph Smith to build temples like the ancient temple in Jerusalem, but due to the poverty of the Church members, the early temples were not covered with gold as was Solomon's temple. They were, however, built with the finest materials and the most excellent workmanship that the members could produce at that time. The first temple was constructed in Kirtland, Ohio, and the next was in Nauvoo, Illinois. The inscription over the door to the temples read, "House of the Lord, Holiness to the Lord." Today over 120 temples are spread across the world, and Latter-day Saints of all nations can come to receive temple blessings.

It is in the temples that sacred instruction is given, in an ordinance called the endowment, where worthy members of the Church make sacred covenants to live a life of holiness, with the blessing of eternal life promised for enduring to the end and keeping these covenants. Some people believe that the endowment is the secret teachings that Jesus gave to his apostles in the forty days after his resurrection.

In the temple, husbands and wives are sealed together in eternal marriages as they kneel across an altar set between two opposite mirrors that project the couple's reflections into a seemingly infinite vanishing point. Children born to parents prior to their sealing are then sealed to the father and mother in an eternal family. Children born after this sealing are "born in the covenant" and are automatically sealed to the family. In the basement of these temples is the baptismal font, where the ordinance of baptism for the dead is performed.

OTHER HEAVENLY VISITATIONS

In the Kirtland Temple, on April 3, 1836, Joseph Smith and Oliver Cowdery beheld visions of the prophets Moses, Elias, and Elijah, as recorded in Doctrine and Covenants, section 110:

> After this vision closed, the heavens were again opened unto us; and Moses appeared before us, and committed unto us the keys of the gathering of Israel from the four parts of the earth, and the leading of the ten tribes from the land of the north.
>
> After this, Elias appeared, and committed the dispensation of the gospel of Abraham, saying that in us and our seed all generations after us should be blessed.
>
> After this vision had closed, another great and glorious vision burst upon us; for Elijah the prophet, who was taken to heaven without tasting death, stood before us, and said:
>
> Behold, the time has fully come, which was spoken of by the mouth of Malachi—testifying that he [Elijah] should be sent, before the great and dreadful day of the Lord come—

> To turn the hearts of the fathers to the children, and the children to the fathers, lest the whole earth be smitten with a curse—
>
> Therefore, the keys of this dispensation are committed into your hands; and by this ye may know that the great and dreadful day of the Lord is near, even at the doors. (D&C 110:11–16)

Every year at a certain feast, the Jews set a place at the table for Elijah's promised return, but Joseph Smith testifies that he has already returned for the purpose of bringing salvation to those who have died without the knowledge of the gospel or the saving ordinance of baptism by an authorized servant of the Lord. This restored doctrine is the motivation behind the unparalleled effort of the LDS Church in preserving and searching family histories and genealogies so that our ancestors can be given the sacred ordinances of baptism vicariously while they wait in spirit prison for the opportunity to move into paradise.

CONCLUSIONS

Because of the apostasy foretold by the apostles in the New Testament, there had to be a restoration before the Second Coming of Christ to prepare the world to receive him when he comes. The long-awaited restoration of all things has occurred, and the gospel is now being spread throughout the world by missionaries of The Church of Jesus Christ of Latter-day Saints. In addition to the appearance of Heavenly Father and Jesus Christ, Joseph Smith was visited by ancient prophets and apostles, who appeared as resurrected beings to restore the true priesthood keys for the ordinances of salvation and for the gathering of Israel. This enabled work for the salvation for the dead who died without the saving ordinances of the gospel through no fault of their own. These incredible claims of heavenly visitations are hard for some to believe, but when considered, they are absolutely necessary to prepare the earth for the Lord's promised Second Coming. This restoration of doctrine and authority should be the most thrilling news of our era, and it should be earnestly investigated by all who hope for more knowledge from God.

NOTES

1. "Book of Mormon Translations by Joseph Smith," in *Encyclopedia of Mormonism*, ed. Daniel H. Ludlow, 4 vols. (New York: Macmillan, 1992), 1:210.

2. Ibid., 1:212.
3. Ibid., 1:210.
4. Joseph L. Allen, *Exploring the Lands of the Book of Mormon* (Orem, UT: S. A. Publishers, 1989), 14.

CHAPTER 15

VOICES FROM THE DUST

Wherefore the Lord said, Forasmuch as this people draw near me with their mouth, and with their lips do honour me, but have removed their heart far from me, and their fear toward me is taught by the precept of men:

Therefore, behold, I will proceed to do a marvellous work among this people, even a marvellous work and a wonder: for the wisdom of their wise men shall perish, and the understanding of their prudent men shall be hid.

Isaiah 29:13–14

MORE EXCITING THAN THE DISCOVERY OF THE DEAD SEA SCROLLS or the Nag Hammadi codices would be a record of Jesus Christ's visit to the American continent following his resurrection, his teachings to his other sheep there, and a collection of revelations that he gave to prophets on this continent. Imagine the newspaper headlines of such a discovery:

Ancient Buried Records Tell of the Visit of Jesus Christ to Central America

Prophecies of Jesus Christ to Ancient Americans Discovered

The whole Christian world would rush to receive such records. Isaiah prophesied of such a record to be buried by the descendants of Israel, saying, "And thou shalt be brought down, and shalt speak out of the ground, and thy speech shall be low out of the dust, and thy voice shall be, as of one that hath a familiar spirit, out of the ground, and thy speech shall whisper out of the dust" (Isaiah 29:4). Isaiah saw the great apostasy when there would be no prophets on the earth, but then a book would be discovered that would allow the blind to see out of darkness:

> For the Lord hath poured out upon you the spirit of deep sleep, and hath closed your eyes: the prophets and your rulers, the seers hath he covered.
>
> And the vision of all is become unto you as the words of a book that is sealed, which men deliver to one that is learned, saying, Read this, I pray thee: and he saith, I cannot; for it is sealed:
>
> And the book is delivered to him that is not learned, saying, Read this, I pray thee: and he saith, I am not learned. . . .
>
> And in that day shall the deaf hear the words of the book, and the eyes of the blind shall see out of obscurity, and out of darkness.
>
> The meek also shall increase their joy in the Lord, and the poor among men shall rejoice in the Holy One of Israel. (Isaiah 29:10–14, 18–19)

Lehi was a descendant of Joseph of Israel, and Moroni, a descendant of this Lehi, buried his people's records written on plates of gold in a hillside in Palmyra, New York. Centuries later, Moroni was sent as a resurrected being to the young boy Joseph Smith to reveal their location. The testimonies of these ancient Americans speak out of the ground through these buried records to open eyes that have been blinded by spiritual darkness and confusion due to centuries without a prophet on the earth.

Nonbelievers often stop their study of the Book of Mormon after hearing of the miraculous and incredible story of how Joseph Smith obtained this sacred record. However, the old adage, "You cannot judge a book by its cover," could not be more profound than when applied to the Book of Mormon, whose cover includes the title and the phrase, "Another Testament of Jesus Christ." Between the covers of the Book of Mormon, in addition to the religious history of the ancient inhabitants of the American continent, is a wealth of geographical, social, cultural, and physical information that describes the origin of these three civilizations. It describes great civilizations, temples, highways, and wars among the people. It identifies the source of the Hebrew and Egyptian cultures found in Central America.

There is an abundance of evidence from Central America that supports the validity of the Book of Mormon as a description of the ancient inhabitants of that land, but the real truth comes only from the Holy Ghost, according to the following promise made by Moroni, the last of the ancient prophets to write in the book.

> And when ye shall receive these things, I would exhort you that ye would ask God, the Eternal Father, in the name of Christ, if these things are not true; and if ye shall ask with a sincere heart, with real intent, having faith in Christ, he will manifest the truth of it unto you, by the power of the Holy Ghost.
>
> And by the power of the Holy Ghost ye may know the truth of all things. (Moroni 10:4–5)

SIGNIFICANT SCRIPTURES AND PROPHECIES IN THE BOOK OF MORMON

- Twenty-two chapters of Isaiah written prior to 600 BC, with slight variations from our Old Testament
- The prophecies of Jehovah to ancient American prophets before his birth as Jesus Christ
- The story of the visit of Jesus Christ to the American continent and his teachings here (3 Nephi)
- The lost parable of the olive trees from the ancient prophet Zenos (Jacob 5)
- The principle of free agency, explaining why God allows suffering (2 Nephi 2:11)
- The purpose of man's existence (2 Nephi 2:25)
- The laws of justice and mercy (Alma 42)
- The Atonement of Jesus Christ (2 Nephi 9:4–14; Alma 34:8–17)
- What happens to our spirits after death (Alma 40:11–14)
- What our bodies will be like in the resurrection (Alma 40:23)
- The correct method of baptism (3 Nephi 11:21–28)
- The words of the prayer for blessing the sacrament (Moroni 4–5)
- The gospel of Jesus Christ in his own words (3 Nephi 27:13–21)

- Restrictions on baptizing little children (Moroni 8:1–24)
- The restoration of the house of Israel in the latter days (1 Nephi 15:13–14)
- Salvation by grace or works or both (2 Nephi 25:23)
- The lost sheep Jesus discussed in John 10:16 (3 Nephi 15:11–24)
- The history of the Jaredites, probable ancestors of the Olmecs (Book of Ether)
- The history of the Nephites and Lamanites, probable ancestors of the Mayans (1 & 2 Nephi)
- The history of the Mulekites, who descended from King Zedekiah of Jerusalem, probable ancestors of the Zapotecs (Helaman 6:10)

A MARVELOUS WORK AND A WONDER

> Wherefore the Lord said, Forasmuch as this people draw near me with their mouth, and with their lips do honour me, but have removed their heart far from me, and their fear toward me is taught by the precept of men:
>
> Therefore, behold, I will proceed to do a marvellous work among this people, even a marvellous work and a wonder: for the wisdom of their wise men shall perish, and the understanding of their prudent men shall be hid. (Isaiah 29:13–14)

CONCLUSIONS

The translation of the Book of Mormon from buried, ancient gold plates inscribed in Reformed Egyptian characters, documenting the history of descendants of the ancient tribe of Joseph who migrated to the Americas six hundred years before Christ, is truly a marvelous work and a wonder. Many proud and learned men and women have rejected this book and have failed to understand its profound implications for all the world. Those with humble hearts, who believe that God is still capable of revealing his will to prophets today and of preserving a history of his revelations, have received the sure witness of the Holy Ghost that this book contains the word of God.

CHAPTER 16

EVIDENCES OF THE BOOK OF MORMON

A DETAILED DISCUSSION OF THE EVIDENCES OF THE BOOK OF Mormon is beyond the scope and purpose of this book, but a summary of those evidences is presented here. The types of evidences to be summarized are

- Witnesses
- Dates and Language
- Archaeological Evidence
- Traditions of Mesoamerica (oral traditions, cultural patterns, and written history)
- Geographical Evidence[1]

WITNESSES

Included in the first few pages of the Book of Mormon are the Testimony of Three Witnesses and the Testimony of Eight Witnesses.

The Testimony of Three Witnesses

Oliver Cowdery, David Whitmer, and Martin Harris testified, saying, in part, "And we declare, with words of soberness, that an angel of God came down from heaven, and he brought and laid before our eyes, that we beheld and saw the plates, and the engravings thereon; and we know that it is by the grace of God the Father, and our Lord Jesus Christ, that we beheld and bear record that these things are true. And marvelous it is in our eyes. Nevertheless, the voice of the Lord commanded us that we should bear record of it" (Book of Mormon, Introduction).

The Testimony of Eight Witnesses

Christian Whitmer, Jacob Whitmer, Peter Whitmer Jr., John Whitmer, Hiram Page, Joseph Smith Sr., Hyrum Smith, and Samuel H. Smith all testified that Joseph Smith showed them the plates and allowed them to handle them and view the ancient engravings thereon. (Book of Mormon, Introduction)

The Testimony of Oliver Cowdery

Oliver Cowdery, Joseph Smith's scribe for much of the translation of the Book of Mormon, testified of the appearance of John the Baptist (see chapter 14), who restored the Aaronic Priesthood, and of Peter, James, and John, who restored the Melchizedek Priesthood.

DATES AND LANGUAGES

Central America is the only place on the American continent where there were written languages corresponding to the time periods described in the Book of Mormon. Dates of the Mayan calendar are carved in stone stelae. Archaeologists can trace the migration of the people from dates carved in these stelae as the people migrated across Central America. The Mayan calendar dates time from 3114 BC,[2] which the Mayans believed to be the date of the great flood.

Dr. Joseph Allen, archaeologist, states: "The Mesoamericans adjusted their calendar in 6 AD when a mass planetary conjunction occurred. This adjustment is consistent with the Book of Mormon, wherein it states that nine years after the birth of Christ (4 BC), the people adjusted their calendar system, the beginning of 6 AD or the end of 5 AD."[3]

"And nine years had passed away from the time when the sign was given. . . . Now the Nephites began to reckon their time from this period when the sign was given, or from the coming of Christ." (3 Nephi 2:7–8)

CHIASMS IN THE BOOK OF MORMON

A chiasm is a poetic style of writing commonly used in ancient Hebrew writing. This poetic form is prevalent in the Bible in the original Hebrew and was first noticed by a few nineteenth-century pioneer theologians in Germany and England, but it was not until the 1930s that Nils Lund laid the principle before the world in a convincing way.[4] Chiasms often become obscured in the translation from Hebrew to English. A chiasm is an inverted parallelism, or, in other words, it is a grammatical structure in which you say something and then repeat yourself in reverse order. The word *chiasm* comes from the Greek letter "chi." This letter is used to describe the structure of a Hebraic inverted parallelism.

The most important aspect is emphasized by placing it in the center of the chiasm.

Genesis 7:21–23 (translating literally from Hebrew)

a. There died on the earth
 b. all birds,
  c. cattle,
   d. beasts and creeping things,
    e. man:
     f. all life
      g. died
      g. and was destroyed
     f. Every living thing
    e. both man,
   d. creeping things
  c. cattle,
 b. birds,
a. were destroyed from the earth

The Hebrew Bible is filled with chiasms, since this was a common literary form in ancient Hebrew writing. Because the Book of Mormon was derived from the writings of descendants of Joseph of Egypt, scholars began to search the Book of Mormon for this literary style. They found its use abundant in the Book of Mormon as well.

Mosiah 3:18–19

a. They humble themselves
  b. and become as little children,
    c. and believe that salvation . . . is . . . in and through the atoning blood of Christ, the Lord Omnipotent.
      d. For the natural man
        e. is an enemy to God,
          f. and has been from the fall of Adam,
          f. and will be, forever and ever,
        e. unless he yields to the enticings of the Holy Spirit,
      d. and putteth off the natural man
    c. and becometh a saint through the atonement of Christ the Lord,
  b. and becometh as a child,
a. submissive, meek, humble . . . full of love

There are 961 chiasms in the Book of Mormon. The entire book of 1 Nephi is written on a chiastic structure consisting of 165 elements to the center of the chiasm and 165 elements from the center to the end of the chiasm. Within the book of 1 Nephi, 107 additional chiasms appear.[5]

A BOOK OF MORMON KING'S NAME IS CARVED IN STONE

An Olmec King named U-Kish Kan is identified in a genealogy of the Maya King Pacal carved in stone at Palenque. U-Kish Kan was born on Wednesday, 8 March 993 BC. *Kan* means serpent. One of the meanings of *Kish* is feathered. Now that the Mayan code is being deciphered, the name of U-Kish Kan has been translated as "he of the feathered serpent." In the book of Ether in the Book of Mormon, a Jaredite king, King Kish, lived about the same time. The account in the book of Ether gives little information about King Kish other than his name. He was the son of a righteous king named Corom and the father of a righteous king named Lib (Ether 1:18–19; 10:17–19). Thus, King Kish was apparently one of the Jaredite monarchs.[6]

ARCHAEOLOGICAL EVIDENCE

As stated before, three civilizations in Central America correspond to three migrations described in the Book of Mormon.[7]

Archaeology Name	Book of Mormon Name	Time Period (Archaeology & Book of Mormon)
Olmecs/Tultecas	Jaredites	2500–600 BC
Mayas	Lamanites/Nephites	600 BC–AD 1519
Zapotecs	Mulekites	580 BC–200 BC

Until 1956, scholars believed that the Mayas were the oldest civilization in Central America. But with the discovery of huge sculpted heads buried beneath the earth in the region of San Andres Tuxla, Veracruz, Mexico, archaeologists learned of a much earlier civilization they labeled as Olmecs, which they have dated to 2500 BC.[8]

Dr. Joseph Allen, in *Exploring the Lands of the Book of Mormon*, states, "The Zapotec civilization had its beginnings in the Valley of Oaxaca [Mexico] about 500 BC. As determined by culture patterns, language, and date correlations, the early Zapotecs may have been a part of the Mulekite culture."[9] The Book of Mormon states that Mulek was a son of King Zedekiah, King of Judah during the Babylonian captivity in 587 BC. (See Helaman 6:10.)

These three civilizations (Mayas, Zapotecs, and Olmecs) known to archaeologists by modern names correspond in both dates and likely locations to three tribes described in the Book of Mormon. The Book of Mormon's description of these tribes' movements correspond remarkably well with the movements tracked by these cultures' records carved in stone stelae as they moved across the continent.

OLMECS/TOLTECS CORRESPOND TO THE JAREDITES

The Book of Mormon says that the Jaredites came from Jerusalem at the time of the tower of Babel.[10] In the book *The Americas before*

Columbus, compiled by Dewey Farnsworth, he quotes an ethnological report by Lowrey in *Schoolcraft's Ethnological Researches,* about the aborigines of America, which concludes "that the first settlement was made shortly after the confusion of the building of the Tower of Babel."[11] In the same book, Farnsworth quotes Herbert Howe Bancroft, who states, "The Toltecs claim to have come to America at the time of the confusion of tongues. . . . The Yucatans have a tradition that they came originally from the far east, passing through the sea."[12]

MAYAS CORRESPOND TO THE NEPHITES AND LAMANITES

The Book of Mormon account tells that Lehi left Jerusalem in 600 BC and that his descendents broke into two factions. The followers of his son Nephi became known as Nephites, and the followers of his son Laman became known as Lamanites. The Book of Mormon describes centuries of wars between the Nephites and the Lamanites and explains that the Lamanites eventually destroyed the Nephite civilization in about AD 400.

Tour guides in the city of Tikal, an ancient Maya city-state in the Peten Jungle of Guatemala, lead tours to the Lost World, whose ruins date to 600 BC, and tell that the main temples in the central plaza were built between AD 400 and 900 by wicked priests who began the practice of human sacrifice to pagan gods and ruled over the common people. The Book of Mormon record concludes with the destruction of the Nephites by the Lamanites about AD 400.

The Maya Civilization Appeared Suddenly in 600 BC

Farnsworth quotes Dr. Morley of Carnegie Institute, who wrote, "With records cut in imperishable stone, the Mayas suddenly made their appearance upon the historical scene on August 6, 613 BC. Why on August 6, 613 BC? Where were the Mayas on August 5th? Nobody knows. . . . They may as well have dropped down from Mars or some other planet on the 6th day of August."[13]

Hebrew Culture before the Spanish Conquest

The Book of Mormon says that Lehi and his sons brought the record of the Jews, including the writings of Isaiah, written on plates of brass. In *The Americas before Columbus,* Farnsworth quotes Alvin

Coulton, a man who lived with many of the Indian tribes and learned many of their legends:

> The story of the flood is widely current among the American Indians. A man (Noach) with certain other people, escaped in a boat filled with various animals and birds. . . . Jacob and his twelve sons are found in the legends of the American Indians. Some of the tribes used to build an altar of twelve stones in memory of a great ancestor.[14]

Lehi, the first Hebrew prophet in the Book of Mormon, was a trader by occupation and traded with the Egyptians. In *The Americas before Columbus,* Farnsworth cites the opinion of archaeologist George Jones, who states in separate articles that the ancient inhabitants of America seem to represent both Hebrew and Egyptian cultures:

> What nation of ancient history can claim and identify those customs and observances as their own, if not the Hebrew? (Jones, History of Ancient America, 21)

> And as if in direct copy of the Egyptian, we have shown that the size of the pyramidal base at Copan is identical with that of the Pyramid of the Nile—while that at Cholula, in Mexican America, is exactly twice the base measurement. It is scarcely possible that these dimensions should have been accidental in construction. (Jones, History of Ancient America, 126)[15]

Jack West, in *The Trial of the Stick of Joseph,* cites conclusions of Professor Marett, who found in a tomb in Monte Alban artifacts and sculpture work that were, "on the one hand, absolutely Egyptian," and he gives many reasons. Then, on the other hand, he found artifacts and sculpture work in the same tomb, made out of the same materials, and as nearly as he could tell, done by the same artisans, that were "just as positively Hebrew."[16]

An incense burner from Monte Alban Period I, 500 BC to 100 BC, is similar to the types of urns from Jerusalem dating to the same time period. The Hebrews used incense burners in offering sacrifices.[17]

Temples and Pyramids in Central America

Temples and pyramids cover the land of Guatemala and southern Mexico. Tikal, a huge Maya city-state, has sections dating from 600 BC to AD 900.

TEMPLE 1 AT TIKAL (SCAFFOLDING WAS FOR THE RESTORATION OF ERODED STONES). PHOTO TAKEN BY ROBERT L. SMITH.

The Book of Mormon has several accounts of people meeting near temples. Temples were built with limestone, which, because of rain, decays into dust upon which grass and trees grow, forming mounds. Tikal terrain is flat, but mounds like the one below are everywhere. Only the vertical walls of the ancient temples reveal the ruins buried beneath vegetation that makes them appear like strange hills on flat land.

Unnamed Pyramid Mound at Tikal, showing grass except on vertical walls. Photo taken by Robert L. Smith.

Because of the decay of the limestone from which the temples were built, later civilizations built taller temples on the ruins of temples from civilizations from an earlier century. The Temple of the Lost World in Tikal has been excavated to show that it is build upon an earlier temple that dates to 600 BC.

Temple 5C-54 (the Lost World Pyramid). Part of a large E-Group complex dating to the Preclassic. Tikal, Peten, Guatemala. Restored west face. Photo by Simon Burchell. Used with permission.

Great Cities Sunken and Destroyed at the Time of the Crucifixion of Christ

The Book of Mormon tells that prophets in the Americas knew of the birth of Christ in Jerusalem and that he would be crucified for the sins of the world. It also tells of great destruction, volcanic eruptions, earthquakes, and hurricanes, and cities swallowed in the lakes and seas at the time of the death of Jesus Christ in Jerusalem. Sunken, buried cities have been found under Lake Atitlán in Guatemala, which is surrounded by three volcanoes.

LAKE ATITLÁN IN GUATEMALA, THOUGHT BY SOME TO BE THE WATERS OF MORMON. PHOTO TAKEN BY ROBERT L. SMITH.

Costly Apparel

The Book of Mormon tells us that "the people of the church began to wax proud . . . for they began to wear very costly apparel" (Alma 4:6). These "tipicos" (pictured) worn by most Guatemalan women—even while working in the fields—cost 80 to 100 dollars, which is a year's wages to these women.

Colorful tipicos worn by Guatemalan women are examples of costly apparel. Photo taken by Joshua D. Smith in Quetzaltenango, Guatemala.

TRADITIONS OF MESOAMERICA

Fernando de Alva Ixtilxochitl (pronounced Ish'-til-sho-chitil') was born of Spanish and Mexican royalty and lived from AD 1578 to 1650.[18] He was the most prolific early writer on the history of Mexico, and he wrote a detailed history of his ancestors in which he affirmed that his source material consisted of native painted records of the Mexicans. His works were first published between 1832 and 1848, after the publication of the Book of Mormon in 1830. In them he tells of a legend of a Great White God, named Quetzalcoatl, who visited his ancestors and promised to return someday. Quetzalcoatl is described by Ixtilxochitl:

Creator of all things
Born of a virgin
White or wearing a white robe
Performed miracles
Taught ordinance of baptism
Prophesied of future events
Universal god
Great destruction at his death
Cross was a symbol
Sent out disciples
Promised he would come a second time
New star associated with his birth
His children will become lords and heirs of the earth[19]

GEOGRAPHICAL EVIDENCE

The Book of Mormon is filled with geographical descriptions of a narrow neck of land between two larger bodies of land. It talks of the "land northward," the "land southward," the "land north," and "land south." It describes the "sea east" and the "sea west." Central America, or Mesoamerica—consisting of southern Mexico, Guatemala, Belize, Honduras, and El Salvador—fits the descriptions of the lands of the Book of Mormon.

There are many more striking similarities between Book of Mormon geographical descriptions and the terrain of Mesoamerica, but this depth is sufficient to establish credible evidence that Mesoamerica is a likely candidate for the land of the Book of Mormon, based on the fact pointed out by Dr. Joseph Allen that Mesoamerica is the only place where a written language existed during the time period of the Book of Mormon, and that a multitude of civilizations found there correspond remarkably in their history and movements to those described in the Book of Mormon.

Archaeology is a science that attempts to reconstruct history where no written or oral history exists. It involves systematic recovery and examination of material evidence, such as graves, buildings, tools, and pottery, remaining from past human life and culture. It is a painstaking process of digging in the earth for buried artifacts in hopes of finding evidence of a previous civilization and of finding articles or relics that might give some clues about the people who left them. Using the scientific method, archaeologists postulate a theory for the origin of their findings and test this theory based on a priori accepted findings to see if the theory fits the hypothesis for the culture being studied. When new evidence is unearthed, the theory may need to be modified to fit with the new findings. Archaeology is not an exact science; therefore, a great deal of interpretation and opinion is required to come to conclusions about the meaning of the artifacts and their relationship to the area, time period, and application of the civilization that created them.

Anthropology is the scientific study of the origin and the physical, social, and cultural development and behavior of humans. Since all recorded human history has included some form of the religious beliefs of the cultures being documented, anthropology and archaeology must consider the religious beliefs of the cultures being investigated. Indeed, such scientific study would be incomplete without considering the religious beliefs of these cultures.

Some of the history of the Mayas is carved in stone stelae, which give an account of their rulers back to AD 250, but little history exists before that time. But a religious history, if it existed, could be of great benefit to the scientific method of investigation. If such a history exists, however, archaeological investigation may serve to corroborate the religious history, lending credence where some skeptics may doubt its authenticity.

Such is the case with the Book of Mormon. The Book of Mormon purports to be a religious history of the ancient inhabitants of the American continent. The Book of Mormon, translated by Joseph Smith in 1830, long before archaeological discoveries in the Americas were available for publication, tells of great highways and aqueducts, fortified cities, the building of ancient temples, and cities buried under lakes and oceans by earthquakes and volcanoes at the time of the crucifixion of Jesus Christ in Jerusalem.

CONCLUSIONS

There is no physical proof that Joseph Smith saw God the Father and Jesus Christ in a vision, that he received the gold plates of the Book of Mormon from a resurrected being, or that he received the priesthood from the resurrected John the Baptist, but there is overwhelming evidence that the history of the ancient inhabitants of America and the places and civilizations described in the Book of Mormon are real places and real people. There is no way that Joseph Smith could have had such detailed knowledge of archaeological evidence as a young farm boy in New York in 1830. But more important, the doctrines taught in the Book of Mormon are consistent with the teachings in the Bible, and they clarify missing or misunderstood principles of salvation. Physical evidence is never conclusive and is insufficient to convince men or women to believe in the visitation of resurrected beings; the only sure source of truth is the Holy Ghost, who reveals truth to those who sincerely seek it by diligently searching and praying for answers.

NOTES

1. Joseph L. Allen, *Exploring the Lands of the Book of Mormon* (Orem, UT: S. A. Publishers, 1989), v.

2. Ibid., 14.
3. Ibid., 22.
4. John W. Welch, "Chiasmus in the Book of Mormon," *The New Era*, Feb. 1972, 6.
5. Richard K. Miner, *Chiastic Literary Structures in the Book of Mormon*, taken from H. Clay Gorton, "A new Witness for Christ-Chiastic structures in the Book of Mormon", posted on the Ancient America Foundation (AAF) website: http://www.ancientamerica.org/library/index.php3?id=/4.%20Featured%20Articles.
6. Bruce Warren, *New Evidences of Christ in America* (Arlington, VA: Stratford Books, 1999), 18–20.
7. Allen, *Exploring the Lands of the Book of Mormon*, 14
8. Ibid., 57.
9. Ibid., 85.
10. See Ether 1:33.
11. Dewey Farnsworth, *The Americas Before Columbus* (El Paso, TX: El Paso Publishing, 1947), 4. He quotes "Lowry, in his reply . . . to official inquiries respecting the aborigines of America concludes concerning the people of the western continent, 'That the first settlement was made shortly after the confusion of the building of the tower or Babel'" (Schoolcraft's Ethnological Researches, vol. 3, 1853).
12. Dewey Farnsworth, *The Americas Before Columbus* (El Paso, TX: El Paso Publishing, 1947), 10, quoting Herbert Howe Bancroft, *Native Races*, 5 vols., 1893.
13. Dewey Farnsworth, *The Americas Before Columbus* (El Paso, TX: El Paso Publishing, 1947), 12.
14. Ibid., 26.
15. Dewey Farnsworth, *The Americas Before Columbus* (El Paso, TX: El Paso Publishing, 1947), 18 (quotes George Jones, *History of Ancient America*, 21) and 22 (quotes George Jones, *History of Ancient America*, 126).
16. Jack West, *Trail of the Stick of Joseph*, (Sacramento, CA: Rich Publishing, 1972), 62.
17. Allen, *Exploring the Lands of the Book of Mormon*, 88.
18. Ibid., 137.
19. Ibid., 159.

CHAPTER 17

IN SEARCH OF TRUTH

And by the power of the Holy Ghost ye may know the truth of all things.

Moroni 10:5

LAPSES IN THE RECORDED HISTORY OF THE WORLD ARE THE CATAlysts for adventure seekers and historians who spend their lives in a quest for truth about the past. Solving the mystery of lost civilizations motivates archaeologists to dig in dirt all their lives, hoping to uncover some great secret about the past. We look to the past to understand our heritage, to glimpse the evolution of knowledge from primitive men to great scientists and philosophers, and to discover ourselves in relation to world history.

Piecing together the history of the Judeo-Christian religion reveals a continuous cycle of prophets who gave their lives to reveal the word of a loving God to his children on earth, followed by periods of prosperity and righteousness, followed by rebellion and rejection of the prophets, resulting in devastation and captivity. Gospel principles revealed to one generation were lost to their descendants for many generations and had to be restored again by prophets sent by God.

The hunger for truth about the purpose of life, the nature of God, and our future after death can be satisfied only by the "Bread of Life," who is Jesus Christ. The revelations of God to men and women on the earth are not limited to prophets and are not limited to any specific period of time. The Holy Ghost, the third member of the Godhead, is the personal messenger of Heavenly Father and Jesus Christ to any and all who call upon them in humble and sincere prayer. This is the ultimate source of all truth. This truth is more powerful and more revealing than any of the greatest discoveries of modern science. The knowledge gained from this source is surer and more convincing than any tangible evidence that can be seen or heard or held.

The truth is that there was a plan developed in heaven before the creation of the earth, and all the spirit sons and daughters of Heavenly Father gathered to learn and choose their eternal destinies. The plan was for God's spirit children to be sent to the earth to gain physical bodies and to learn by faith to keep the commandments God revealed through his prophets. Heavenly Father had a glorified body of flesh and bones like ours (except that ours is not yet glorified), and we were to be created in his image, both spiritually in heaven and physically on earth. We desired to be like him, and like any loving parent, he wanted to bless us with all that he has. But he knows that we must learn through experiences to make correct choices to grow in wisdom and righteousness. In order for us to understand righteousness, we needed to sin, and sin was brought about by temptations to misuse the gift of agency that we would be given. To appreciate joy, it was necessary for us to experience sadness; to appreciate health and well being, we needed to go through periods of sickness; and to understand and appreciate eternal life, we needed to experience physical death. This physical death is the separation of the spirit and the mortal body. But to become like Heavenly Father, we needed a glorified and immortal body, which we would receive in the resurrection, which was planned from the foundation of the world.

The key to this plan was agency, or freedom of choice. The first choice was whether to follow Jesus Christ or Lucifer, both sons of Heavenly Father. Lucifer's plan was to force us all to obey God's commandments so that we would all return to heaven, but Lucifer wanted all the glory for becoming our savior and wanted to overthrow the throne of God. But Jesus Christ, the Firstborn Son of Heavenly Father, agreed to go to earth and offer himself as a sacrifice for the sins of all people so that he could balance the scales of justice and mercy. God's eternal laws required rewards for righteousness and punishments for wickedness, but the only perfect person to live on this earth agreed before the creation to pay for the sins of all mankind, on the conditions of faith and repentance, so that we can all be brought back to live with Heavenly Father. Jesus also agreed to give all of the glory to the Father. In order to bring about our eternal lives, Jesus came to earth as we all do—as a child of a mortal mother—but he was also the Son of an immortal Heavenly Father. He experienced all of the pains, suffering, temptations, ridicule, and heartache that we go through, so he is capable of understanding our experiences. To bring about our eternal lives, he overcame two types of death. He overcame the physical death by the resurrection, which is a free gift to all who come to this earth. "For as in Adam, all die, even so in Christ, shall all become alive" (1 Corinthians 15:22). He overcame the spiritual death, which is the separation from God, by suffering in the Garden of Gethsemane and on the cross for all of our sins so that upon our faith, repentance, and baptism, we can be washed clean and be worthy to live with him in the kingdom of his Father.

The Bible tells that one-third of the spirits in the pre-earth life chose to follow Lucifer (Revelation 12:4). Modern revelation explains that this was because of Satan's promise to bring back everyone, that one soul would not be lost. This brought about the War in Heaven described in the Book of Revelation, where Lucifer and his angels were cast down to the earth, never to have the opportunity to have bodies and continue their eternal progression. Those spirits who followed Jesus chose to risk temptations, with the hope of eternal exaltation in Heavenly Father's kingdom, based on the Savior's promise to forgive their transgressions if they repent and are baptized and strive to endure to the end of their lives in keeping the commandments. Heavenly Father promised to send prophets to teach righteous living and to teach of the Messiah, who would someday come into the world to atone for their sins. However, many people would be murdered or accidentally killed or suffer early deaths by disease or infirmities. Many would be deceived by false prophets and false teachers who would lead them to commit sins without a complete knowledge of the commandments of God or who would teach them to worship false gods without their knowledge of the true God. God allows sin and wickedness on the earth because of the sacred gift of agency, but he also provides for the eternal welfare of those who suffer as the victims of the sins of others.

Our loving Heavenly Father prepared a plan whereby those who lived and died on this earth without a chance to hear and understand the fulness of the gospel in this life would be taught the correct principles in the spirit world, where all spirits go to await the resurrection. Those who are taught and believe and who would have accepted the gospel in this life if it had been presented to them correctly will benefit from the Atonement of the Savior and will move from the spirit prison to spirit paradise to await the resurrection. Because baptism on earth is a requirement for all to enter into the kingdom of heaven, the ordinance of baptism for the dead was introduced to the apostles, but this principle was lost for centuries before it was restored to the earth again.

The Bible teaches that the kingdom of heaven is divided into at least three kingdoms: the celestial kingdom is likened unto the glory of the sun, the terrestrial kingdom is compared to the glory of the moon, and the telestial kingdom is compared to the glory of the stars. Paul said, "I knew a man in Christ . . . caught up to the third heaven" (2 Corinthians 12:2). Those who repent and are baptized and endure to the end in keeping the commandments, repenting when they sin, are heirs of the celestial kingdom, where Heavenly Father and Jesus Christ dwell eternally.

Those who inherit the terrestrial kingdom are those righteous men and women who were good and kind but who did not have strong testimonies of Jesus Christ after being taught about him.

Those who inherit the telestial kingdom are the wicked of the earth who knew the truth but chose to follow Satan and sinned without repentance. The Atonement of the Savior is not effective for them, so they must suffer for their own sins, "Which suffering caused myself, even God, the greatest of all, to tremble because of pain, and to bleed at every pore, and to suffer both body and spirit—and would that I might not drink the bitter cup, and shrink" (D&C 19:18). But after they have paid the price of suffering for their own sins, they will become the heirs of the telestial kingdom, which is their hell, since they will not be able to progress eternally and will be condemned to live with others like them who chose wickedness after being taught correctly and who rejected the Atonement of the Savior.

Sincere seekers of truth should rejoice at the very thought that God may have sent prophets to the earth in our lifetimes and should eagerly investigate any such claims to see if they bear any fruit, for the Savior said, "By their fruits ye shall know them" (Matthew 7:16–20).

Moroni, the last prophet to write in the Book of Mormon, challenged our generation to read this record of the ancient prophets of God on the American continent and to ponder and pray about the things that we read:

> And when ye shall receive these things, I would exhort you that ye would ask God, the Eternal Father, in the name of Christ, if these things are not true; and if ye shall ask with a sincere heart, with real intent, having faith in Christ, he will manifest the truth of it unto you, by the power of the Holy Ghost. And by the power of the Holy Ghost ye may know the truth of all things. (Moroni 10:5–6)

I repeat this challenge to all sincere seekers of truth. Ancient manuscripts and discoveries of lost or hidden records may reveal mysteries about past generations and may shed new light upon previously obscure cultures, but the great source of truth that stands the test of time is the personal revelation that comes from the Holy Ghost after sincere investigation of prophetic writings and after sincere prayer to learn of their truth.

About the Author

Robert L. Smith has been a convert to The Church of Jesus Christ of Latter-day Saints since 1971. He has served as a bishop and is presently serving as a seminary teacher. He speaks at youth and single adult conferences on archeological evidences of the Book of Mormon and has published articles on related subjects on the Ancient America Foundation (AAF) website, and in numerous issues of the Internet-based news magazine *The New Archaeology Review.* His first book, *In Search of Truth: From the Creation to the Restoration*, is a result of extensive research and study of acclaimed current and past LDS authors on the history of the early Church established by Jesus Christ and his apostles and the subsequent apostasy leading to the Protestant Reformation and the restoration of the gospel by the Lord through Joseph Smith.

0 26575 10513 1